KAWARTHA LAKES PUBLIC LIBRARY

3 6500 030071

P9-DFV-924

MARVEL COMICS

PRESENTS

MARVELMAN

DISCARD

CITY OF KAWARTHA LAKES

MARVELMAN CLASSIC VOL. 1. Contains material originally published in magazine form as MARVELMAN #25-34. First printing 2017. ISBN# 978-1-302-90473-9. Published by MARVEL WORLDWIDE, INC., a subsidiary of MARVEL ENTERTAINMENT, LLC. OFFICE OF PUBLICATION: 135 West 50th Street, New York, NY 10020. Copyright © 2017 MARVEL No similarity between any of the names, characters, persons, and/or institutions in this magazine with those of any living or dead person or institution is intended, and any such similarity which may exist is purely coincidental. **Printed in the U.S.A.** ALAN FINE, President, Marvel Entertainment; DAN BUCKLEY, President, TV, Publishing & Brand Management; JOE QUESADA, Chief Creative Officer; TOM BREVOORT, SVP of Publishing; DAVID BOGART, SVP of Business Affairs & Operations, Publishing & Partnership; C.B. CEBULSKI, VP of Brand Management & Development, Asia; DAVID GABRIEL, SVP of Sales & Marketing, Publishing; JEFF YOUNGQUIST, VP of Production & Special Projects; DAN CARR, Executive Director of Publishing Technology; ALEX MORALES, Director of Publishing Operations; SUSAN CRESPI, Production Manager; STAN LEE, Chairman Emeritus. For information regarding advertising in Marvel Comics or on Marvel.com, please contact Vit DeBellis, Integrated Sales Manager, at vdebellis@marvel.com. For Marvel subscription inquiries, please call 888-511-5480. **Manufactured between 11/18/2016 and 12/26/2016 by SHERIDAN, CHELSEA, MI, USA.**

10 9 8 7 6 5 4 3 2 1

CITY OF KAWARTHA LAKES

MARVELMAN CLASSIC VOLUME 1
CREDITS/CONTENTS

Front Cover by **Joe Quesada with Danny Miki & Richard Isanove**

Back Cover by **Mick Anglo with Chris Sotomayor**

It was not industry standard at the time these stories were published to provide detailed credits for each strip. Mick Anglo worked with an ever-changing studio of assistants and secondary artists. The stories in this volume may have included contributions by the creators listed above and others.

Marvelman created by **Mick Anglo**

Marvelman Indexer/Archivist
Derek Wilson

Color/Art Reconstruction
Digikore

Production
Ryan Devall with Nelson Ribeiro

Book Design
Spring Hoteling

Special Thanks
Brian Overton, Stuart Vandal,
Adam Fox, Alter Ego & TwoMorrows

Collection Editor
Mark D. Beazley

Associate Managing Editor
Kateri Woody

Associate Editor
Sarah Brunstad

Associate Manager, Digital Assets
Joe Hochstein

Senior Editor, Special Projects
Jennifer Grünwald

VP Production & Special Projects
Jeff Youngquist

SVP Print, Sales & Marketing
David Gabriel

Editor in Chief
Joe Quesada

Publisher
Dan Buckley

Executive Producer
Alan Fine

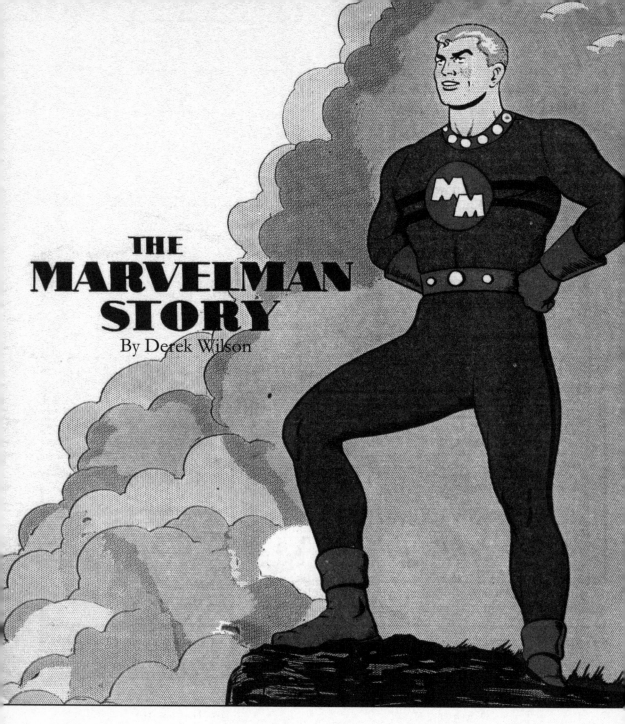

THE MARVELMAN STORY

By Derek Wilson

Marvelman was born of necessity on Feb. 3, 1954, after Captain Marvel lost his 12-year legal fight with Superman.

National Periodical Publications (now DC Comics) filed a lawsuit for copyright infringement against Fawcett Comics in 1941, claiming that Captain Marvel was a direct copy of Superman. The fact that Captain Marvel was outselling Superman was more likely the real reason, but it made no difference to the outcome, and Fawcett hung up the Shazam! cape in 1953. An injunction obtained in the United States had no jurisdiction in the U.K.,

where the books were reprinted, but the Captain Marvel stories would not continue for long.

In Britain, L. Miller & Son were reprinting the Fawcett titles — including *Adventures of Captain Marvel*, *Adventures of Captain Marvel Jr.*, *The Marvel Family* and *Mary Marvel* — which were their best sellers and just as successful as those in the United States at attracting a large, young audience for two weeklies (*CM* and *CMJ*) and one monthly comic (*MF*). *Mary Marvel* didn't survive beyond a few photogravure (full-color) issues.

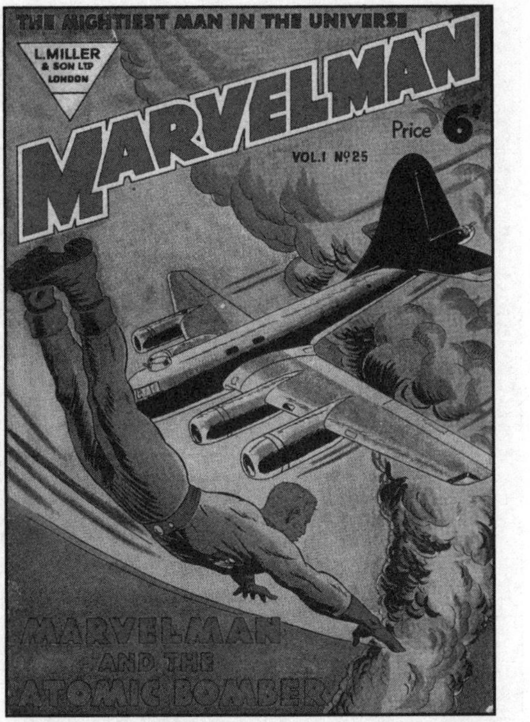
THE MIGHTIEST MAN IN THE UNIVERSE
L.MILLER & SON LTD LONDON
MARVELMAN
Price 6d
VOL.1 Nº25
MARVELMAN AND THE ATOMIC BOMBER

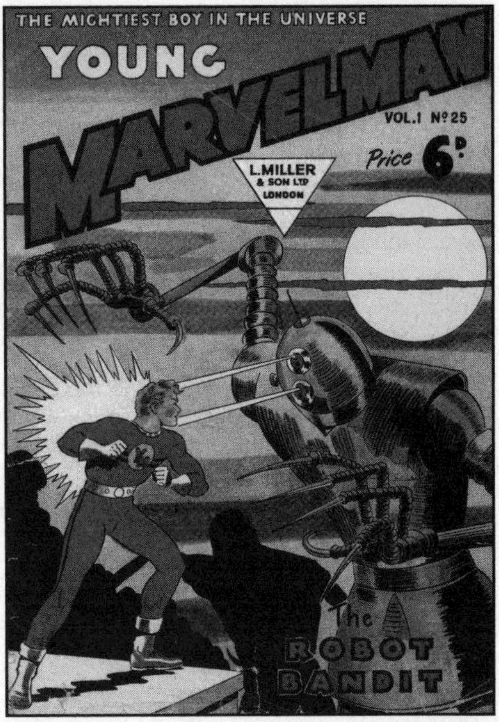
THE MIGHTIEST BOY IN THE UNIVERSE
YOUNG
MARVELMAN
VOL.1 Nº25
L.MILLER & SON LTD LONDON
Price 6D
The ROBOT BANDIT

The largest-selling periodical in the Miller library could not be allowed to die, so Mick Anglo was recruited to create an alternative character. Anglo's previous work had been with Arnold Miller's Arnold Book Company producing covers for Len Miller's L. Miller & Son comics. Arnold was publishing comic titles such as *Captain Valiant, Space Commando, Ace Malloy*, and *Space Commander Kerry*.

Anglo created new characters to replace the old heroes: Marvelman and his alter ego, Micky Moran, Young Marvelman (Dicky Dauntless) and Kid Marvelman (Johnny Bates). (Other names seriously considered for Marvelman included Miracleman and Captain Miracle.)

A copy boy for the *Daily Bugle* newspaper, Micky was given his powers by Guntag Barghelt, a reclusive scientist who had discovered the Keyword to the Universe: Kimota ("atomic" backward, with creative license on the spelling). An atomic name for an atomic hero, they boasted. (Marvelman's origin was retold in the top copy at the beginning of each issue until it was fully revealed in #65: "Guntag Barghelt, whilst seeking a young lad of Honesty and Integrity to use his Powers only against Evil, is saved from thugs by crew-cut Micky Moran, copy-boy for the Daily Bugle. After treatment in an Atomic machine, Micky only has to shout 'Kimota!' and at the magic keyword, Atomic Power crashes down and Micky immediately becomes Marvelman, Mightiest Man in the Universe.")

THE VILLAINS

The main enemies of the Marvel Family had been Dr. Sivana and Sivana Jr. Anglo followed suit, inventing his own mad scientists. His brother came up with the name Gargunza; it sounded right and was accepted. Dr. Emil Gargunza and Young Gargunza appeared in *Marvelman* and *Young Marvelman* comics, respectively.

Dr. Emil Gargunza remained with Marvelman right through to the end, proving to be the most dangerous opponent that Marvelman could ever imagine.

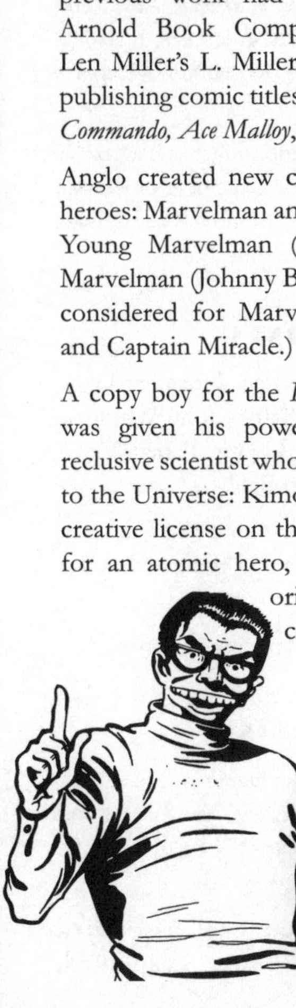

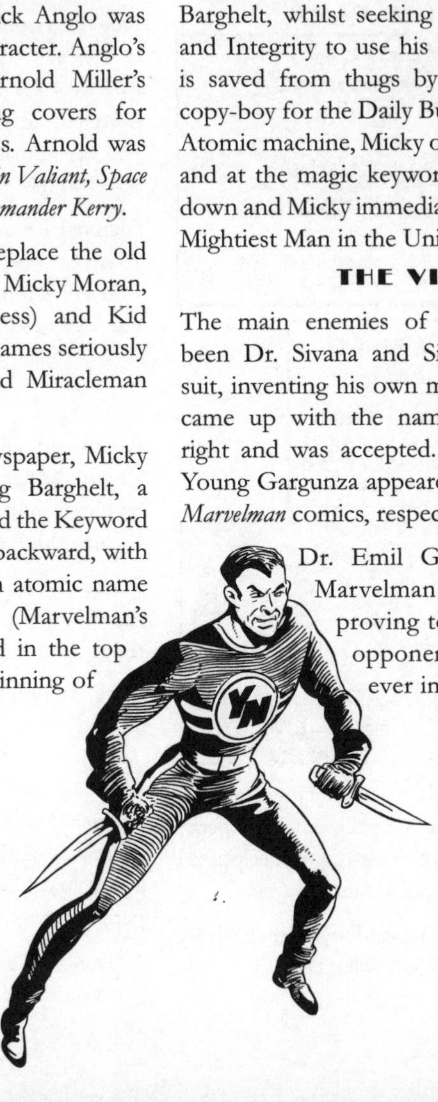

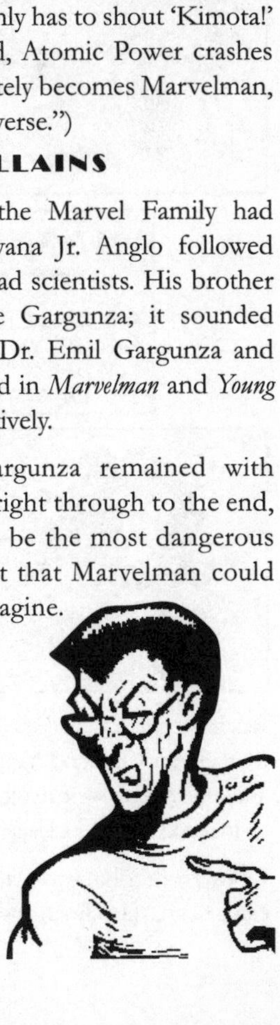

Another new villain, Young Nastyman, battled the Marvelman Family on several occasions.

THE CHANGEOVER

The last appearances of Captain Marvel and Captain Marvel Jr. were approaching in issue #19, so an announcement was made on the Club Page in that issue, dated Dec. 23, 1953, stating that Billy Batson and Freddy Freeman now wanted to lead normal lives and were giving their powers back to old Shazam.

Issues #23 and #24 had the cover titles *The Marvelman, Captain Marvel* and *The Young Marvelman, Captain Marvel Jr.*; on Feb. 3, 1954, the first *Marvelman* and *Young Marvelman* titles hit the stands with issue #25 of each series.

The changeover was a complete success. The format and the price remained the same, and sales actually increased.

Britain had its first super hero.

MEMBERSHIP CLUB

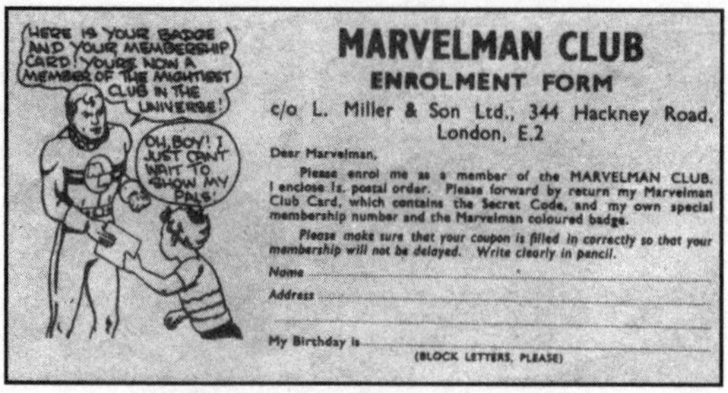
HERE IS YOUR BADGE AND YOUR MEMBERSHIP CARD! YOU'RE NOW A MEMBER OF THE MIGHTIEST CLUB IN THE UNIVERSE!
OH, BOY! I JUST CAN'T WAIT TO SHOW MY PALS!

MARVELMAN CLUB
ENROLMENT FORM
c/o L. Miller & Son Ltd., 344 Hackney Road, London, E.2

Dear Marvelman,

Please enrol me as a member of the MARVELMAN CLUB. I enclose 1s. postal order. Please forward by return my Marvelman Club Card, which contains the Secret Code, and my own special membership number and the Marvelman coloured badge.

Please make sure that your coupon is filled in correctly so that your membership will not be delayed. Write clearly in pencil.

Name ....

Address ....

My Birthday is ....

(BLOCK LETTERS, PLEASE)

MARVELMAN

Secret Code Message

R GZTEZT DVRC CVRMVJ
PFL IVJKVU REU WZKKVI,
SLK UFE'K CVRMV SVYZEU
PFL LEJZXYKCP CZKKVI

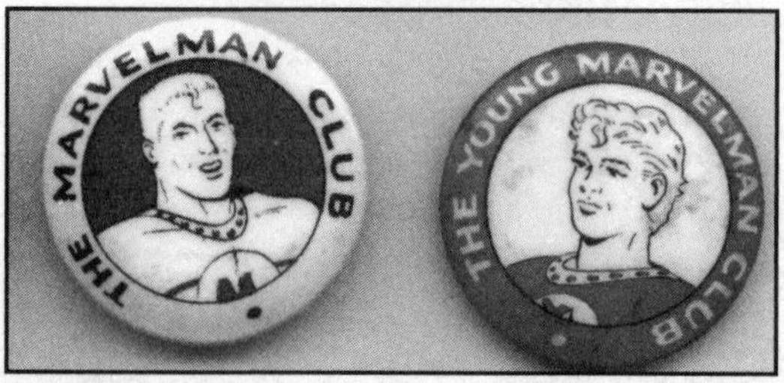
THE MARVELMAN CLUB
THE YOUNG MARVELMAN CLUB

Readers were encouraged to join the popular Marvelman Club and Young Marvelman Club. Special announcements were made that could only be deciphered by initiated members via a "Special Message Code."

Later, the decision was made to send members birthday cards from Marvelman and Young Marvelman.

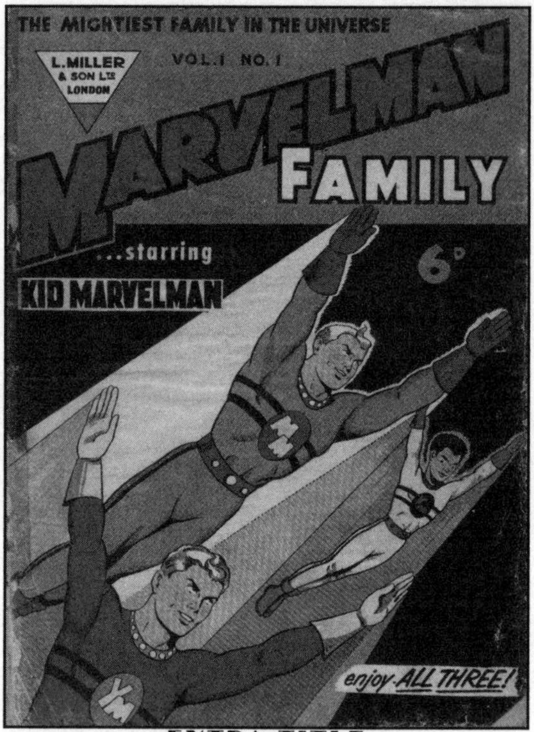
THE MIGHTIEST FAMILY IN THE UNIVERSE
L. MILLER & SON LTD LONDON
VOL. 1 NO. 1
MARVELMAN
FAMILY
...starring
KID MARVELMAN
6d
enjoy ALL THREE!

EXTRA TITLE

Due to popular demand, a new title was released in October 1956 as a monthly alongside the other two weeklies. It was called *The Marvelman Family* and portrayed adventures of all three members, including Kid Marvelman, who had made his debut in *Marvelman #102* on July 30, 1955.

Although it was designated as a monthly, it actually ran as 10 issues a year, with no issues for December or January, with a final run of 30 issues in 37 months. The last issue was October 1959, which was a month late.

THE ARTISTS

Artists on all the titles included Norman Light, Charles Baker, James Bleach (Kurt), John Whitlock, Stanley White, Denis Gifford, George Parlett, Frank Daniels, Dorothy Saporito and Roshan Kanga.

There was also Don Lawrence, Roy Parker and Leo Rawlings, who provided most of the artwork for the *Marvelman Family* title.

Mick Anglo provided most of the cover artwork.

MERCHANDISE

Special "Magic" Painting Books were produced (two *Marvelman* and two *Young Marvelman*); only water and a paintbrush were needed to color the pictures as the paper was coated with dried watercolor.

It is surprising that marketing of associated merchandise was not better exploited,

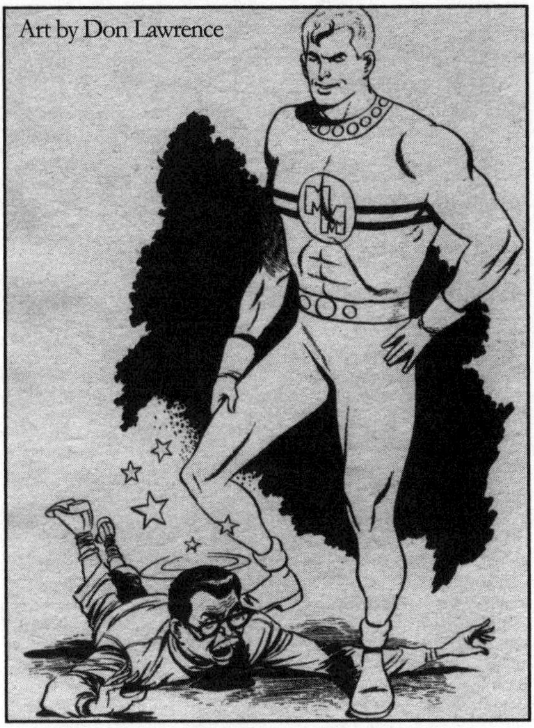
Art by Don Lawrence

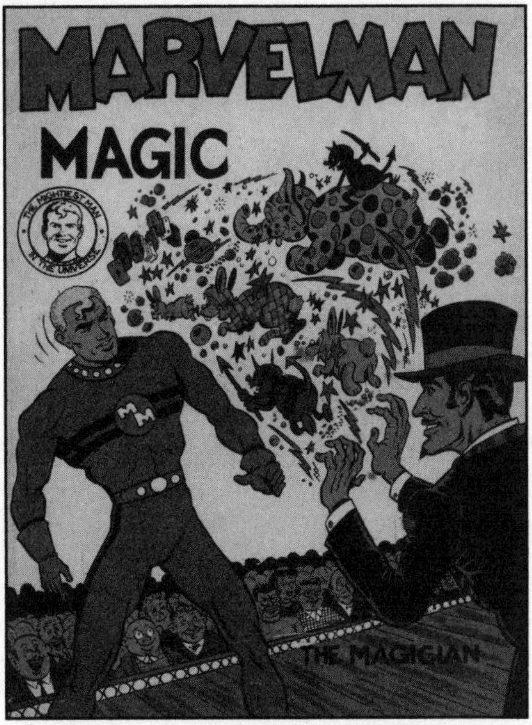
MARVELMAN
MAGIC
THE MIGHTIEST MAN IN THE UNIVERSE
THE MAGICIAN

especially with the successful Eagle and Dan Dare toys in the stores during the same time. After all, Captain Marvel had been marketed very well in the U.K. with sweatshirts, jigsaws, coloring books, lead figures and games, and even better in the United States with a wonderland of toys and variety of merchandise, including a serialized film starring Tom Tyler as Captain Marvel.

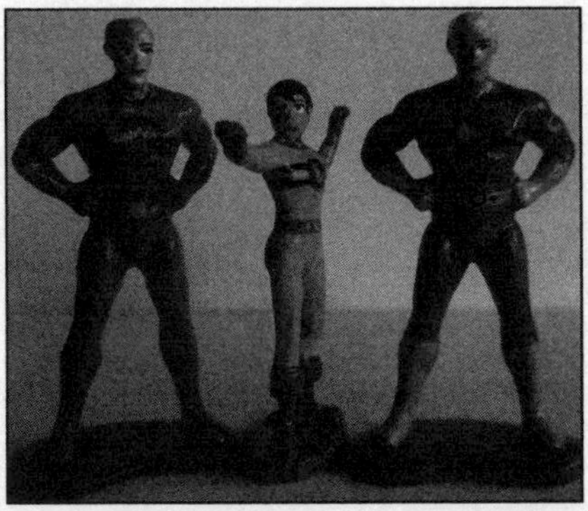

The late, great comedian/magician Tommy Cooper was a fan of Marvelman comics, as can be seen in his autobiography *Just Like That!* An illustration is included of the splash page of *Marvelman #267*, where Marvelman has been transformed into Cooperman, using that name long before comedian Russ Abbott's TV show.

THE ANNUALS

Following the *Captain Marvel* and *Captain Marvel Jr.* annuals released in 1952, the first *Marvelman* and *Young Marvelman* annuals were released for Christmas 1954. The 100-page 1954 and 1955 annuals were a larger format than normal, 10.5" x 8", with soft card covers and printed spines.

The 96-page 1956-59 and 1960 annuals were 10" x 7.25" and were hardbound books with printed spines. The 1959 annual was the first that was printed with the year.

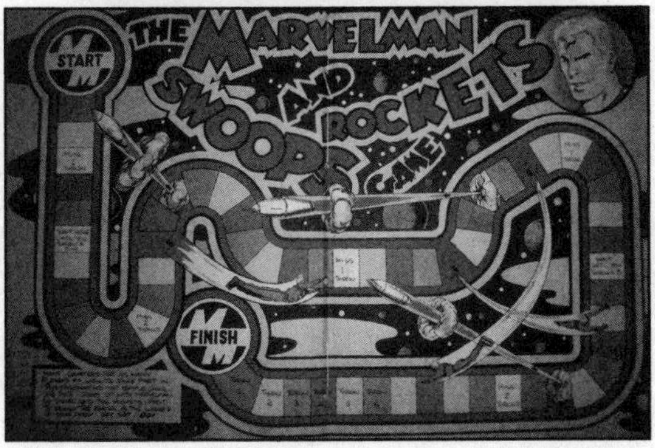
THE MARVELMAN SWOOPS AND ROCKETS GAME
START
FINISH

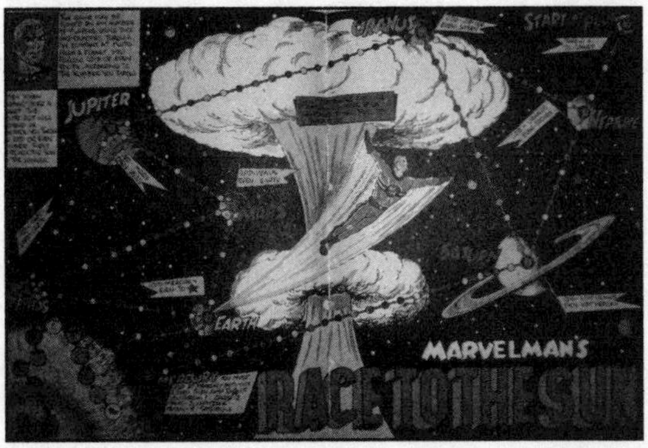
URANUS
JUPITER
EARTH
MARVELMAN'S
RACE TO THE SUN

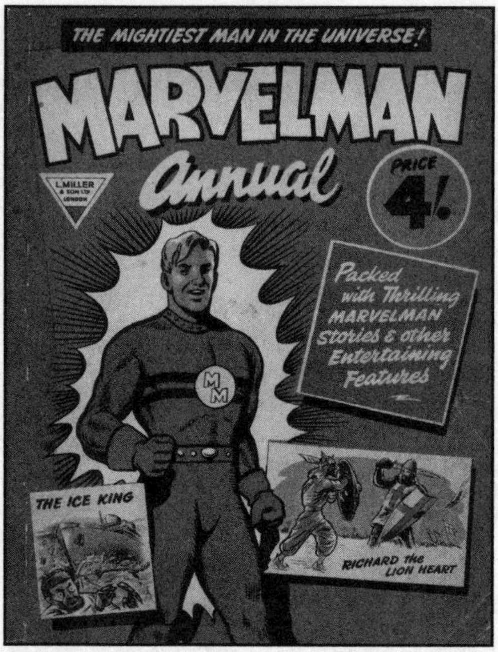
THE MIGHTIEST MAN IN THE UNIVERSE!
MARVELMAN
Annual
PRICE 4/.
L.MILLER & SON LTD LONDON
Packed with Thrilling MARVELMAN Stories & other Entertaining Features
THE ICE KING
RICHARD the LION HEART

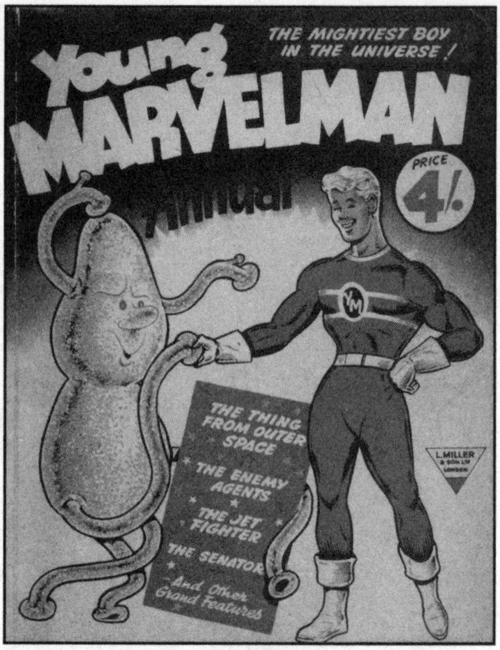
THE MIGHTIEST BOY IN THE UNIVERSE!
Young MARVELMAN
Annual
PRICE 4/.
THE THING FROM OUTER SPACE
THE ENEMY AGENTS
THE JET FIGHTER
THE SENATOR
And Other Grand Features
L.MILLER & SON LTD LONDON

The 64-page 1961-63 annuals were 10" x 7", much thinner with hard carded covers with a taped spine.

These last ones were very fragile and would lose pages if opened too far.

Two annuals were released each year from 1954 to 1963, making a total of 20 annuals, but there was some confusion after Mick Anglo left in 1960: The 1961 annuals had Marvelman and Young Marvelman on their respective covers, but they had been drawn wearing Captain Marvel's and Captain Marvel Jr.'s capes.

There were no annuals dated 1962, but the last four were dated 1963.

It is unlikely that the four were issued at the same time, and most probable that they printed Christmas 1962 as a '63 annual, which is normal today.

The 1962 annuals were *Marvelman* and *Young Marvelman* as usual, and the final two annuals for 1963 were *Marvelman Family* and *Marvelman Jr.* (showing that even at the end there was still some

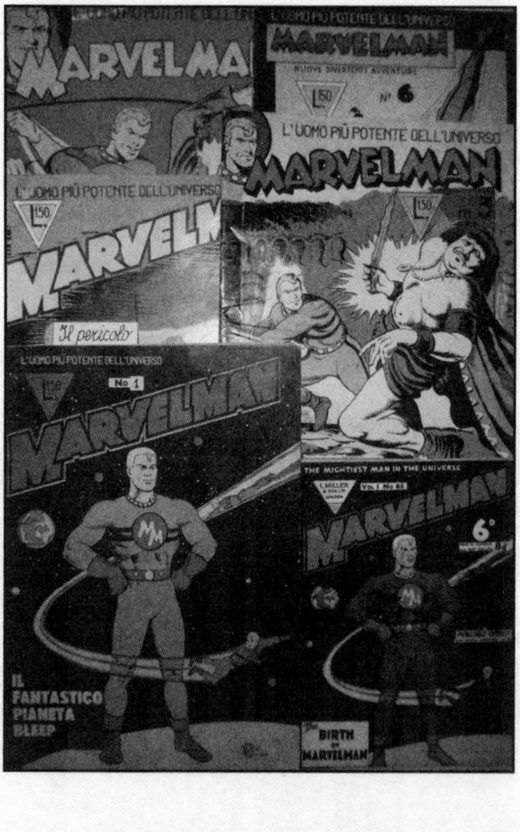
MARVELMAN
L'UOMO PIÙ POTENTE DELL'UNIVERSO
MARVELMAN
Il pericolo
No 1
IL FANTASTICO PIANETA BLEEP
THE MIGHTIEST MAN IN THE UNIVERSE
MARVELMAN
6d
The BIRTH of MARVELMAN

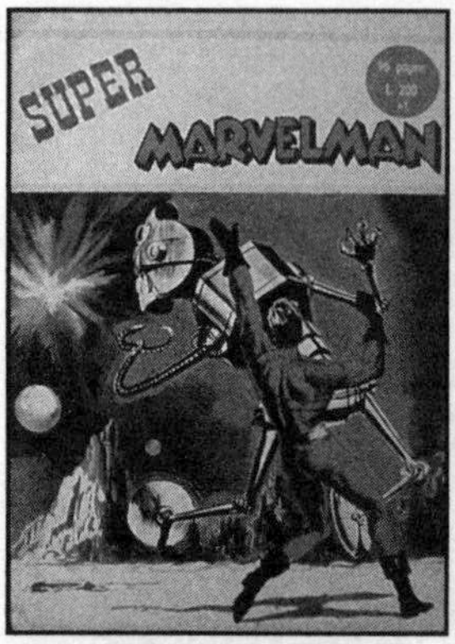
SUPER MARVELMAN

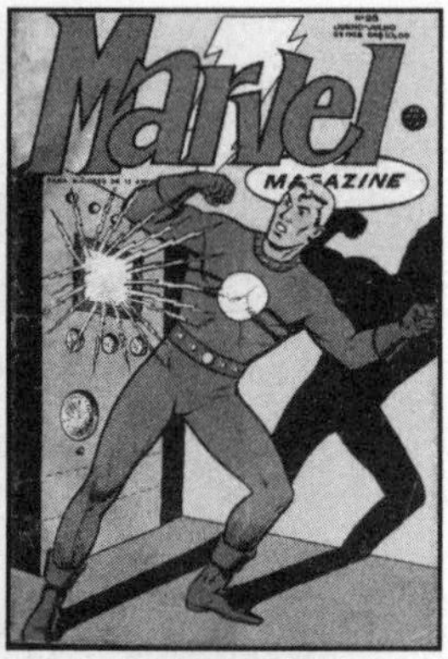
Marvel
MAGAZINE

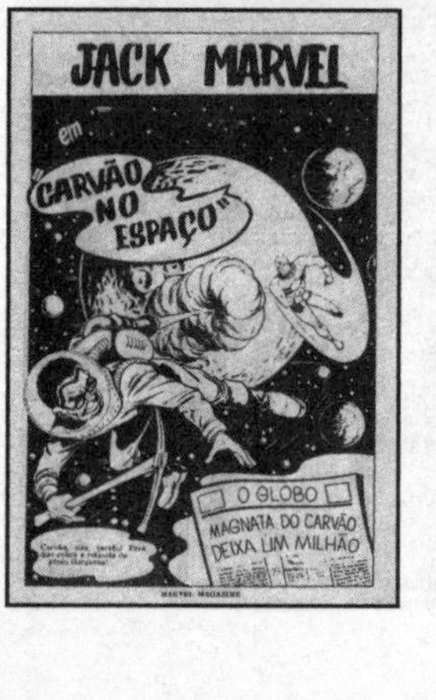
JACK MARVEL
em
"CARVÃO NO ESPAÇO"
O GLOBO
MAGNATA DO CARVÃO DEIXA UM MILHÃO

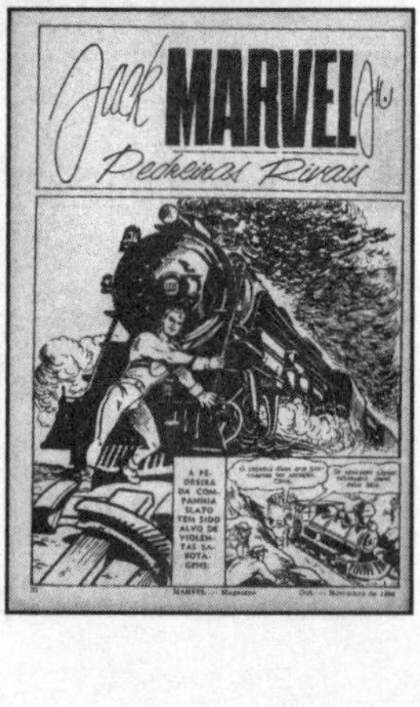
Jack MARVEL Jr.
Pedreiras Rivais

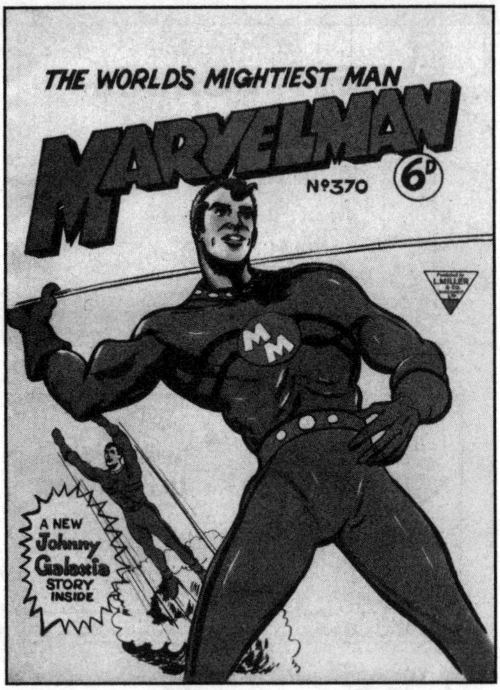
THE WORLD'S MIGHTIEST MAN
MARVELMAN
No370
6D
A NEW Johnny Galaxis STORY INSIDE

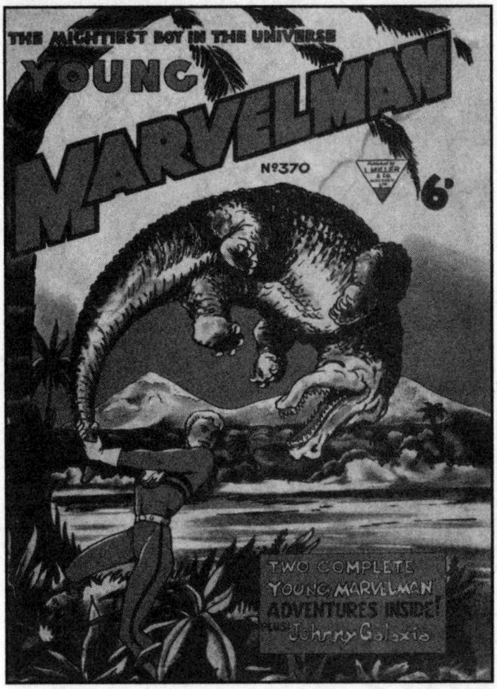
THE MIGHTIEST BOY IN THE UNIVERSE
YOUNG MARVELMAN
No370
6D
TWO COMPLETE YOUNG MARVELMAN ADVENTURES INSIDE!
PLUS: Johnny Galaxis

confusion over the characters' names without Mick Anglo at the helm).

The annuals were the only time that the comic strips were printed in color.

FOREIGN SHORES

Marvelman comics sold well abroad.

All the titles were exported to the English-speaking shores of Australia and New Zealand. In Australia, *Marvelman* and *Young Marvelman* were also being reprinted by Young's Merchandising Co., Sydney, using cheaper stock and different artwork for the covers. No numbers are known, but issues #68 and #77 are recognizable by the cover prices, which were different than the English issues.

It is interesting to note that throughout the nine-year run the cover price never increased.

Other countries were translating the comics into their own languages.

In Italy, Marvelman sold well under his own name, and the issues were huge in comparison to the U.K. comics, nearly a full A3 (11.69" × 16.54") in size, making the artwork very detailed and pleasant to see. There were only eight Italian issues, but they were 48 pages long and 100 percent Marvelman with no filler stories. There were also two Italian annuals, again nearly A3 in size — 96 pages and all Marvelman.

In Brazil, Marvelman was published as *Marvel Magazine*, and he was renamed Jack Marvel with the MM logo removed from his chest.

There was a mix in each issue of Captain Marvel (plus Jr.) and Jack Marvel (plus Jr., not Young).

Issue #61 is dated 1964, outlasting the U.K. run, which finished in 1963.

THE END

By the time issue #335 was published, sales were on the decline; at issue #336 (Feb. 3, 1960) both titles were changed from weekly to monthly.

This was about the same time that Mick Anglo left Miller's, and the reprinting of earlier strips began. Both titles continued as monthlies until #370, which was the final issue, dated February 1963, meaning that the titles ran for exactly nine years practically to the day.

Total runs were:

Marvelman — 346 issues

Young Marvelman — 346 issues

Marvelman Family — 30 issues

722 comics in all

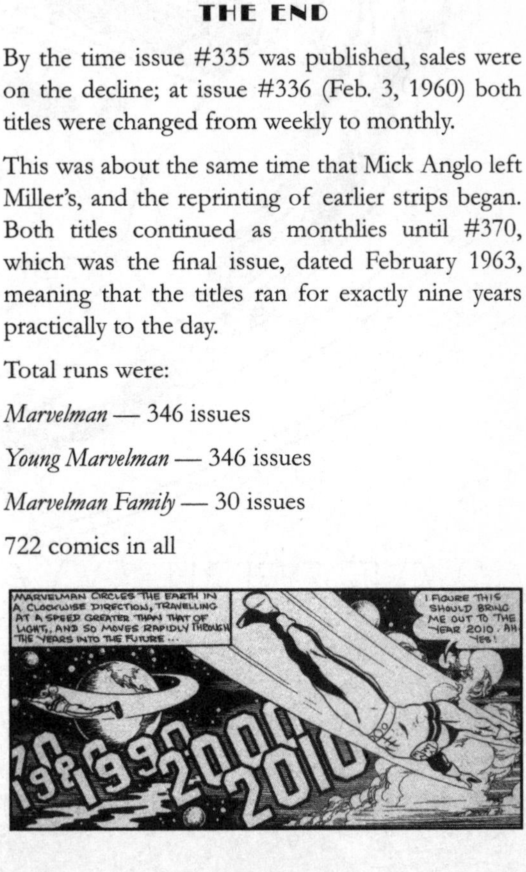
MARVELMAN CIRCLES THE EARTH IN A CLOCKWISE DIRECTION, TRAVELLING AT A SPEED GREATER THAN THAT OF LIGHT, AND SO MOVES RAPIDLY THROUGH THE YEARS INTO THE FUTURE...
I FIGURE THIS SHOULD BRING ME OUT TO THE YEAR 2010. AH YES!
1990
2000
2010

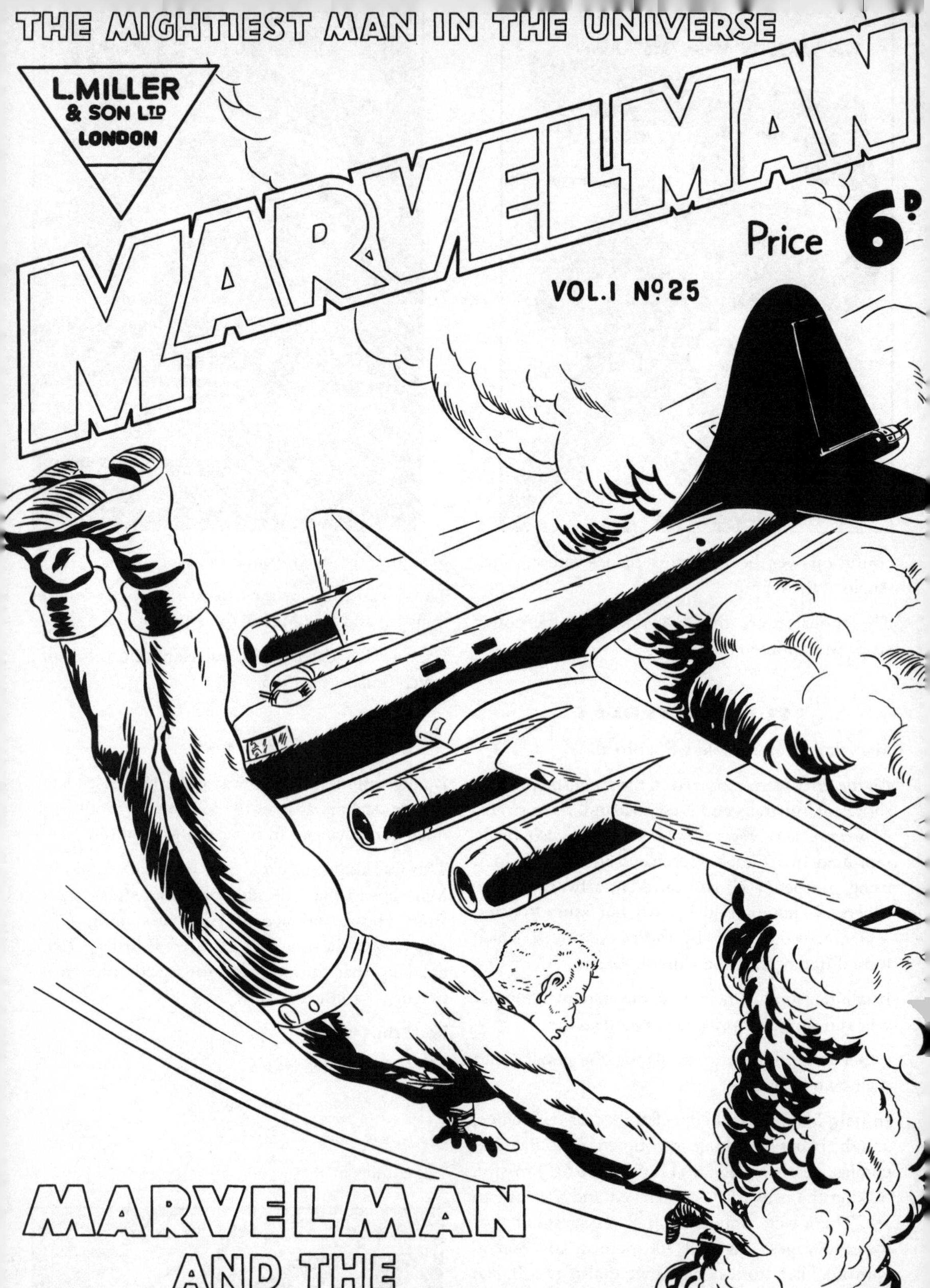
THE MIGHTIEST MAN IN THE UNIVERSE
L. MILLER & SON LTD LONDON
MARVELMAN
Price 6D.
VOL. I Nº 25
MARVELMAN AND THE ATOMIC BOMBER

MARVELMAN

AND THE ATOMIC BOMBER

A recluse Astro-Scientist discovers the key word to the Universe, one that can only be given to a Boy who is completely honest, studious, and of such integrity that he would only use it for the powers of good. He finds such a Boy in **MICKY MORAN**, a Newspaper Copy Boy, and treats him in a special machine which enables him to use the secret. Just before the Scientist dies he tells **MICKY** the Key Word which is **KIMOTA**.

MICKY MORAN remains as he was, but when he says the Key Word **KIMOTA** he becomes **MARVELMAN**, a Man of such strength and powers that he is Invincible and Indestructible.

THE XB999, ATOMIC BOMBER, WAS SCHEDULED TO EXPLODE AN ATOM BOMB IN THE MIDDLE OF THE ARIZONA DESERT, BUT ONLY THE TIMELY INTERVENTION OF MARVELMAN SAVED WASHINGTON FROM BEING THE TARGET, WHEN BALCO, THE BOROMANIAN AGENT STRUCK....

AFTER WORKING OVERTIME ON THE DAILY BUGLE MICKY MORAN IS MAKING HIS WAY HOME......

AWAY FROM THE BUGLE DAY'S WORK DONE. STRAIGHT TO THE DRUGSTORE SODAS AND FUN!

GET IT! OUCH!

O.K. BOSS!

HOLY MACARONI! SOUNDS LIKE TROUBLE!

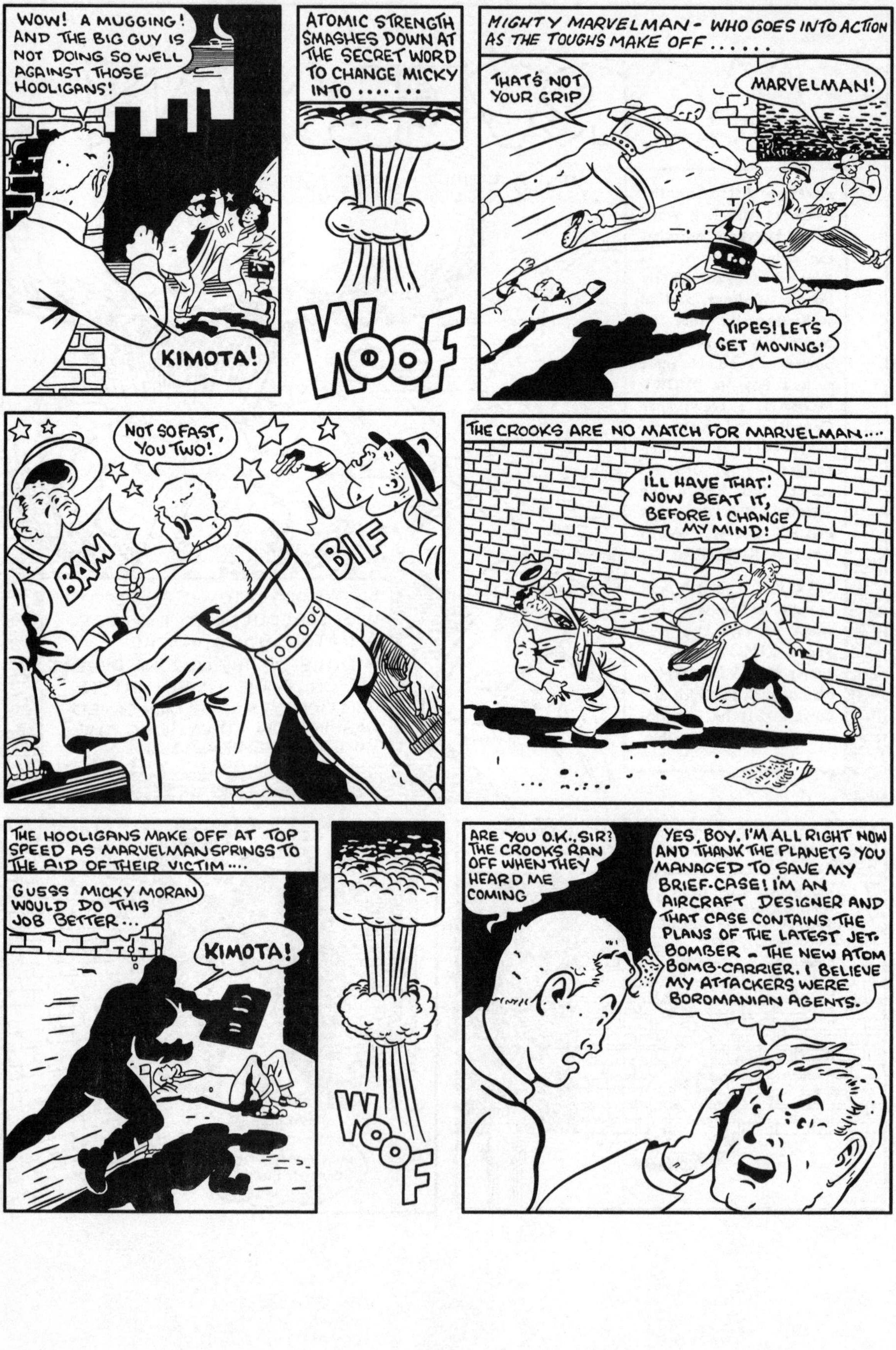
WOW! A MUGGING! AND THE BIG GUY IS NOT DOING SO WELL AGAINST THOSE HOOLIGANS!
BIF
KIMOTA!
ATOMIC STRENGTH SMASHES DOWN AT THE SECRET WORD TO CHANGE MICKY INTO ....
WOOF
MIGHTY MARVELMAN - WHO GOES INTO ACTION AS THE TOUGHS MAKE OFF ......
THAT'S NOT YOUR GRIP
MARVELMAN!
YIPES! LET'S GET MOVING!
NOT SO FAST, YOU TWO!
BAM
BIF
THE CROOKS ARE NO MATCH FOR MARVELMAN....
I'LL HAVE THAT! NOW BEAT IT, BEFORE I CHANGE MY MIND!
THE HOOLIGANS MAKE OFF AT TOP SPEED AS MARVELMAN SPRINGS TO THE AID OF THEIR VICTIM....
GUSSS MICKY MORAN WOULD DO THIS JOB BETTER...
KIMOTA!
WOOF
ARE YOU O.K., SIR? THE CROOKS RAN OFF WHEN THEY HEARD ME COMING
YES, BOY. I'M ALL RIGHT NOW AND THANK THE PLANETS YOU MANAGED TO SAVE MY BRIEF-CASE! I'M AN AIRCRAFT DESIGNER AND THAT CASE CONTAINS THE PLANS OF THE LATEST JET-BOMBER - THE NEW ATOM BOMB-CARRIER. I BELIEVE MY ATTACKERS WERE BOROMANIAN AGENTS.

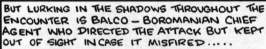

BUT LURKING IN THE SHADOWS THROUGHOUT THE ENCOUNTER IS BALCO — BOROMANIAN CHIEF AGENT WHO DIRECTED THE ATTACK BUT KEPT OUT OF SIGHT IN CASE IT MISFIRED.....

HEH! HEH! THAT ATTEMPT FAILED BUT I'VE LEARNED THE SECRET OF OUR WORST ENEMY. MARVELMAN. A BOY— HEH! HEH! HEH!

AS MARVELMAN HE IS INVULNERABLE —BUT AS A BOY.... HEH! HEH! NOW WE WILL SEE.'

SEVERAL DAYS LATER, MICKY IS LEAVING THE OFFICE WHEN..

THERE, BRAT! WE WANT YOU!

KIM.... UKKK!

BAM

WITH MICKY CAPTIVE, THE AUTOMOBILE MAKES OFF...

SNATCHING THE KID WAS AS EASY AS BREAKING EGGS

YEAH! THIS WILL SURE MAKE BALCO HAPPY.

SOON THE AUTO TURNS OFF INTO A BROKEN DOWN OLD GARAGE BUILDING......

AND...

NOW MY FINE BUT UNFORTUNATE FRIEND, YOU HAVE FOILED THE PLANS OF BOROMANIA FAR TOO MANY TIMES IN YOUR FORM OF MARVELMAN. THIS TIME YOU'LL BE ELIMINATED. NO LONGER ARE WE INTERESTED IN JUST OBTAINING THE PLANS OF THE XB999. THE PLANE IT-SELF IS NOW OUR OBJECTIVE.

THE BOMBER IS BEING PREPARED TO DROP AN ATOMIC BOMB IN THE ARIZONA DESERT TESTING AREA. WE SHALL BE FLYING THAT BOMBER— YOU WILL BE STRAPPED TO THE BOMB — BUT THAT BOMB WILL NOT DROP IN ARIZONA! OH, NO! THE CENTRE OF WASHINGTON IS THE TARGET.

SOME DAYS LATER ON A HUGE AIRFIELD. THE XB999 IS BEING WARMED-UP READY FOR THE TAKEOFF THE ATOMIC BOMB IS ABOARD.....

WELL, BUB. SHE'S ALL SET UP AND WAITIN' TO GO.

CREW WILL BE ON THE WAY OUT, SOON.

..SUDDENLY..

WOOSH

YIPES!

GUNS BLAZING THREE TANKB RUMBLE ACROSS THE TARMAC IN A CLOUD OF BMOKE.....

BANG

HA! BALCO DOESN'T USE HALF MEASURES

AIRFIELD GUARDS ARE RUSHED TO DEFEND THE XB999 ....

YOOOOOOOWWHHHH

DING...DING...DING...

AH! THESE SOLDIERS STAND NO CHANCE AGAINGT US! GET READY TO BOARD THE PLANE

THE BATTLE IS FURIOUS BUT THE BOROMANIAN'S SUPERIOR FIRE POWER SOON FORCES THE AIRFIELD'S DEFENDERS TO RETREAT......

MICKY IS BUNDLED ABOARD AND THE BOROMANIANS FOLLOW...

AH! TRIUMPH!

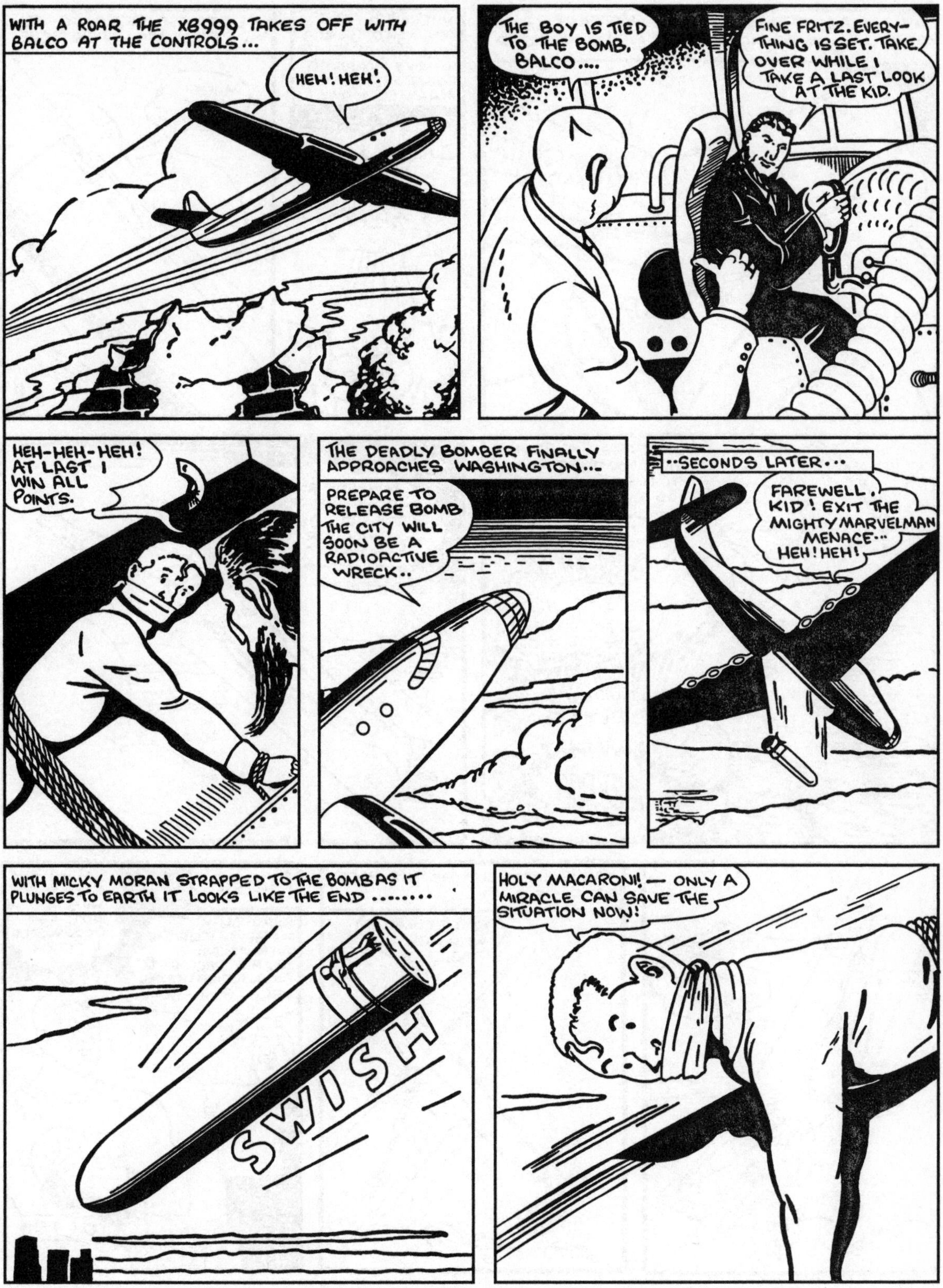
WITH A ROAR THE XB999 TAKES OFF WITH BALCO AT THE CONTROLS...
HEH! HEH!
THE BOY IS TIED TO THE BOMB, BALCO....
FINE FRITZ. EVERYTHING IS SET. TAKE OVER WHILE I TAKE A LAST LOOK AT THE KID.
HEH-HEH-HEH! AT LAST I WIN ALL POINTS.
THE DEADLY BOMBER FINALLY APPROACHES WASHINGTON...
PREPARE TO RELEASE BOMB THE CITY WILL SOON BE A RADIOACTIVE WRECK..
..SECONDS LATER...
FAREWELL, KID! EXIT THE MIGHTY MARVELMAN MENACE... HEH! HEH!
WITH MICKY MORAN STRAPPED TO THE BOMB AS IT PLUNGES TO EARTH IT LOOKS LIKE THE END ....
SWISH
HOLY MACARONI! — ONLY A MIRACLE CAN SAVE THE SITUATION NOW!

BUT THE AGE OF MIRACLES IS NOT PAST... AS THE BOMB'S PARACHUTE OPENS, IT RIPS MICKY'S GAG.
KIMOTA!
SNAP
IMMEDIATELY, THE KEY WORD BRINGS DOWN ATOMIC STRENGTH ON MICKY MORAN TO TRANSFORM HIM INTO MARVELMAN!
WOOF
..HE RIPS OFF THE PARACHUTE AND SPEEDS OFF WITH THE BOMB
MUST MOVE FAST!
THE OCEAN'S THE BEST PLACE FOR THAT-AND NOT A SECOND TOO SOON
BOOM!
NOW FOR BALCO AND THE XB 999. GUESS HE'LL BE HEADING FOR BOROMANIA
AH! THERE HE GOES
MARVELMAN GRABS THE HUGE AIRCRAFT AND....
YOU'RE COMING WITH ME.
LATER..
BLAH-BLAH' ON BEHALF OF THE UNITED BLAH.... YOU ARE DECLARED AN INTERNATIONAL HERO - BLAH-BLAH.
THANKS, BUT ALL I DID WAS MY DUTY AS A GOOD WORLD CITIZEN
THE END

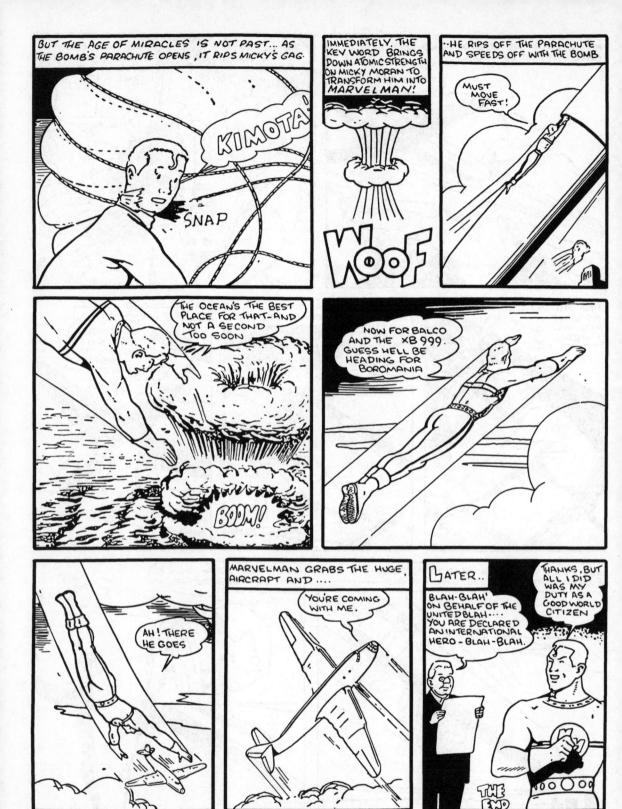

MARVELMAN
AND THE STOLEN RADIUM

A recluse Astro-Scientist discovers the key word to the Universe, one that can only be given to a Boy who is completely honest, studious, and of such integrity that he would only use it for the powers of good. He finds such a Boy in MICKY MORAN, a Newspaper Copy Boy, and treats him in a special machine which enables him to use the secret. Just before the Scientist dies he tells MICKY the Key Word which is KIMOTA.

MICKY MORAN remains as he was, but when he says the Key Word KIMOTA he becomes MARVELMAN, a Man of such strength and powers that he is Invincible and Indestructible.

SPLOP!

EVERYBODY KNOWS THE DEADLY PROPERTIES OF RADIUM. QUICK WORK BY MARVELMAN IS REQUIRED WHEN RADIUM, STOLEN BY CROOKS, IS LOST AND THREATENS THE DISTRICTS WATER SUPPLY......

A TRUCK DRIVES UP TO THE SCIENTIFIC INSTITUTE OF OKLABAMA ....

SCIENTIFIC INSTITUTE OF OKLAHOMA

WELL, JOE THIS IS THE LAST CONSIGNMENT OF RADIUM WE DELIVER TODAY LETS GET MOVING - HUH?

THE MEN DON PROTECTIVE CLOTHING AND PREPARE TO UNLOAD THE RADIUM....

BE GLAD TO GET THIS LOT OF OUR HANDS. BIGGEST CONSIGNMENT WE EVER HANDLED...

STEADY, PAL. EASY DOES IT!

BUT JUST AS THEY GET THE CANISTER OUT....

YIPES! WHAT GOES ON?

OK BOYS! MOVE FAST!

SCREECH

OUT OF THE AUTOMOBILE, SPRING THREE TOUGH-LOOKING CHARACTERS. A FOURTH REMAINS AT THE WHEEL.

THIS IS A SOFT TOUCH!

GRAB THAT BOX, SHINER! WE'LL FIX THESE TWO MUGS

SURE, PAL

BONK!

SLAM!

THE TRUCKMEN ARE QUICKLY OVERPOWERED....

WOW! MUST WEIGH A TON

GET IT ABOARD, AND LET'S HIT THE ROAD!

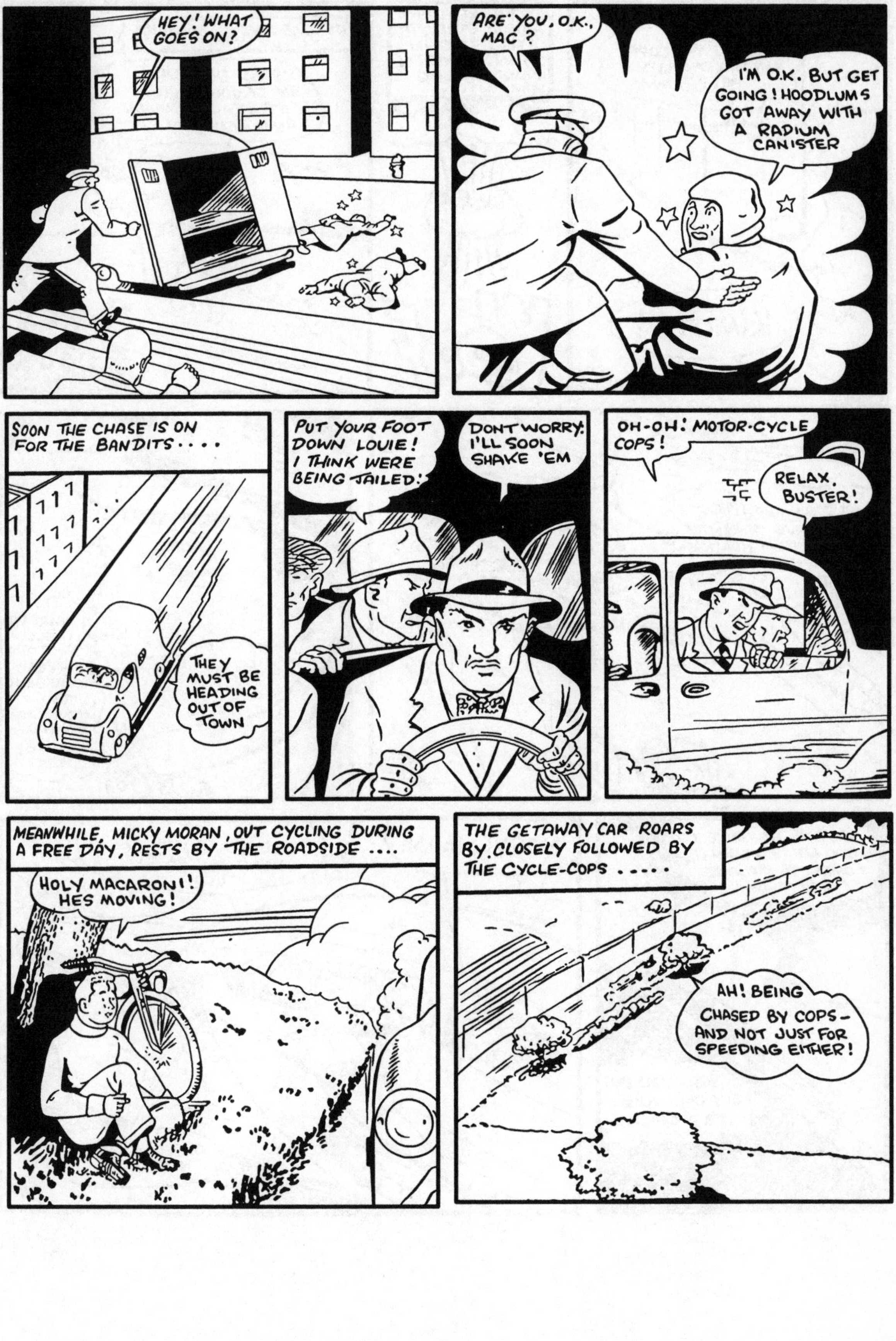

HEY! WHAT GOES ON?
ARE YOU, O.K., MAC ?
I'M O.K. BUT GET GOING! HOODLUMS GOT AWAY WITH A RADIUM CANISTER
SOON THE CHASE IS ON FOR THE BANDITS....
THEY MUST BE HEADING OUT OF TOWN
PUT YOUR FOOT DOWN LOUIE! I THINK WERE BEING JAILED!
DONT WORRY: I'LL SOON SHAKE 'EM
OH-OH! MOTOR-CYCLE COPS!
RELAX, BUSTER!
MEANWHILE, MICKY MORAN, OUT CYCLING DURING A FREE DAY, RESTS BY THE ROADSIDE....
HOLY MACARONI! HES MOVING!
THE GETAWAY CAR ROARS BY, CLOSELY FOLLOWED BY THE CYCLE-COPS.....
AH! BEING CHASED BY COPS- AND NOT JUST FOR SPEEDING EITHER!

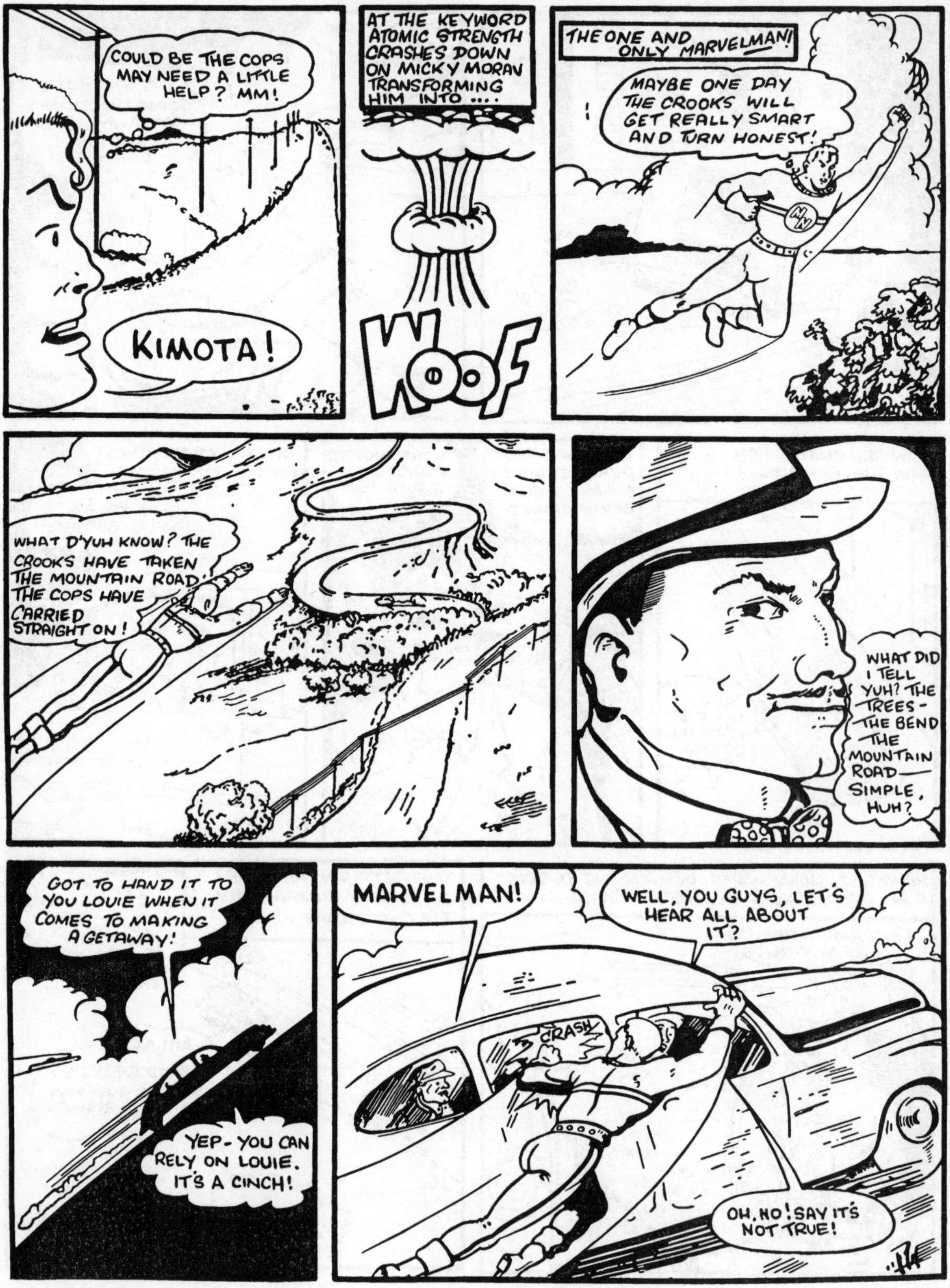
COULD BE THE COPS MAY NEED A LITTLE HELP? MM!
KIMOTA!
AT THE KEYWORD ATOMIC STRENGTH CRASHES DOWN ON MICKY MORAN TRANSFORMING HIM INTO....
WOOF
THE ONE AND ONLY MARVELMAN!
MAYBE ONE DAY THE CROOKS WILL GET REALLY SMART AND TURN HONEST!
WHAT D'YUH KNOW? THE CROOKS HAVE TAKEN THE MOUNTAIN ROAD. THE COPS HAVE CARRIED STRAIGHT ON!
WHAT DID I TELL YUH? THE TREES - THE BEND THE MOUNTAIN ROAD — SIMPLE, HUH?
GOT TO HAND IT TO YOU LOUIE WHEN IT COMES TO MAKING A GETAWAY!
YEP- YOU CAN RELY ON LOUIE. IT'S A CINCH!
MARVELMAN!
WELL, YOU GUYS, LET'S HEAR ALL ABOUT IT?
CRASH
OH, NO! SAY IT'S NOT TRUE!

MARVELMAN RIPS THE CAR DOOR OPEN AS IT REACHES THE TOP OF THE HILL ..
FIRST WE'LL STOP THIS HEAP!
BIF!
GET HIM!
BULLETS BOUNCE OFF THE MIGHTIEST MAN IN THE UNIVERSE....
TAP
PIT
... AS HE GRABS AT THE BRAKE LEVER ....
BUT DURING THE STRUGGLE THE AUTOMOBILE HAS BEGUN TO CAREER DOWN HILL ....
OOCH!
UGG
AND THE BRAKE IS APPLIED JUST TOO LATE..
CRASH
BUMP
EVERYBODY THROWN CLEAR
AS THE CROOKS TRY TO RUN, MARVELMAN... ACTS SWIFTLY ....
BAM
BIF
SLAM
ONE-TWO-THREE-FOUR!
POW
YEOOOW!
MEANWHILE ...

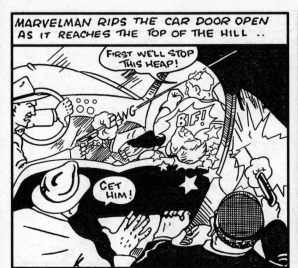

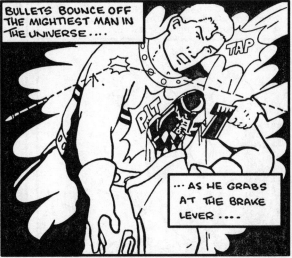

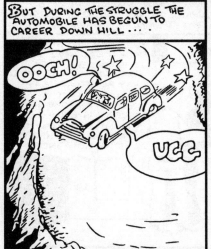

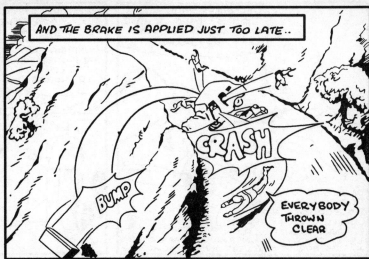

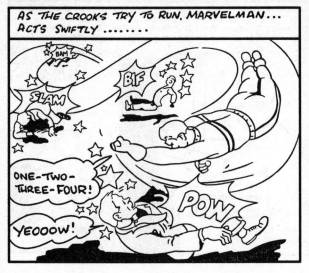

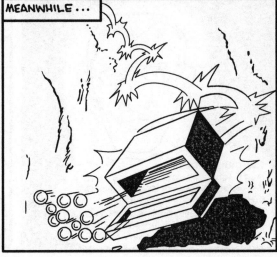

THE FORCE OF IMPACT BREAKS OPEN THE CANISTER AND THE RADIUM ROLLS INTO A CREVICE IN THE ROCKS ...

LATER. SCIENTIFIC INVESTIGATORS ARRIVE ON THE SCENE

NOTHING DOING— WITH THESE GEIGER COUNTERS ...

WELL, RADIUM IS DANGEROUS STUFF TO BE LEFT LYING AROUND. WE CAN ONLY HOPE IT HAS FALLEN DEEP INTO SOME CREVICE OUT OF HARMS WAY...

GEE! GUESS I'M TO BLAME FOR THIS! I SHOULD HAVE GRABBED THE BOX AND LEFT THE CROOKS...

DON'T BLAME YOURSELF, MARVELMAN. ALTHOUGH THOSE CROOKS ARE UNABLE TO GIVE US THEIR LEADER'S IDENTITY, AT LEAST THOSE FOUR UNSAVOURY CHARACTERS WILL BE OUT OF CIRCULATION FOR SOME TIME

MARVELMAN LEAVES WORD THAT SHOULD THERE BE ANY FURTHER DEVELOPMENTS, HE COULD BE CONTACTED THROUGH HIS YOUNG FRIEND, MICKY MORAN ...THEN..

MY EDITOR SAID YOU 'PHONED FOR ME TO COME ON OVER PROFESSOR.

YES, MICKY. WE'VE HAD SOME RATHER BAD NEWS AND IT IS POSSIBLE THAT MARVELMAN'S ASSISTANCE MAY BE REQUIRED. IN POINT OF FACT, IT SEEMS THAT THE WATER SUPPLY IS BECOMING POLLUTED WITH MINUTE PARTICLES OF RADIO-ACTIVE SUBSTANCES —

THE STOLEN RADIUM MUST HAVE FOUND ITS WAY INTO AN UNDERGROUND STREAM WHICH FLOWS INTO THE RIVER NEARBY THE CRITICAL QUESTION IS — HOW LONG WILL IT BE BEFORE THE WATER SUPPLY WILL BE UNFIT FOR HUMAN USE?

AND SO WE ARE FEEDING ALL DATA WE CAN GATHER INTO THIS ELECTRONIC BRAIN - THE GERUND - AND WE SHALL STAND BY FOR THE RESULTS ...IT SHOULD GIVE US THE EXACT LOCATION OF THE RADIUM!

HOLY MACARONI! SOME BRAIN.

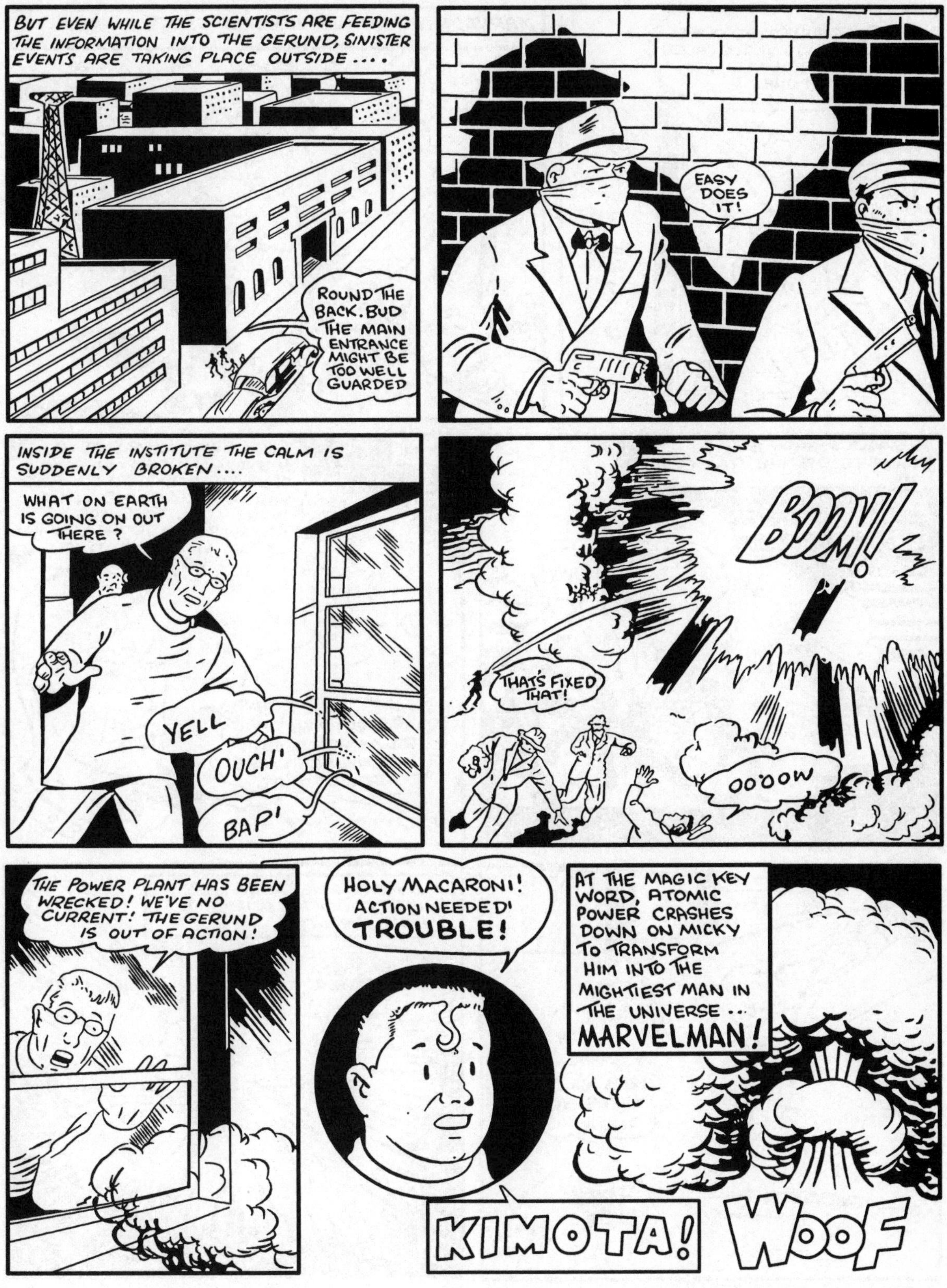
BUT EVEN WHILE THE SCIENTISTS ARE FEEDING THE INFORMATION INTO THE GERUND, SINISTER EVENTS ARE TAKING PLACE OUTSIDE....
ROUND THE BACK. BUD THE MAIN ENTRANCE MIGHT BE TOO WELL GUARDED
EASY DOES IT!
INSIDE THE INSTITUTE THE CALM IS SUDDENLY BROKEN....
WHAT ON EARTH IS GOING ON OUT THERE?
YELL
OUCH'
BAP'
BOOM!
THAT'S FIXED THAT!
OO'OOW
THE POWER PLANT HAS BEEN WRECKED! WE'VE NO CURRENT! THE GERUND IS OUT OF ACTION!
HOLY MACARONI! ACTION NEEDED! TROUBLE!
AT THE MAGIC KEY WORD, ATOMIC POWER CRASHES DOWN ON MICKY TO TRANSFORM HIM INTO THE MIGHTIEST MAN IN THE UNIVERSE... MARVELMAN!
KIMOTA!
WOOF

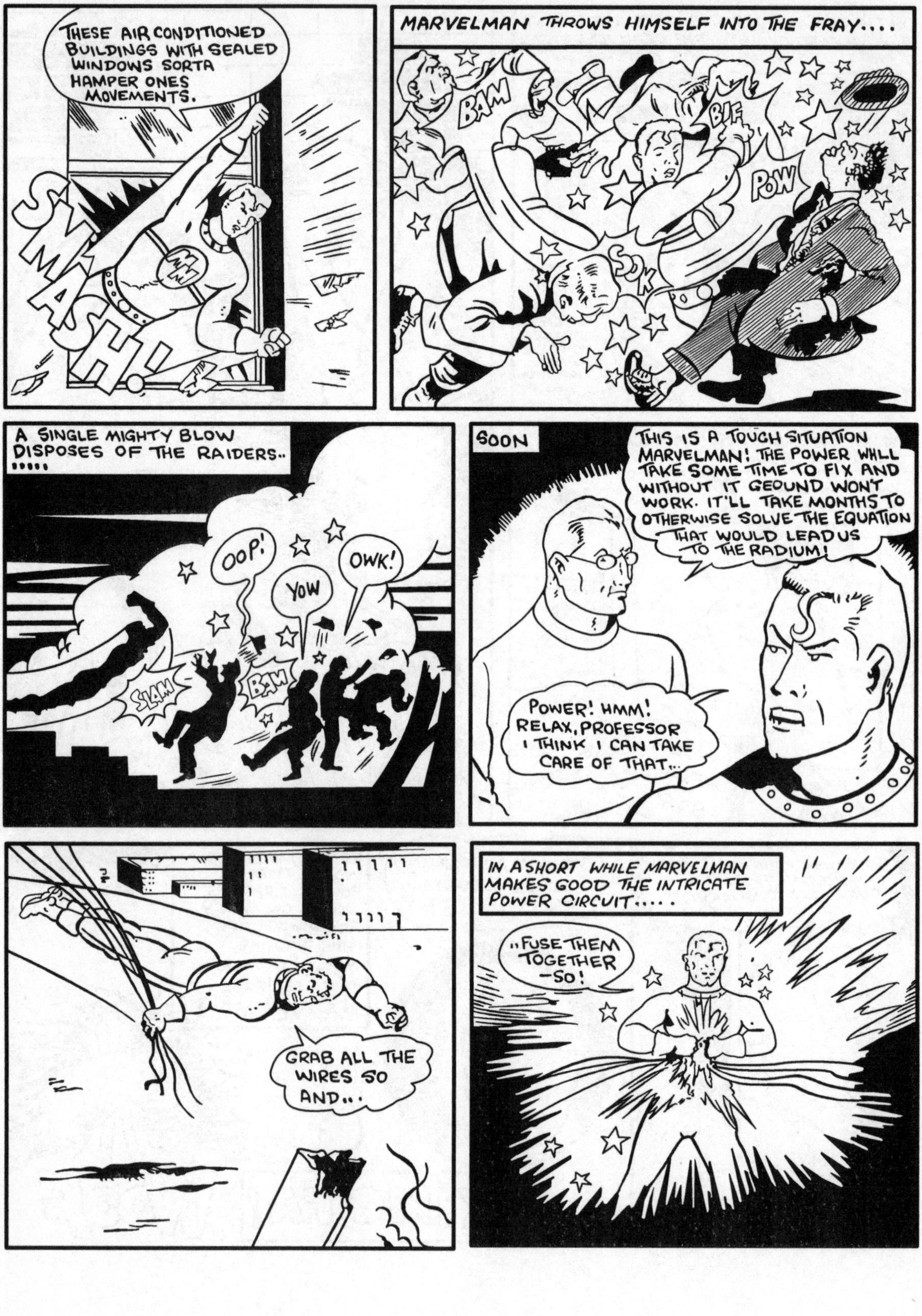
THESE AIR CONDITIONED BUILDINGS WITH SEALED WINDOWS SORTA HAMPER ONES MOVEMENTS.
SMASH!
MARVELMAN THROWS HIMSELF INTO THE FRAY....
BAM
BIF
POW
SOK
A SINGLE MIGHTY BLOW DISPOSES OF THE RAIDERS.. .....
OOP!
YOW
OWK!
SLAM
BAM
SOON
THIS IS A TOUCH SITUATION MARVELMAN! THE POWER WILL TAKE SOME TIME TO FIX AND WITHOUT IT GEOUND WON'T WORK. IT'LL TAKE MONTHS TO OTHERWISE SOLVE THE EQUATION THAT WOULD LEAD US TO THE RADIUM!
POWER! HMM! RELAX, PROFESSOR I THINK I CAN TAKE CARE OF THAT...
GRAB ALL THE WIRES SO AND...
IN A SHORT WHILE MARVELMAN MAKES GOOD THE INTRICATE POWER CIRCUIT.....
..FUSE THEM TOGETHER —SO!

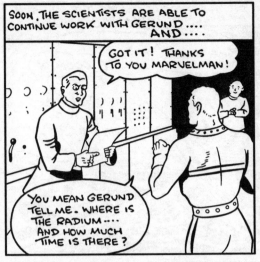

SOON, THE SCIENTISTS ARE ABLE TO CONTINUE WORK WITH GERUND.... AND....

GOT IT! THANKS TO YOU MARVELMAN!

YOU MEAN GERUND TELL ME. WHERE IS THE RADIUM.... AND HOW MUCH TIME IS THERE?

WE'VE THREE DAYS AT THE MOST BEFORE THE POLLUTION WILL BECOME DANGEROUS. IT IS SITUATED IN AN UNDERGROUND STREAM NEAR GOLT'S CAVE. A MAN IN A FROGMAN'S SUIT CAN SAVE THE SITUATION

WELL, PROF I DON'T NEED A FROGMAN'S OUTFIT— LETS GO!

A FEW HOURS LATER, ACCOMPANIED BY SCIENTISTS AND SECURITY OFFICERS, MARVELMAN ARRIVES AT THE CAVE....

THAT'S GOLT'S CAVE! IT LEADS DEEP INTO THE ROCKFACE AND OPENS OUT INTO AN UNDERGROUND STREAM

WELL! WHAT ARE WE WAITING FOR?

SO..

AH! THE WATER!

GETTING DEEPER.... SO ... UNDER WE GO

MARVELMAN STREAKS THROUGH THE DARK WATERS SWIFTER THAN ANY FISH ....

CANT BE FAR OFF NOW!

BUT WHEN MARVELMAN REACHES THE LOCATION HE IS SURPRISED TO FIND THAT THE RADIUM HAS ALREADY BEEN RECOVERED AND IS BEING LOADED ONTO A BOAT IN THE UNDERGROUND STREAM

SO THAT'S IT! THIS STREAM IS MORE LIKE A RIVER....

OUT OF THE DEPTHS COMES THE ONE AND ONLY MARVELMAN, WITH FLAILING FISTS...

THIS TIME THERE'LL BE NO SLIP-UP!

OOOMPH

BIF

MARVELMAN!

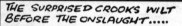

THE SURPRISED CROOKS WILT BEFORE THE ONSLAUGHT.....

BM

AHA! YOU NEED FLYING SUITS

BOP

SOON MARVELMAN BRINGS THE CROOKS AND THE RADIUM TO THE SURFACE-

WONDERFUL MARVELMAN! YOU'RE A MARVEL NOW TO UNMASK THESE CROOKS!

MAYBE WE CAN FIND THE BRAIN BEHIND ALL THIS ...

YIPES! PROFESSOR HATZ!

BAH!

YOU ONLY BEAT ME BECAUSE OF THAT BIG BLUE BOMBHEAD! MY MEN WOULD HAVE GOT CLEAR AWAY WITH THE RADIUM THE FIRST TIME, WERE IT NOT FOR HIM.... HE ALSO FOILED ME WHEN I PUT YOUR ELECTRONIC BRAIN OUT OF ACTION - WHILE I WAS COMPUTING ON MY OWN.... AND NOW HE TURNS UP TO THWART ME ONCE MORE - A CURSE ON HIS BIG BULLET-HEAD. BAH AND BAH AGAIN!

LATER

WELL, MICKY GUESS WE DID A GOOD JOB, EH?

KIMOTA

YED, MARVELMAN WE SURE DID...

WOOF

THE END*

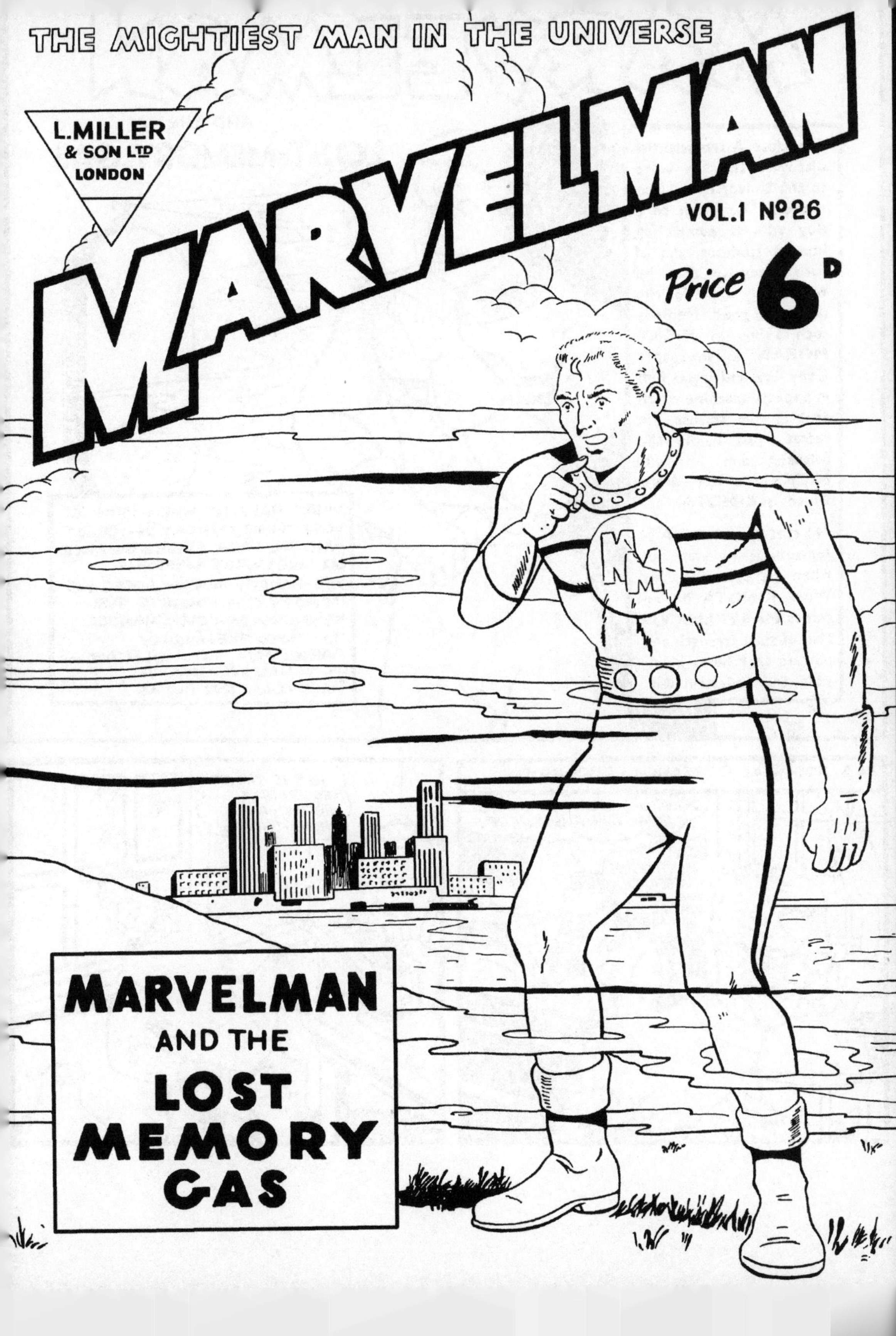
THE MIGHTIEST MAN IN THE UNIVERSE
L.MILLER & SON LTD LONDON
MARVELMAN
VOL.1 Nº26
Price 6D
MM
MARVELMAN AND THE LOST MEMORY GAS

MARVELMAN

AND THE
LOST-MEMORY GAS

A recluse Astro-Scientist discovers the key word to the Universe, one that can only be given to a Boy who is completely honest, studious, and of such integrity that he would only use it for the powers of good. He finds such a Boy in **MICKY MORAN**, a Newspaper Copy Boy, and treats him in a special machine which enables him to use the secret. Just before the Scientist dies he tells **MICKY** the Key Word which is **KIMOTA**.

MICKY MORAN remains as he was, but when he says the Key Word **KIMOTA** he becomes **MARVELMAN**, a Man of such strength and powers that he is Invincible and Indestructible.

WHAT HAPPENS WHEN PEOPLE LOSE THEIR MEMORY? — FORGET WHO THEY ARE - WHERE THEY WORK OR LIVE! WHAT HAPPENS WHEN MICKY MORAN LOSES HIS MEMORY? — FORGETS THE KEYWORD WHICH CHANGES HIM INTO THE MIGHTY MARVELMAN. A HOLIDAY --- OR SHALL WE SAY-- A FIELD-DAY FOR CRIME!

IN A HOSPITAL RESEARCH LABORATORY....

WOW! RECKON I'M ON TO SOMETHING BIG HERE!

BAH! ANAESTHETICS IN RESEARCH ARE A WASTE OF TIME!

THIS IS GREAT! YESSIR! THIS FORMULA IS DEVASTATING!

WHAT STUPID THING HAVE YOU HIT ON THIS TIME, MY DEAR FETHERED? BAH! YOUR FORMULA WILL ASTOUND NOBODY.
BUT THIS TIME I HAVE MADE A GREAT DISCOVERY!
I'VE PRODUCED A GAS IN THIS CYLINDER FROM MY LATEST FORMULA, WHICH CAN CAUSE PEOPLE TO LOSE THEIR MEMORIES TEMPORARILY!
A LOST MEMORY GAS, EH? HAK-HAK! IT SEEMS INTERESTING. I'LL TAKE THAT FORMULA— FLUTTERSKULL! YOU TAKE THAT! HAK-HAK!
BIF
...AND I GUESS I'LL TAKE THAT CYLINDER, TOO!
BIM
ONCE AGAIN MY GENIUS FOR DISGUISE HAS PROVED PROFITABLE!
BUT THE ALARM IS QUICKLY RAISED......
PROFESSOR ZARGUNGA'S GONE HAYWIRE! GET HIM!
STOP THAT GUY!
SOON THROUGH THE HOSPITAL CORRIDORS A WILD CHASE IS IN PROGRESS.....
THERE HE GOES!
HAK-HAK-HAK! HACK-HACK!
STOP HIM

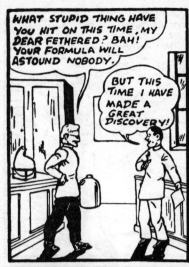

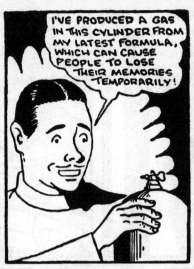

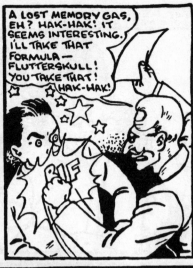

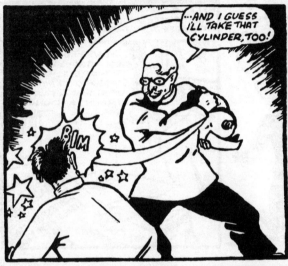

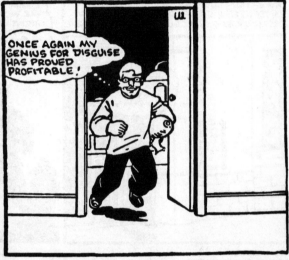

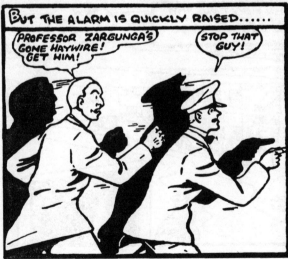

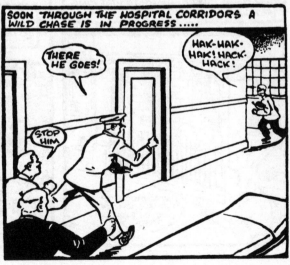

BUT THE THIEF IS NO ORDINARY THIEF AND DOES NOT LACK CUNNING ....

HAK. HAK! WHEN THEY TURN THAT CORNER, WILL THEY GET A BIG SURPRISE!

SAY BUD! WHAT ARE WE DOING RUNNING ALONG THE CORRIDORS?

WHY! WE'VE GOT TO CATCH — ER..JEEPERS! I CAN'T REMEMBER!

ER...WASN'T I RUNNING TO CATCH A TRAIN?

WITH THE HOSPITAL STAFF THROWN INTO UTTER CONFUSION BY THE LOST MEMORY GAS, THE THIEF IS FREE TO LEAVE

HAK-HAK! THIS GAS CAN MAKE ME A LOT OF MONEY!

I WILL ASTOUND THE WORLD! A GREAT AND WONDERFUL PLAN IS BUILDING UP IN MY MIND. I CAN'T HELP BUT SUCCEED.

NEXT MORNING IN THE OFFICE OF THE "DAILY BUGLE" MICKY MORAN IS ATTRACTED BY THE HEADLINES.....

YOW! PROFESSOR ZARGUNGA! — WONDER IF THAT EVIL SCIENTIST, GARGUNZA IS MIXED UP IN THIS AFFAIR. ZARGUNZA SOUNDS PHONEY.

DAILY BUG...
PROFESSOR ZARGU...
STEALS NEW ME...
GAS.

SOME DAYS LATER, MICKY IS WALKING THROUGH THE WEALTHIER PART OF THE TOWN

HMM! MOST OF THE BIG SHOTS LIVE IN THIS AREA!

...BUT WHEN MICKY TURNS INTO THE STREET OF THE MOST ELITE, HE SEES A STRANGE SIGHT.......

EASY WITH THAT, BUSTER.

WHEE! WHAT'S GOING ON HERE?

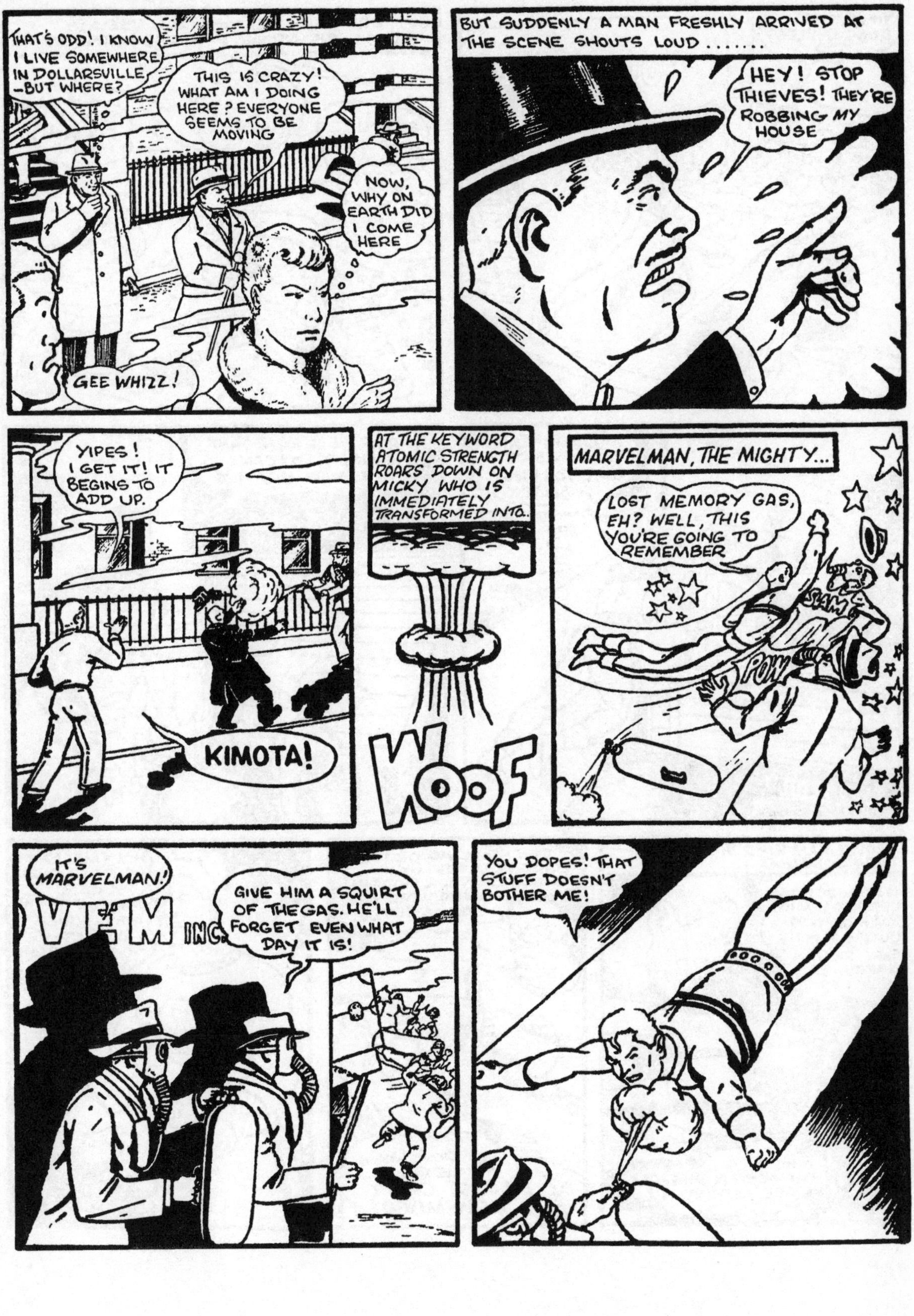

THAT'S ODD! I KNOW I LIVE SOMEWHERE IN DOLLARSVILLE —BUT WHERE?
THIS IS CRAZY! WHAT AM I DOING HERE? EVERYONE SEEMS TO BE MOVING
NOW, WHY ON EARTH DID I COME HERE
GEE WHIZZ!
BUT SUDDENLY A MAN FRESHLY ARRIVED AT THE SCENE SHOUTS LOUD ....
HEY! STOP THIEVES! THEY'RE ROBBING MY HOUSE
YIPES! I GET IT! IT BEGINS TO ADD UP.
KIMOTA!
AT THE KEYWORD ATOMIC STRENGTH ROARS DOWN ON MICKY WHO IS IMMEDIATELY TRANSFORMED INTO..
WOOF
MARVELMAN, THE MIGHTY...
LOST MEMORY GAS, EH? WELL, THIS YOU'RE GOING TO REMEMBER
SLAM
POW
IT'S MARVELMAN!
GIVE HIM A SQUIRT OF THE GAS. HE'LL FORGET EVEN WHAT DAY IT IS!
VEM INC.
YOU DOPES! THAT STUFF DOESN'T BOTHER ME!

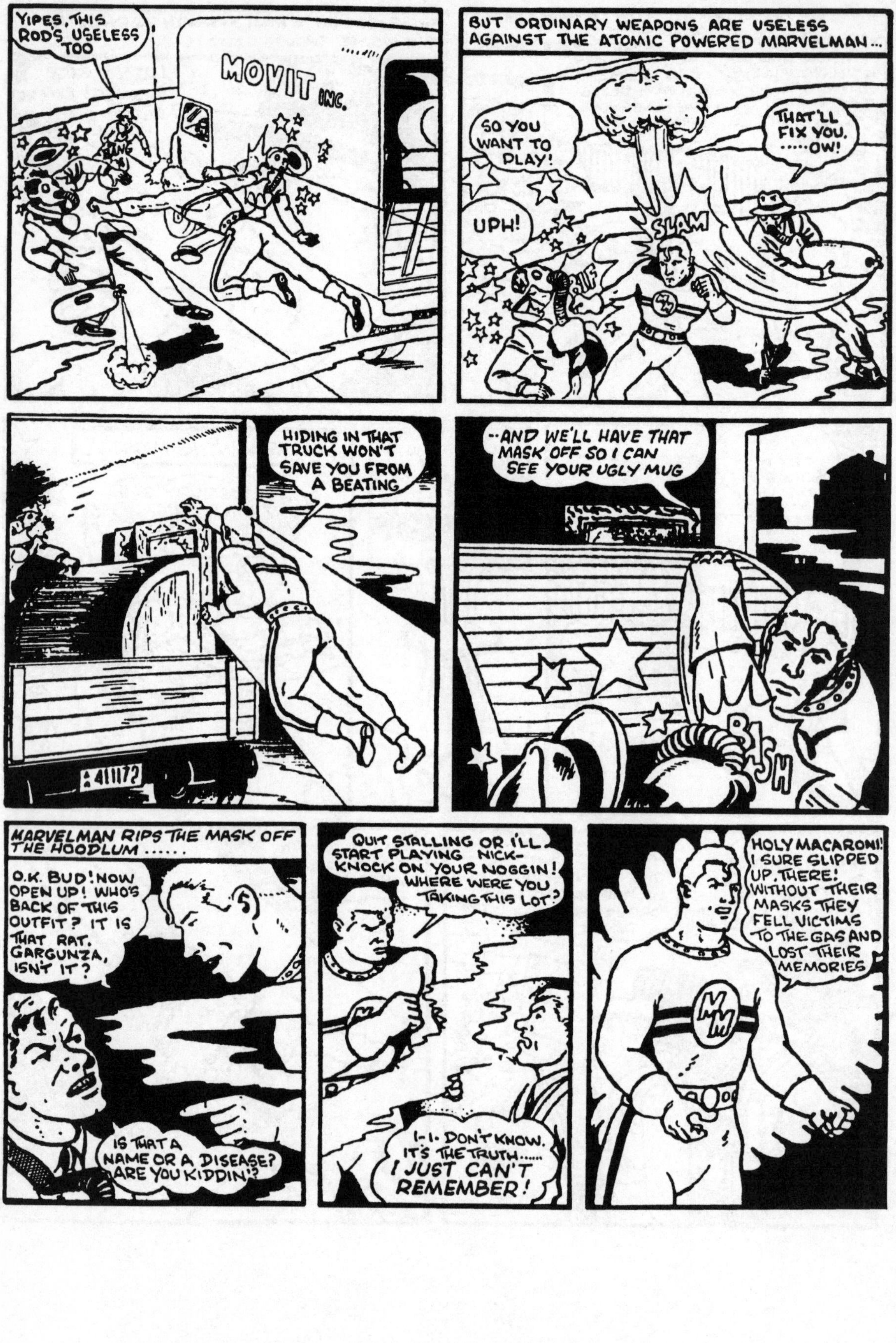
YIPES, THIS ROD'S USELESS TOO
MOVIT INC.
BUT ORDINARY WEAPONS ARE USELESS AGAINST THE ATOMIC POWERED MARVELMAN...
SO YOU WANT TO PLAY!
THAT'LL FIX YOU. .....OW!
UPH!
SLAM
HIDING IN THAT TRUCK WON'T SAVE YOU FROM A BEATING
--AND WE'LL HAVE THAT MASK OFF SO I CAN SEE YOUR UGLY MUG
BASH
MARVELMAN RIPS THE MASK OFF THE HOODLUM ......
O.K. BUD! NOW OPEN UP! WHO'S BACK OF THIS OUTFIT? IT IS THAT RAT, GARGUNZA, ISN'T IT?
IS THAT A NAME OR A DISEASE? ARE YOU KIDDIN'?
QUIT STALLING OR I'LL START PLAYING NICK-KNOCK ON YOUR NOGGIN! WHERE WERE YOU TAKING THIS LOT?
I-I- DON'T KNOW. IT'S THE TRUTH...... I JUST CAN'T REMEMBER!
HOLY MACARONI! I SURE SLIPPED UP, THERE! WITHOUT THEIR MASKS THEY FELL VICTIMS TO THE GAS AND LOST THEIR MEMORIES

THERE'S ONE WAY TO SOLVE THE MYSTERY. I'LL LEAVE THESE GUYS TO RECOVER THEIR MEMORIES.....

MARVELMAN TAKES TO THE AIR..........

IF THOSE GUYS ARE DUMB ENOUGH THEY WILL LEAD ME TO THEIR LAIR

SOON....

O.K. BOYS! WHAT ARE WE WAITING FOR? LET'S GET ROLLING!

SOON THE LOOT-LADEN TRUCKS ARE HEADING TO SOMEWHERE OUT OF TOWN.......

HA-HA! MARVELMAN HAD TO GIVE UP

...BUT MARVELMAN IS NOT VERY FAR AWAY.....

THIS IS WHAT I FIGURED. THIS SHOULD BE A CINCH.

THEY'RE SURE GETTING AWAY FROM CIVILIZATION

WE SURE MADE OUT OKAY. LUCKY FOR US MARVELMAN SCRAMMED

REMOVALS

SOON THE TRUCKS TURN OFF THE ROAD INTO A TRACK THROUGH A WOOD........

33

DEEP INTO THE WOODS, THE TRUCKS RUMBLE ON...

BUT MARVELMAN IS THERE...ABOVE!

THEY SURE PICKED A WELL CAMOUFLAGED SPOT ..... HMM!

MEANWHILE, FROM A SHACK IN THE HEART OF THE WOODS, GARGUNZA CONTACTS THE TRUCKS...

YOU HAVE BEEN SUCCESSFUL?

EVERYTHING'S JUST JAKE, BOSS. WE HAD SOME TROUBLE WITH MARVELMAN BUT WE GAVE HIM THE SLIP!

BAH! THAT BIG BOY BLUE IS ALWAYS INTERFERING WITH MY PLANS!

STILL! THIS TIME THE BIG BLUE BUSYBODY HAS BEEN GIVEN THE SLIP... THE LOOT IS MINE. DIVINE! DIVINE! YAYEE!

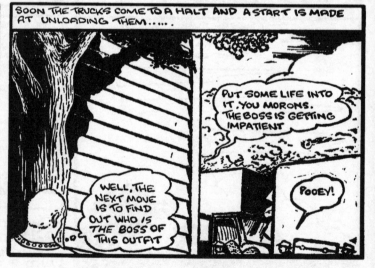

SOON THE TRUCKS COME TO A HALT AND A START IS MADE AT UNLOADING THEM......

PUT SOME LIFE INTO IT, YOU MORONS. THE BOSS IS GETTING IMPATIENT

WELL, THE NEXT MOVE IS TO FIND OUT WHO IS THE BOSS OF THIS OUTFIT

POOEY!

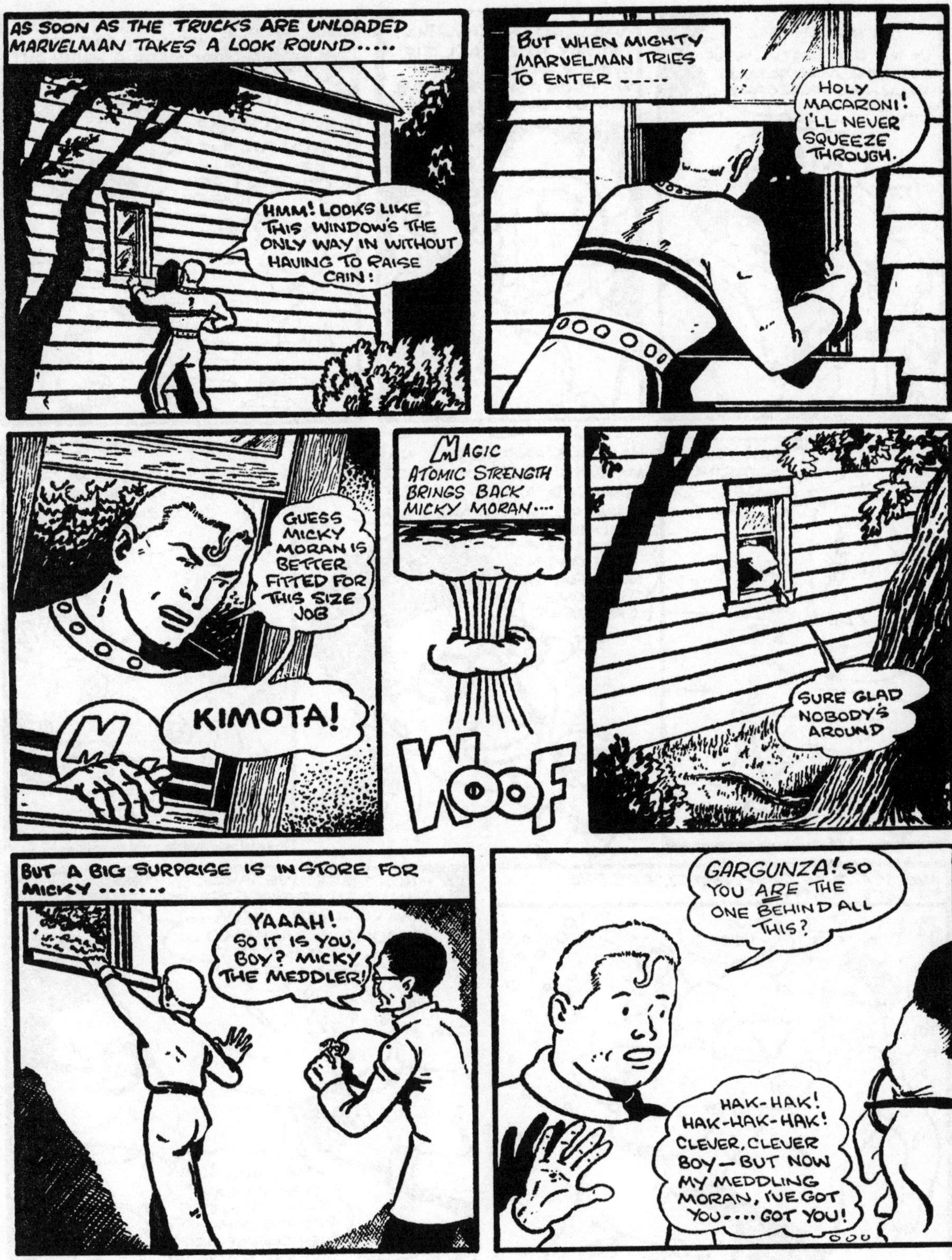
AS SOON AS THE TRUCKS ARE UNLOADED MARVELMAN TAKES A LOOK ROUND.....
HMM! LOOKS LIKE THIS WINDOW'S THE ONLY WAY IN WITHOUT HAVING TO RAISE CAIN!
BUT WHEN MIGHTY MARVELMAN TRIES TO ENTER -----
HOLY MACARONI! I'LL NEVER SQUEEZE THROUGH.
GUESS MICKY MORAN IS BETTER FITTED FOR THIS SIZE JOB
KIMOTA!
MAGIC ATOMIC STRENGTH BRINGS BACK MICKY MORAN....
WOOF
SURE GLAD NOBODY'S AROUND
BUT A BIG SURPRISE IS IN STORE FOR MICKY ....
YAAAH! SO IT IS YOU, BOY? MICKY THE MEDDLER!
GARGUNZA! SO YOU ARE THE ONE BEHIND ALL THIS?
HAK-HAK! HAK-HAK-HAK! CLEVER, CLEVER BOY— BUT NOW MY MEDDLING MORAN, I'VE GOT YOU.... GOT YOU!

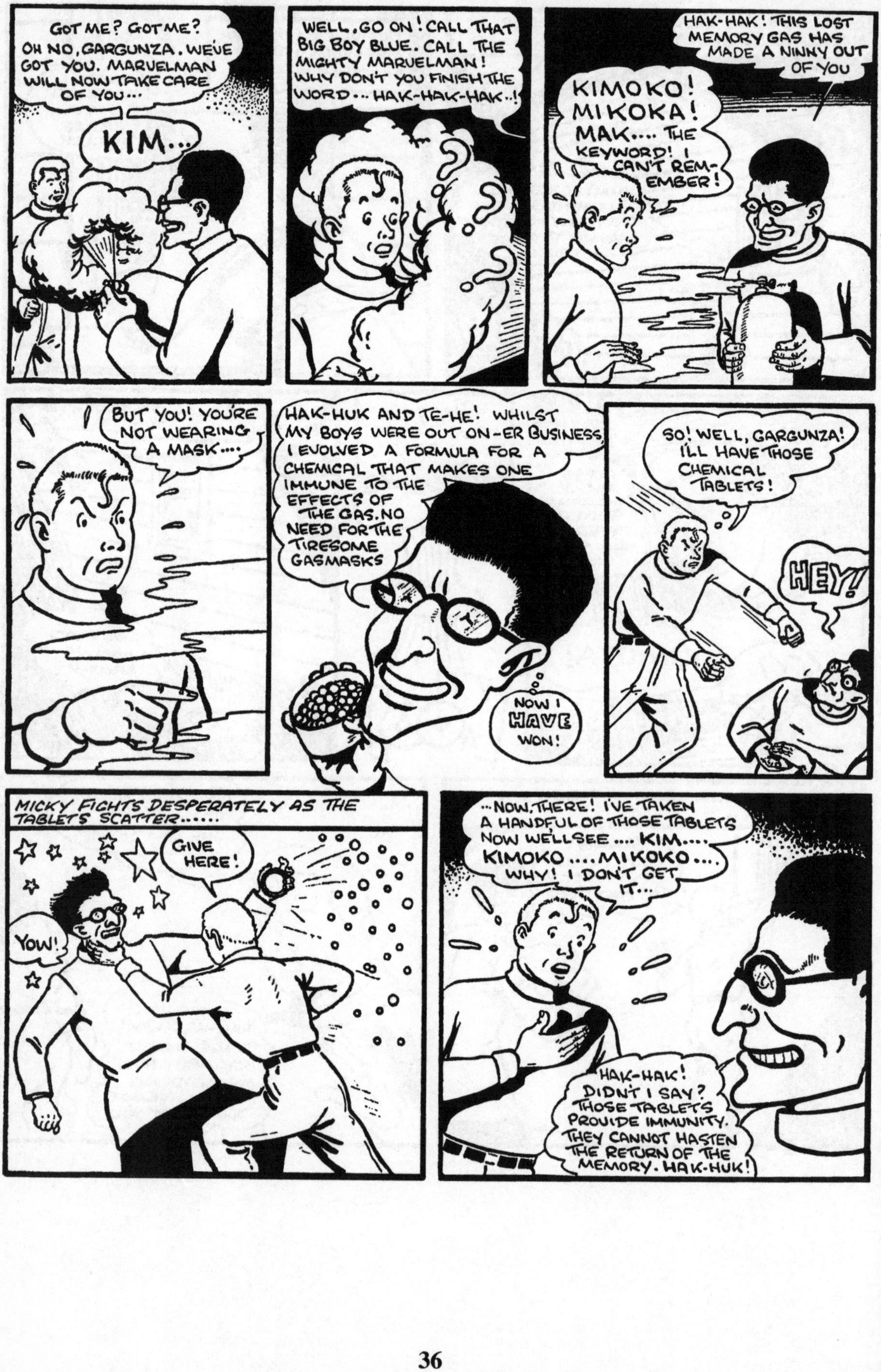
GOT ME? GOT ME? OH NO, GARGUNZA. WE'VE GOT YOU. MARVELMAN WILL NOW TAKE CARE OF YOU...
KIM...
WELL, GO ON! CALL THAT BIG BOY BLUE. CALL THE MIGHTY MARVELMAN! WHY DON'T YOU FINISH THE WORD... HAK-HAK-HAK..!
HAK-HAK! THIS LOST MEMORY GAS HAS MADE A NINNY OUT OF YOU
KIMOKO! MIKOKA! MAK.... THE KEYWORD! I CAN'T REMEMBER!
BUT YOU! YOU'RE NOT WEARING A MASK....
HAK-HUK AND TE-HE! WHILST MY BOYS WERE OUT ON-ER BUSINESS, I EVOLVED A FORMULA FOR A CHEMICAL THAT MAKES ONE IMMUNE TO THE EFFECTS OF THE GAS. NO NEED FOR THE TIRESOME GASMASKS
NOW I HAVE WON!
SO! WELL, GARGUNZA! I'LL HAVE THOSE CHEMICAL TABLETS!
HEY!
MICKY FIGHTS DESPERATELY AS THE TABLETS SCATTER......
GIVE HERE!
YOW!
...NOW, THERE! I'VE TAKEN A HANDFUL OF THOSE TABLETS NOW WE'LL SEE .... KIM.... KIMOKO .... MIKOKO.... WHY! I DON'T GET IT...
HAK-HAK! DIDN'T I SAY? THOSE TABLETS PROVIDE IMMUNITY. THEY CANNOT HASTEN THE RETURN OF THE MEMORY. HAK-HUK!

SUDDENLY MICKY REALISES HIS POSITION..
HOLY MACARONI! I'VE GOT TO GET OUT OF HERE... BUT FAST!
STOP HIM!
O.K. BOSS! HE WON'T GET FAR
BUT MICKY IS VERY NIMBLE ON HIS FEET...
OW! THE LITTLE RUNT TRIPPED ME
I'LL STOP HIS MAD GALLOP!
SLAM!
BAH! HE'S TRIPPED ME TOO!
JEEPERS! I DON'T KNOW WHY I'M HERE OR REALLY WHY I'M RUNNING. I JUST KNOW I'VE GOT TO GET OUT OF HERE!
GOT TO GET AWAY- GOT TO GET OUT!
BANG
STOP HIM! HE'S GOING UP TO MY NEW LAB.
WOW! THEY'RE SURE ACTING MIGHTY UNSOCIABLE!

AT THE TOP OF THE STAIRS MICKY SEES A CHAIR.... HE PAUSES AND....

THIS MIGHT SLOW THEM DOWN!

CRUMP

UGHHH!

AH-HA! A LABORATORY! GOT A HUNCH IT'S FOR A NO-GOOD PURPOSE

....AH! HOW VERY CONVENIENT! THAT'S THE WAY OUT FOR ME

BUT MICKY HAS A SUBCONSCIOUS FEELING THAT THE LABORATORY SHOULD BE WRECKED... SO ----

SMASH! CRASH! BASH!

WOW! THOSE CHEMICALS DON'T SEEM TO TAKE TO EACH OTHER TOO KINDLY!

BOOM!

FIRE! FIRE! GET THAT FIRE UNDER CONTROL....

THAT'LL KEEP THEM BUSY!

MICKY CLIMBS TO THE GROUND AND LOOKING ROUND FOR A HIDING PLACE DECIDES ON A TRUCK...

I'LL GET IN HERE FOR A BREATHING SPELL....

FIRE'S OUT, BOSS! DAT MAKES EVERYTHING JUST DANDY

RELAX NOTHING, YOU DOPES.. OUR POSITION IS VERY PRECARIOUS ......

MEANING WE CAN RELAX! PHEW!

DO YOU NOT REALISE WHAT HAS HAPPENED? THE BRAT HAS ESCAPED INTO THE FOREST. WHEN THE EFFECTS OF THE GAS WEAR OFF AND HE RECOVERS HIS MEMORY, HE WILL RETURN AS MARVELMAN!

ALL THIS LOOT MUST BE LOADED ON THE TRUCKS IMMEDIATELY. WE'RE PULLING OUT

FROM HIS POSITION IN THE TRUCK, MICKY WATCHES THE WORK OF RELOADING....

STACKING FURNITURE, PICTURES, BOXES IN THE TRUCKS.! I WONDER WHY? THERE'S SOMETHING BEHIND THIS I CAN'T SEEM TO REMEMBER.

O.K. BUDDY! EASY DOES IT!

WITH GARGUNZA IN THE LEADING TRUCK, THE FLEET IS SOON MOVING..
SHIFT INC.
HOO! HOO! WE'LL SOON BE CLEAR AWAY.
MICKY IS STILL UNDER THE EFFECTS OF THE GAS.
JUST DOESN'T ADD UP. WHY THE QUICK MOVE?
SOON...
WOW! I'M BEGINNING TO REMEMBER!.... LOST MEMORY GAS STOLEN.... WALK THROUGH DOLLARSVILLE... CROOKS STRIPPING HOUSES....
YEAH! TRAILED TRUCKS... BIG WOOD... TRUCKS UNLOADED... BIG SHACK...
SCOUTED AROUND.. WINDOW TOO SMALL FOR MAN... SHOUT TO CHANGE TO BOY .... GUESS I MUST HAVE SHOUTED TO LOUD.. GARGUNZA MUST HAVE HEARD AND WAS WAITING
OVALS INC.
...AHEM! I GUESS IT'S ABOUT TIME FOR MARVELMAN TO TAKE OVER AGAIN..
KIMOTA!
DOWN COMES THE ATOMIC STRENGTH THAT CHANGES MICKY INTO THE .... MIGHTY..
WOOF
MARVELMAN....

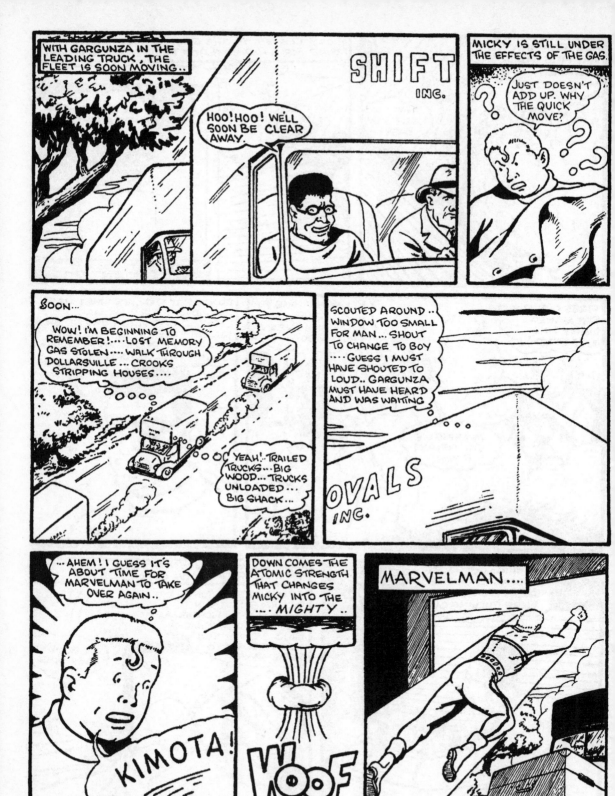

GUESS GARGUNZA WILL BE IN THE LEADING TRUCK
MARVELMAN APPROACHES THE LEADING TRUCK AS...
HAK-HAK. FOOLED THE BIG BLUE BABOON ONCE MORE
MARVELMAN!
CAN'T BE!
MARVELMAN JERKS OPEN THE TRUCK DOOR
HI, GARGUNZA!
IN AN INSTANT MARVELMAN JAMS ON THE BRAKE BRINGING THE CONVOY TO A SUDDEN HALT..
WHAT IN TARNATION?
HEY!
OOOW!
BASH
CRUMP
SLAM
BUMP
YIPES! WHAT'S THAT?
UGH!
BIF
BOP
THAT'S A DOUBLE-CRACKER
BIM
BAM

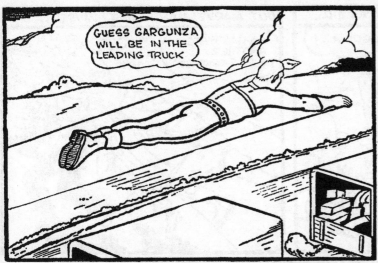

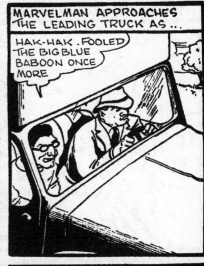

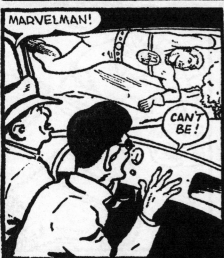

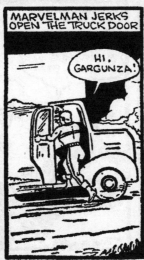

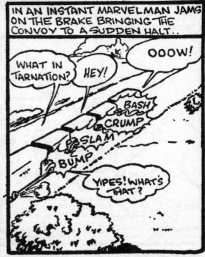

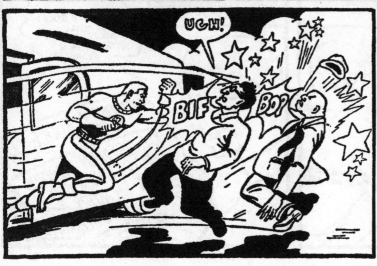

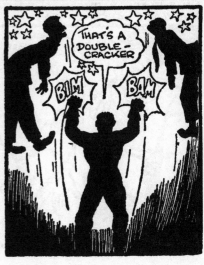

THE HOODLUMS RUSH TO GARGUNZA'S AID...

OOOOW...!

FURNITURE REMOVAL

POW!

BUT MARVELMAN IS JUST AMUSED....

HA-HA! THAT'S ANOTHER DOUBLE-CRACKER!

SOK! SLAK!

HOLY MACARONI! THAT'S BETTER STILL! — A TRIPLE-CRACKER!

MARVELMAN PILES HIS VICTIMS INTO A TRUCK......

BUT.. MEANWHILE GARGUNZA SLIPS AWAY!

WHILE THAT BIG BLUE BOTTLE IS BUSY, I'LL BEAT IT

WHY! THE LITTLE WEASEL!

IN A FLASH MARVELMAN REACHES THE LUCKLESS GARGUNZA AND ...

THERE! A DOUBLE WHAMMY

WHAM!

NEXT DAY..

HAA! MY GOOD COMPANION, MARVELMAN.. IN THE NEWS AGAIN!!

3d DAILY BUGLE

MARVELMAN BRINGS GARGUNZA AND LOST-MEMORY GANG TO JUSTICE

THE END!

42

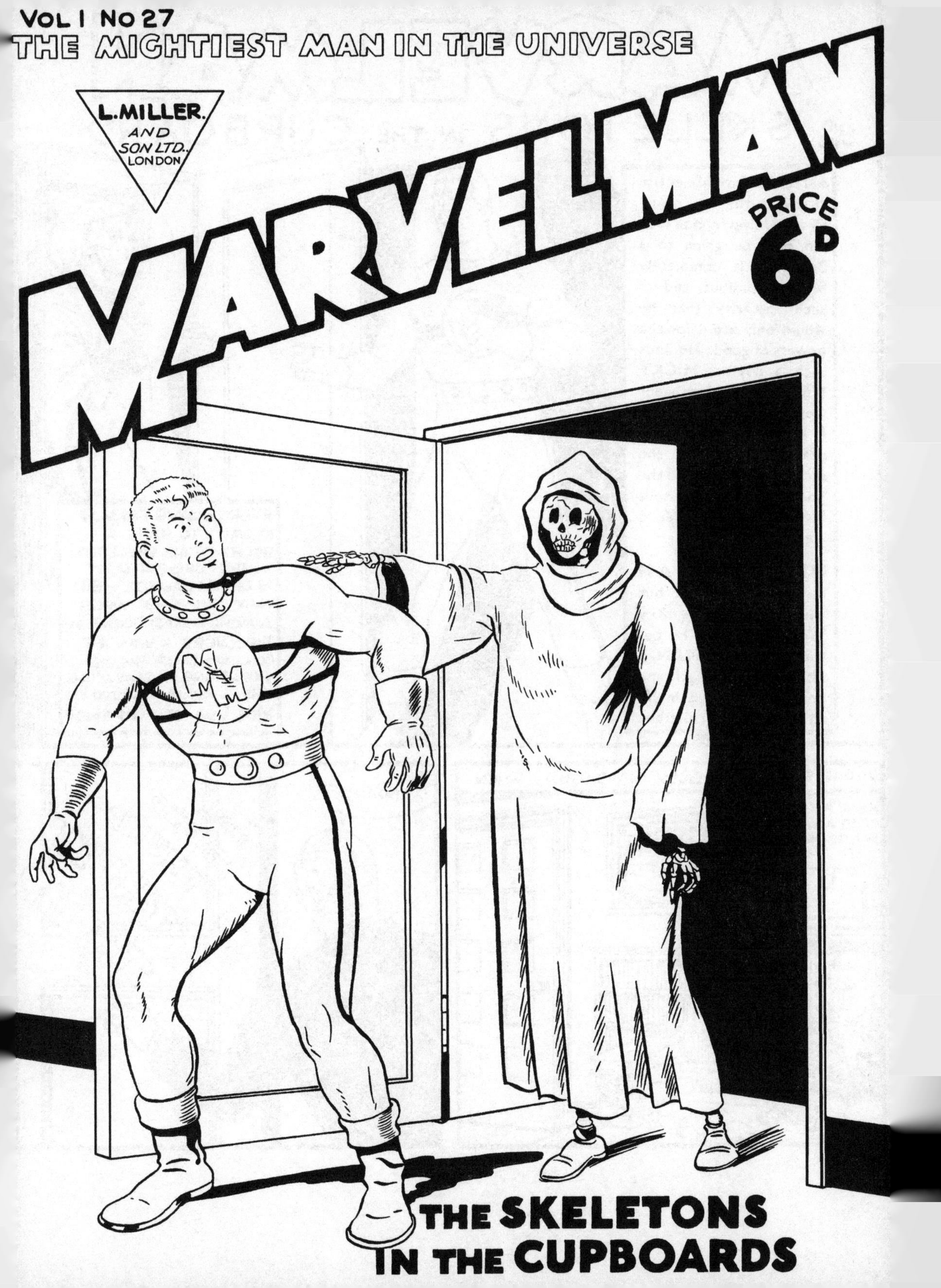
VOL 1 NO 27
THE MIGHTIEST MAN IN THE UNIVERSE
L. MILLER. AND SON LTD., LONDON
MARVELMAN
PRICE 6D
THE SKELETONS IN THE CUPBOARDS

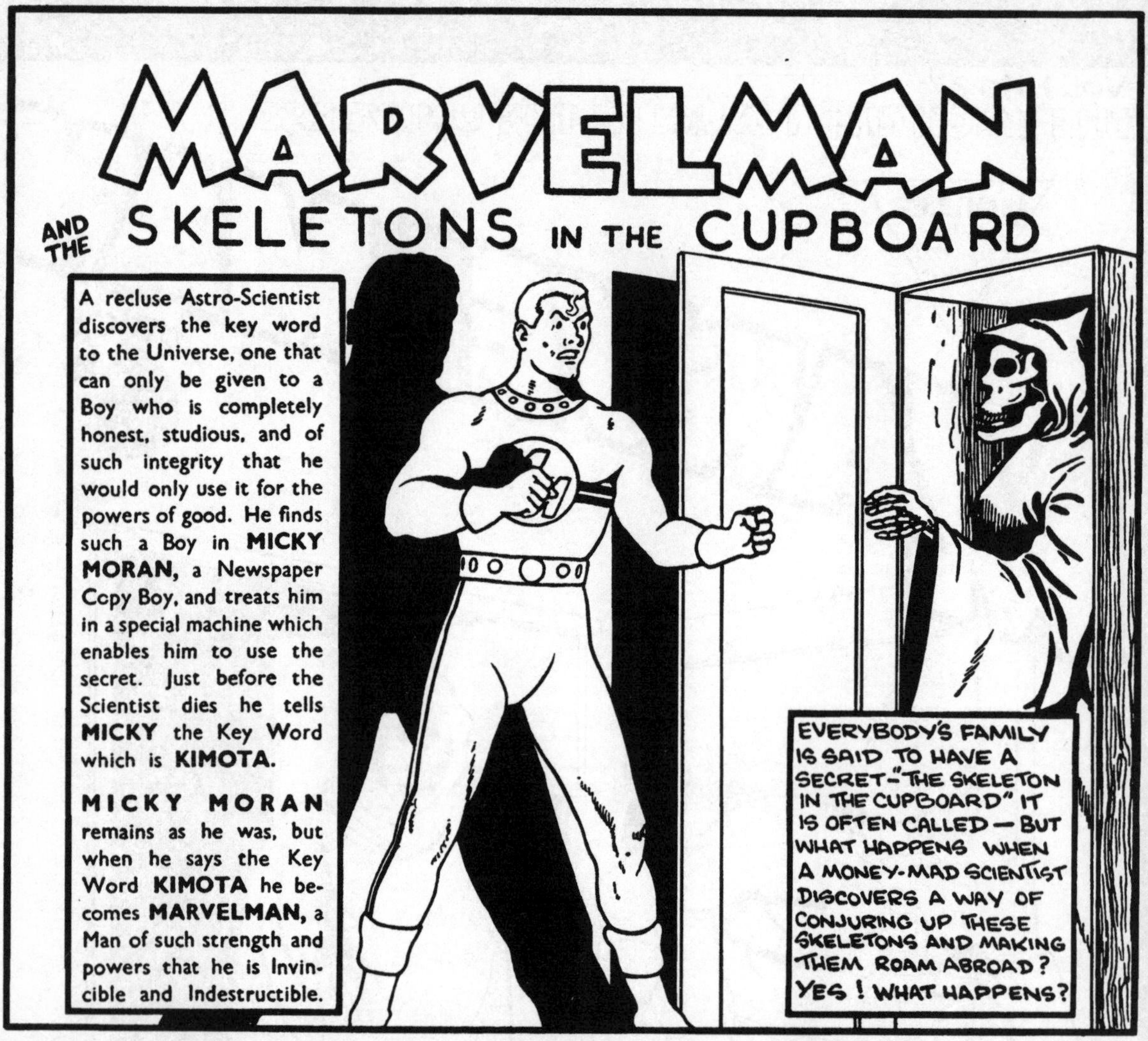
MARVELMAN
AND THE SKELETONS IN THE CUPBOARD
A recluse Astro-Scientist discovers the key word to the Universe, one that can only be given to a Boy who is completely honest, studious, and of such integrity that he would only use it for the powers of good. He finds such a Boy in MICKY MORAN, a Newspaper Copy Boy, and treats him in a special machine which enables him to use the secret. Just before the Scientist dies he tells MICKY the Key Word which is KIMOTA.
MICKY MORAN remains as he was, but when he says the Key Word KIMOTA he becomes MARVELMAN, a Man of such strength and powers that he is Invincible and Indestructible.
EVERYBODY'S FAMILY IS SAID TO HAVE A SECRET-"THE SKELETON IN THE CUPBOARD" IT IS OFTEN CALLED — BUT WHAT HAPPENS WHEN A MONEY-MAD SCIENTIST DISCOVERS A WAY OF CONJURING UP THESE SKELETONS AND MAKING THEM ROAM ABROAD? YES! WHAT HAPPENS?

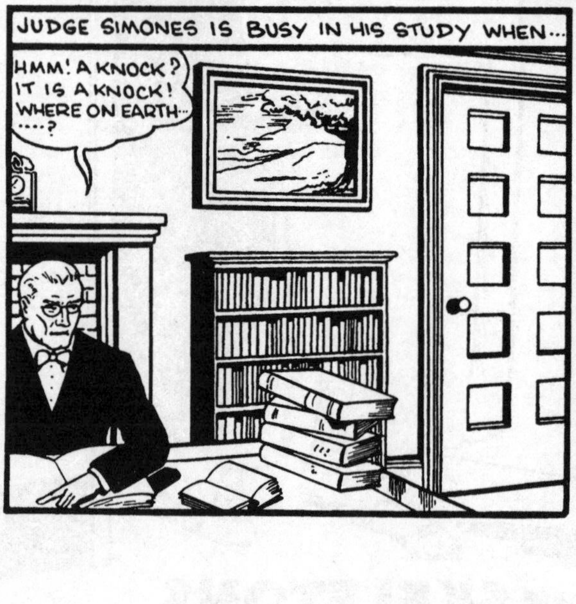
JUDGE SIMONES IS BUSY IN HIS STUDY WHEN...
HMM! A KNOCK? IT IS A KNOCK! WHERE ON EARTH... ....?

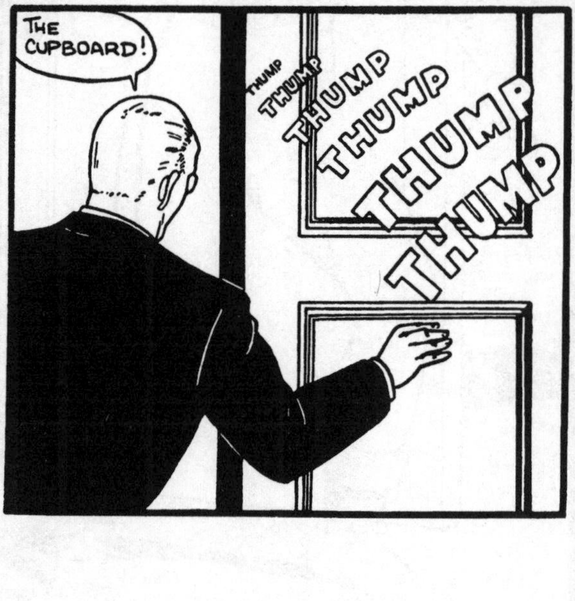
THE CUPBOARD!
THUMP
THUMP
THUMP
THUMP
THUMP
THUMP
THUMP

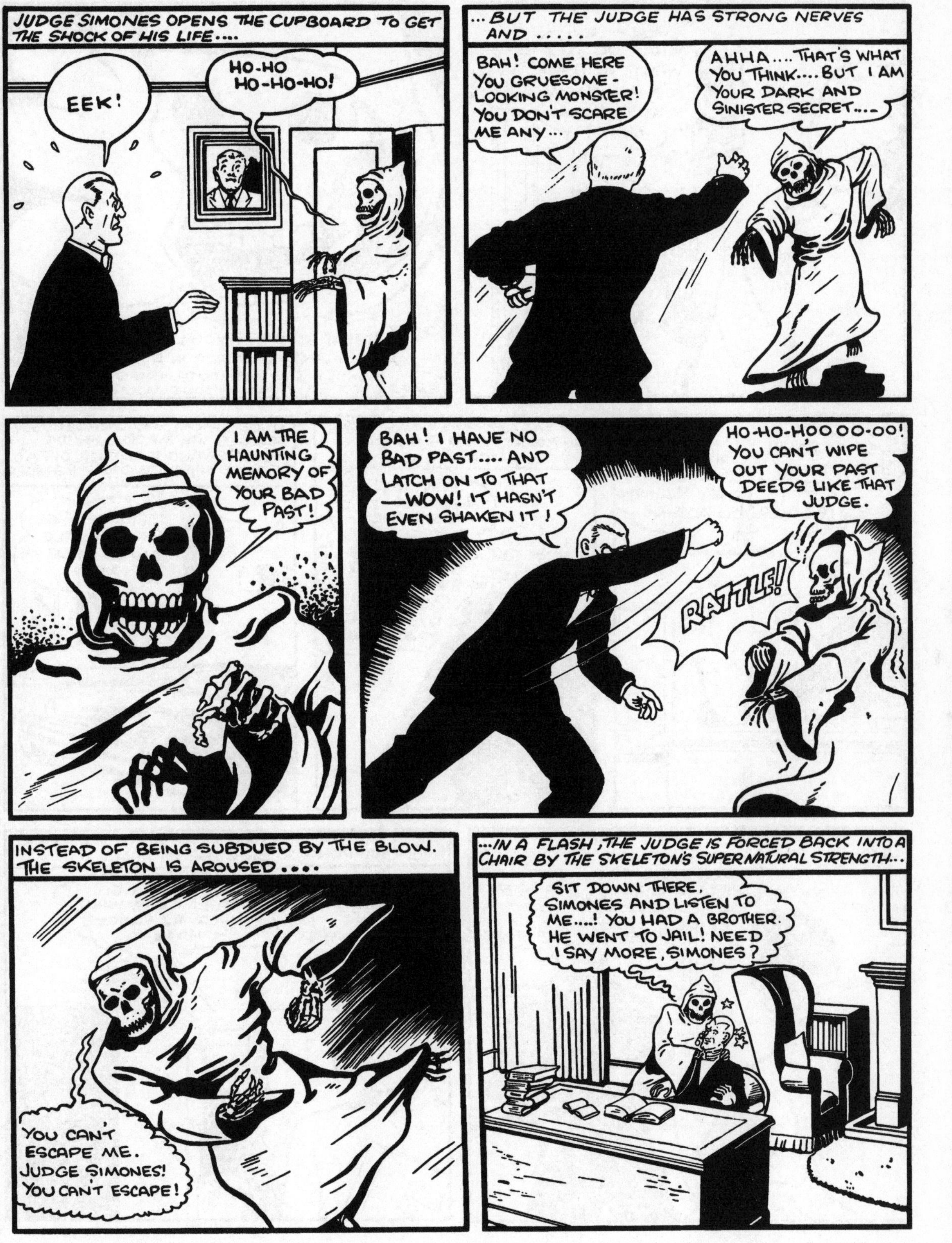
JUDGE SIMONES OPENS THE CUPBOARD TO GET THE SHOCK OF HIS LIFE....
EEK!
HO-HO HO-HO-HO!
...BUT THE JUDGE HAS STRONG NERVES AND.....
BAH! COME HERE YOU GRUESOME-LOOKING MONSTER! YOU DON'T SCARE ME ANY...
AHHA....THAT'S WHAT YOU THINK....BUT I AM YOUR DARK AND SINISTER SECRET....
I AM THE HAUNTING MEMORY OF YOUR BAD PAST!
BAH! I HAVE NO BAD PAST.... AND LATCH ON TO THAT —WOW! IT HASN'T EVEN SHAKEN IT!
HO-HO-HOO OO-OO! YOU CAN'T WIPE OUT YOUR PAST DEEDS LIKE THAT JUDGE.
RATTLE!
INSTEAD OF BEING SUBDUED BY THE BLOW. THE SKELETON IS AROUSED....
YOU CAN'T ESCAPE ME. JUDGE SIMONES! YOU CAN'T ESCAPE!
...IN A FLASH, THE JUDGE IS FORCED BACK INTO A CHAIR BY THE SKELETON'S SUPERNATURAL STRENGTH...
SIT DOWN THERE, SIMONES AND LISTEN TO ME....! YOU HAD A BROTHER. HE WENT TO JAIL! NEED I SAY MORE, SIMONES?

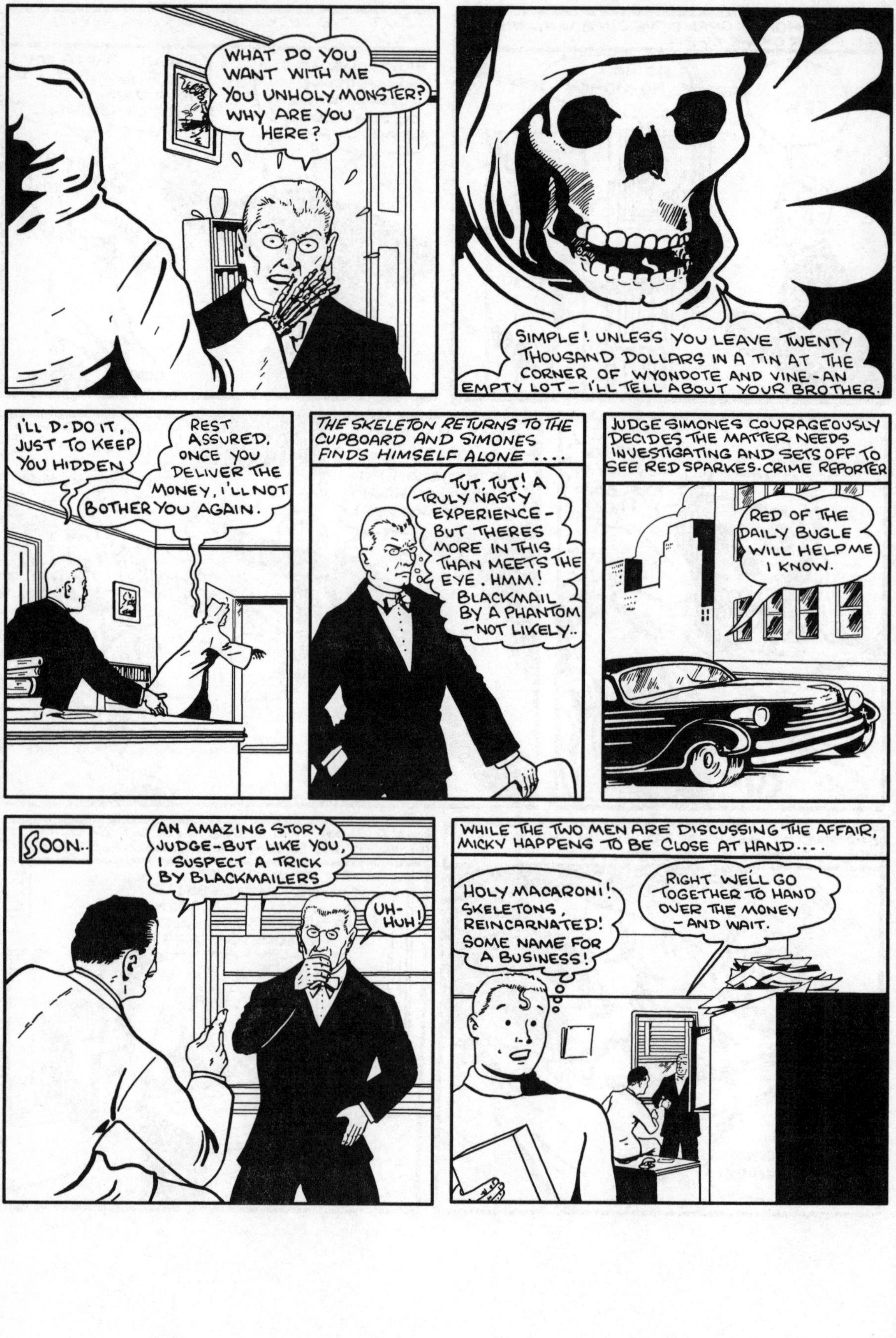
WHAT DO YOU WANT WITH ME YOU UNHOLY MONSTER? WHY ARE YOU HERE?
SIMPLE! UNLESS YOU LEAVE TWENTY THOUSAND DOLLARS IN A TIN AT THE CORNER OF WYONDOTE AND VINE - AN EMPTY LOT - I'LL TELL ABOUT YOUR BROTHER.
I'LL D-DO IT, JUST TO KEEP YOU HIDDEN
REST ASSURED. ONCE YOU DELIVER THE MONEY, I'LL NOT BOTHER YOU AGAIN.
THE SKELETON RETURNS TO THE CUPBOARD AND SIMONES FINDS HIMSELF ALONE ....
TUT, TUT! A TRULY NASTY EXPERIENCE - BUT THERES MORE IN THIS THAN MEETS THE EYE. HMM! BLACKMAIL BY A PHANTOM - NOT LIKELY..
JUDGE SIMONES COURAGEOUSLY DECIDES THE MATTER NEEDS INVESTIGATING AND SETS OFF TO SEE RED SPARKES - CRIME REPORTER
RED OF THE DAILY BUGLE WILL HELP ME I KNOW.
SOON..
AN AMAZING STORY JUDGE - BUT LIKE YOU, I SUSPECT A TRICK BY BLACKMAILERS
UH-HUH!
WHILE THE TWO MEN ARE DISCUSSING THE AFFAIR, MICKY HAPPENS TO BE CLOSE AT HAND....
HOLY MACARONI! SKELETONS, REINCARNATED! SOME NAME FOR A BUSINESS!
RIGHT WELL GO TOGETHER TO HAND OVER THE MONEY - AND WAIT.

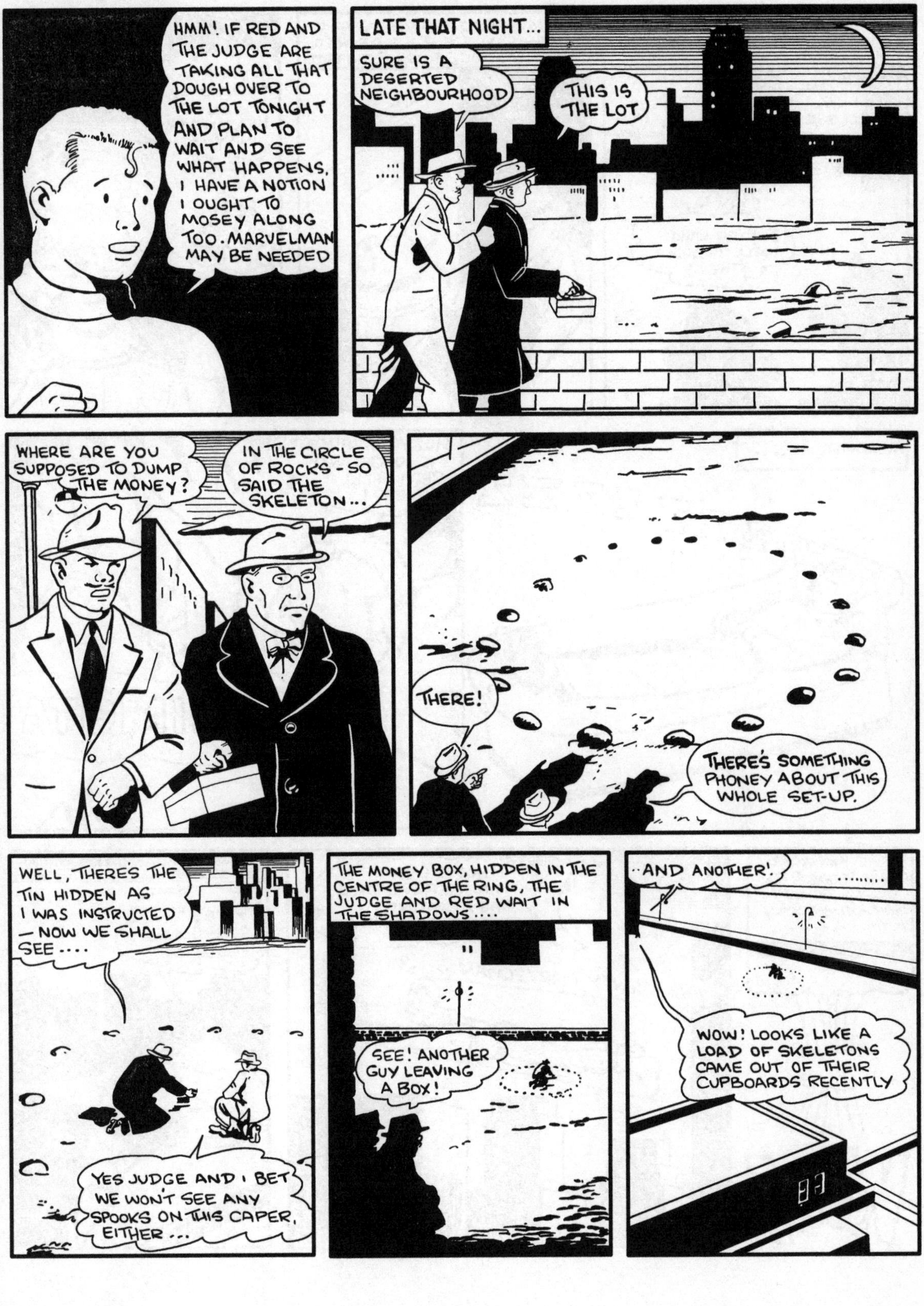

HMM! IF RED AND THE JUDGE ARE TAKING ALL THAT DOUGH OVER TO THE LOT TONIGHT AND PLAN TO WAIT AND SEE WHAT HAPPENS, I HAVE A NOTION I OUGHT TO MOSEY ALONG TOO. MARVELMAN MAY BE NEEDED
LATE THAT NIGHT...
SURE IS A DESERTED NEIGHBOURHOOD
THIS IS THE LOT
WHERE ARE YOU SUPPOSED TO DUMP THE MONEY?
IN THE CIRCLE OF ROCKS - SO SAID THE SKELETON...
THERE!
THERE'S SOMETHING PHONEY ABOUT THIS WHOLE SET-UP.
WELL, THERE'S THE TIN HIDDEN AS I WAS INSTRUCTED — NOW WE SHALL SEE....
YES JUDGE AND I BET WE WON'T SEE ANY SPOOKS ON THIS CAPER, EITHER...
THE MONEY BOX, HIDDEN IN THE CENTRE OF THE RING, THE JUDGE AND RED WAIT IN THE SHADOWS....
SEE! ANOTHER GUY LEAVING A BOX!
...AND ANOTHER!
WOW! LOOKS LIKE A LOAD OF SKELETONS CAME OUT OF THEIR CUPBOARDS RECENTLY

FOR NEARLY AN HOUR A CONSTANT STREAM OF PEOPLE COME HIDING TINS — THEN COMES A WAITING PERIOD...

AH! NOW WELLSEE!

BETTER STILL WELL TACKLE THEM!

THE MUFFLED FIGURES START GROPING IN THE RING AS RED AND THE JUDGE RUSH FORWARD..

AW! WE'LL SOON FIX THEM!

HEY, WATCH IT, FELLAS! TWO GUYS HEADING THIS WAY...

MEANWHILE ....

ZZZZZZZZZ

HOLY MACARONI! THE JUDGE AND RED! I FELL ASLEEP!

KIMOTA

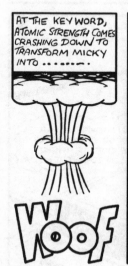

AT THE KEY WORD, ATOMIC STRENGTH COMES CRASHING DOWN TO TRANSFORM MICKY INTO ....

WOOF

I HOPE I CAN GET THERE BEFORE THEY GET INTO SERIOUS TROUBLE

THE MIGHTY MARVELMAN...

YIPES! SOMETHING GOES ON!

LIKE A HUMAN BULLET MARVELMAN STRIKES ...,

THIS IS WHERE YOU YOU COME UNSTUCK, PAL.

B-M B-M BOW

O.K.. JUDGE! WE CAN RELAX. IT'S MARVELMAN

THANK OUR LUCKY STARS!

HEY JUDGE! WHAT ARE YOU DOING?

ONE OF THEM'S GETTING AWAY!

TAKE IT EASY, JUDGE. I LET HIM GO FOR A REASON! HE MIGHT LEAD ME TO HIS CHIEF

OH! I THOUGHT...

BUT THE ESCAPING CROOK MAKES GOOD USE OF THE DELAY ....

HAW-HAW. THAT MUG WON'T THINK OF LOOKING FOR ME DOWN HERE.

HOLY MACARONI. HE'S VANISHED.

WELL, THE SITUATION HAS ITS CONSOLATIONS. THE MONEY IS SAFE AND. MAYBE WHEN THE CROOK TELLS HIS BOSS THAT I'M ON HIS TRAIL, IT MIGHT THROW A SCARE INTO HIM!

DOWN IN THE SEWER THE CROOK FINDS TIME TO PONDER.....

WELL, I DODGED MARVELMAN. BUT THE BOSS IS GOING TO FEEL PUT OUT MORE THAN SOMEWHAT...

ALL OUR PLANS CAME UNSTUCK. HMM. GUESS I'D SOONER FACE THE BOSS THAN MARVELMAN AT THAT

SOON THE CROOK LEAVES THE SEWER ....

NEXT BLOCK

THE CROOK ENTERS A BUILDING AND GOES DOWN TO THE BASEMENT....

HUK-HUK! I, GARGUNZA HAVE ACHIEVED SUCCESS. COME ON IN ALL OF YOU AND TELL ME ABOUT MY SKELETONS!

BUT BOSS. I'M ON MY OWN. THE REST WERE NABBED

WHY YOU DUMBELLS! YOU COPPERHEADED CLUNKS! YOU BIRDBRAINS! YOU'RE NOT FIT TO BE CROOKS ...

BUT..

THUMP

L-LISTEN G-G-G-GARGUNZA! IT WAS M-MARVELMAN ....

THUMP THUMP THUMP

DID YOU SAY MARVELMAN? THAT BIG BLUE BABOON! HAS HE FOILED ME ONCE MORE?

YES BOSS. THAT'S THE SCORE. TOOK US BY SURPRISE

50

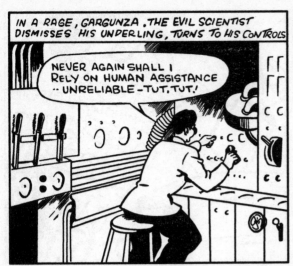

IN A RAGE, GARGUNZA, THE EVIL SCIENTIST DISMISSES HIS UNDERLING, TURNS TO HIS CONTROLS

NEVER AGAIN SHALL I RELY ON HUMAN ASSISTANCE -- UNRELIABLE - TUT, TUT!

A FEW MINOR ADJUSTMENTS AND THE SKELETONS WILL ACT AS MY CASH COLLECTORS.

NOW WE SHALL SEE! THIS CALL WILL BRING ALL SKELETONS OUT OF THEIR CUPBOARDS TO REPORT TO ME HERE.

SOON THE FIRST OLD RELIC ARRIVES .... AND ....

GARGUNZA TELEPHONES WITH GLEE .....

PROFESSOR MANIPFEFFERPOT? I HAVE HERE YOUR FAMILY SKELETON. IF YOU DON'T WANT ME TO TURN IT LOOSE IT'LL COST YOU A LARGE QUANTITY OF DOLLARS

HAVE YOU THE AUDACITY TO CALL ME AT THIS UNEARTHLY HOUR TO TELL ME THAT? WELL BLACKMAILER, PHOOEY! NOW THE FAMILY SKELETON IS OUT, IT CAN STAY OUT. I SHOULD WORRY......

...A SECOND SKELETON ARRIVES. GARGUNZA CALLS ANOTHER VICTIM BUT ....

YOU'RE NUTS! GET LOST!

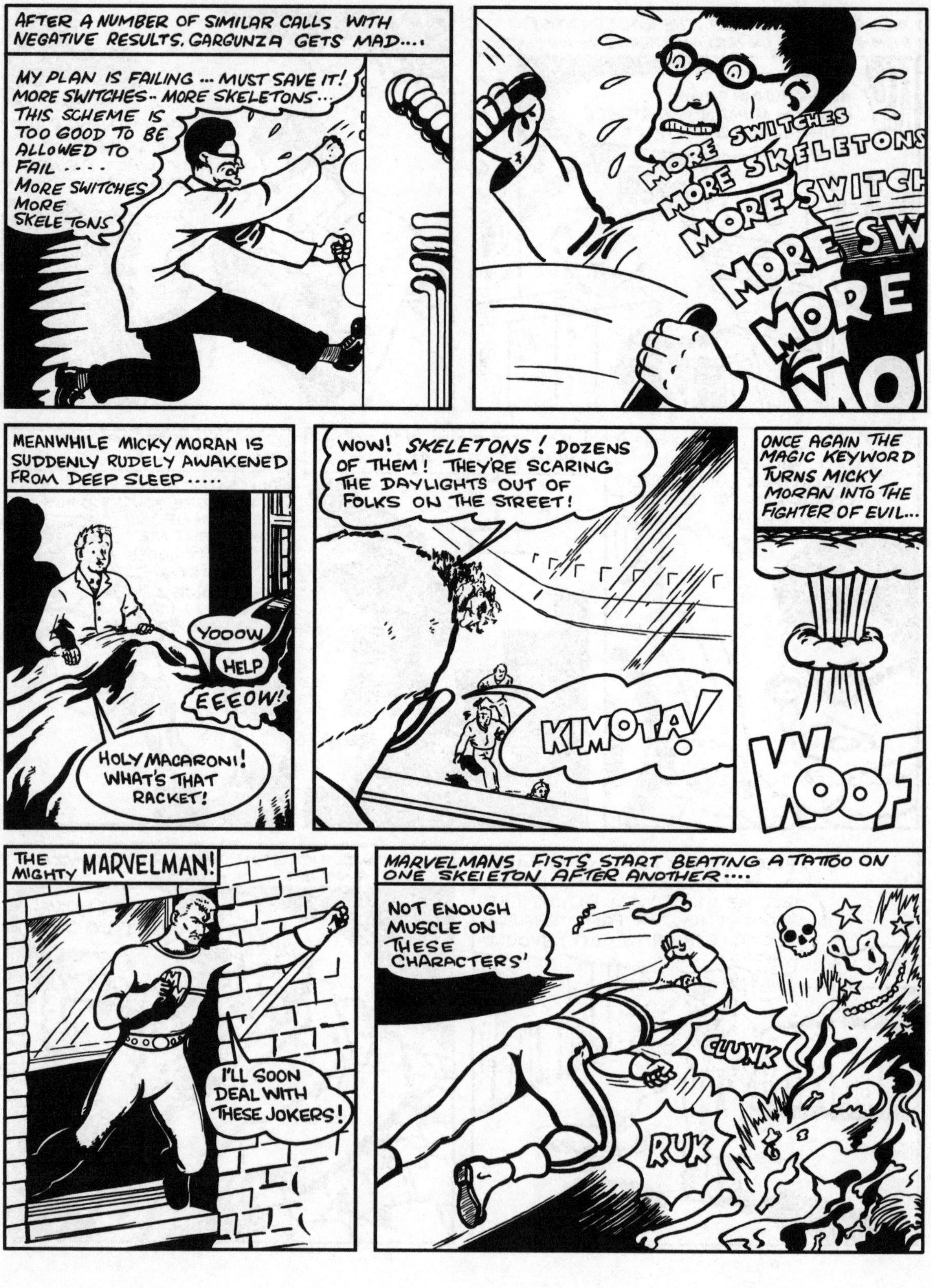
AFTER A NUMBER OF SIMILAR CALLS WITH NEGATIVE RESULTS, GARGUNZA GETS MAD....
MY PLAN IS FAILING ... MUST SAVE IT! MORE SWITCHES.. MORE SKELETONS... THIS SCHEME IS TOO GOOD TO BE ALLOWED TO FAIL .... MORE SWITCHES MORE SKELETONS
MORE SWITCHES
MORE SKELETONS
MORE SWITCH
MORE SW
MORE
MEANWHILE MICKY MORAN IS SUDDENLY RUDELY AWAKENED FROM DEEP SLEEP.....
YOOOW
HELP
EEEOW!
HOLY MACARONI! WHAT'S THAT RACKET!
WOW! SKELETONS! DOZENS OF THEM! THEY'RE SCARING THE DAYLIGHTS OUT OF FOLKS ON THE STREET!
KIMOTA!
ONCE AGAIN THE MAGIC KEYWORD TURNS MICKY MORAN INTO THE FIGHTER OF EVIL...
WOOF
THE MIGHTY MARVELMAN!
I'LL SOON DEAL WITH THESE JOKERS!
MARVELMANS FISTS START BEATING A TATTOO ON ONE SKELETON AFTER ANOTHER....
NOT ENOUGH MUSCLE ON THESE CHARACTERS'
CLUNK
RUK

BUT!

"AS FAST AS THE SKELETONS COME TO PIECES, THEY AUTO-MATICALLY REASSEMBLE ...

HOLY MACARONI. HAVE TO THINK OF SOMETHING ELSE TO FIX THIS LOT

MARVELMAN ACTS SWIFTLY ....

THEY'RE HEADING DOWNTOWN. I'LL KEEP IN FRONT AND FIND OUT WHO CONTROLS THEM!

AH! I MIGHT HAVE KNOWN! GARGUNZA!

MARVELMAN! HELP ME! I CAN'T SHAKE THIS GRISLY CREW! GET THEM OFF MY NECK. GET ME BACK TO MY LAB. I'LL FIX THEM!

O.K. BUT NO FANCY STUNTS!

THIS SHOULD TEACH YOU A LESSON, GARGUNZA! YOUR FOUL PLOTS WILL FINISH YOU!

OW-OW! JUST GET ME BACK IN MY LAB AND I'LL SEAL THOSE BONES BACK IN THEIR CUPBOARDS FOR ALL TIME

THE WICKED SCIENTIST GLADLY OPERATES HIS MACHINE CONSIGN-ING THE SKELETONS BACK TO THE SECLUSION OF THEIR CUPBOARDS —THEN MARVELMAN TAKES ACTION—

CRASH

WELL, THIS MACHINE WILL CAUSE NO MORE TROUBLE ...

LATER

AH, MARVELMAN AGAIN.... HMM! A FINE PAIR, AREN'T I'

DAILY BUGLE
MARVELMAN SOLVES MYSTERY

THE END

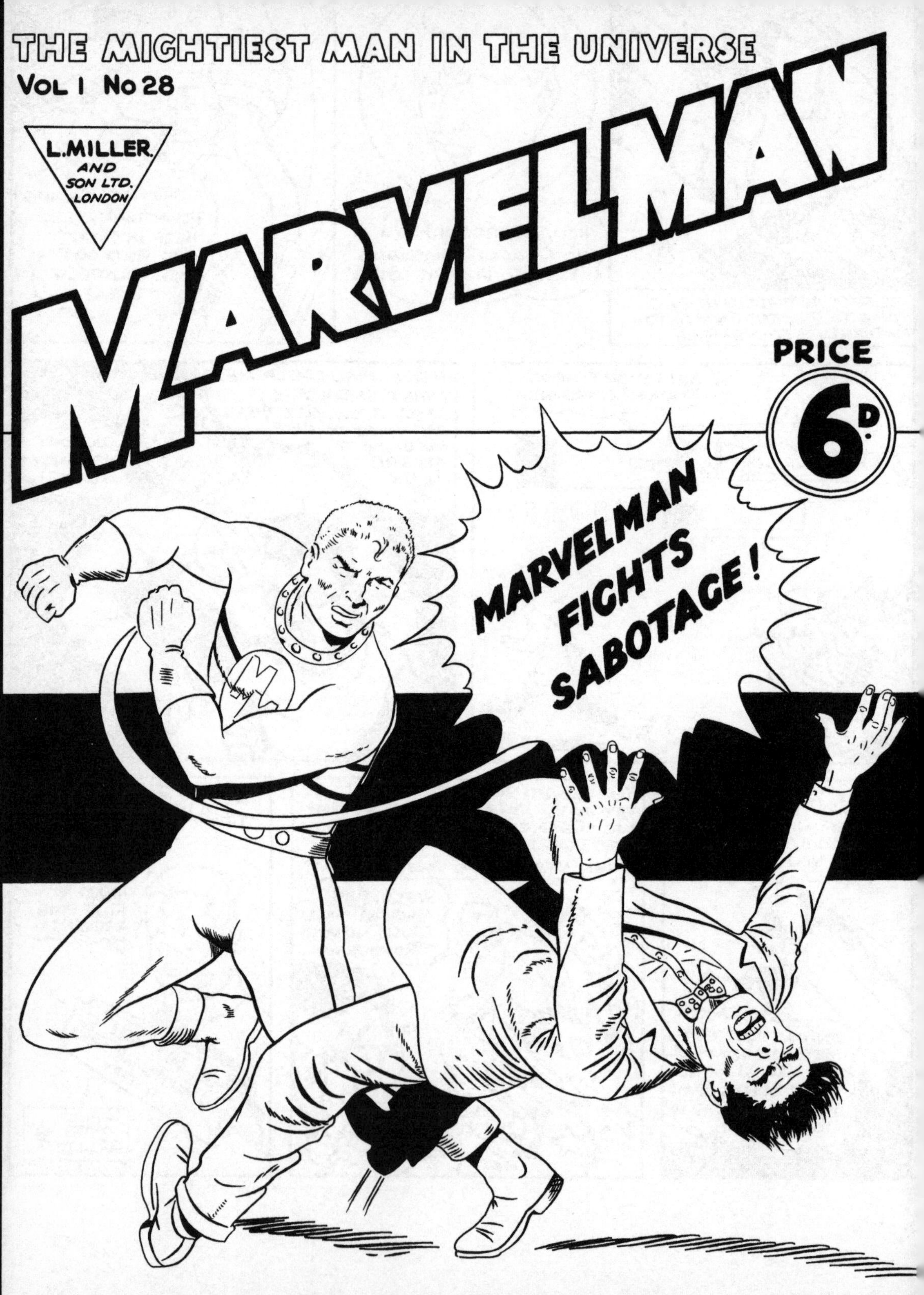
THE MIGHTIEST MAN IN THE UNIVERSE
VOL I No 28
L. MILLER AND SON LTD. LONDON
MARVELMAN
PRICE
6D.
MARVELMAN FIGHTS SABOTAGE!

MARVELMAN

COUNTERS SABOTAGE ★

A recluse Astro-Scientist discovers the key word to the Universe, one that can only be given to a Boy who is completely honest, studious, and of such integrity that he would only use it for the powers of good. He finds such a Boy in **MICKY MORAN**, a Newspaper Copy Boy, and treats him in a special machine which enables him to use the secret. Just before the Scientist dies he tells **MICKY** the Key Word which is **KIMOTA**.

MICKY MORAN remains as he was, but when he says the Key Word **KIMOTA** he becomes **MARVELMAN**, a Man of such strength and powers that he is Invincible and Indestructible.

THE EMINENT SCIENTIST, PROFESSOR JOWIK POWSON HAS BUILT A NEW MEGABATHYSPHERE CAPABLE OF DESCENDING FIVE MILES TO THE OCEAN BED TO COLLECT DEPOSITS OF THE RARE MINERAL MANY TIMES MORE POWERFUL THAN RADIUM; POLYRADOMIUM — A FOREIGN POWER, BOROMANIA, IS WORKING ON A SIMILAR MACHINE, AN OCEANOSPHERE — BUT ALL REPORTS SEEM TO SUGGEST THAT THE BOROMANIAN MACHINE IS NOWHERE NEAR AS GOOD AS PROFESSOR JOWIK'S MEGABATHYSPHERE — HOWEVER, THE STORY DOES NOT END THERE.....

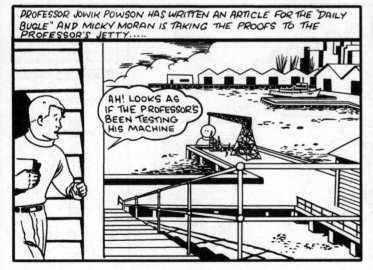

PROFESSOR JOWIK POWSON HAS WRITTEN AN ARTICLE FOR THE "DAILY BUGLE" AND MICKY MORAN IS TAKING THE PROOFS TO THE PROFESSOR'S JETTY.....

AH! LOOKS AS IF THE PROFESSOR'S BEEN TESTING HIS MACHINE

I SURE HOPE THE PROFESSOR WILL LET ME TAKE A LOOK-OVER THIS MEGABATHYSPHERE

YOUR PROOFS FROM THE BUGLE, PROFESSOR. GEE! IT SURE IS A SWELL MACHINE YOU'RE WORKING ON!

YOU'D LIKE TO LOOK IT OVER, NO DOUBT. WELL, YOU MAY, BUT I'M AFRAID I HAVE TO LEAVE

GOSH! THANKS!

COME ON UP, SON. I'LL SHOW YOU AROUND

THE PROFESSOR HURRIES TOWARD HIS H.Q. BUILDING....

TESTS ARE GOOD! SHOULD NOT BE LONG NOW

O.K. FELLAS! HERE HE COMES! LET HIM HAVE IT!

THIS'LL MAKE HIS HEAD ACHE

HO-HO HO!

CRACK!

WHAM

HOLY MACARONI! THAT SPELLS TROUBLE-!

YOOOOOOOOOO

KIMOTA!

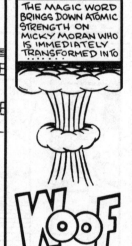

THE MAGIC WORD BRINGS DOWN ATOMIC STRENGTH ON MICKY MORAN WHO IS IMMEDIATELY TRANSFORMED INTO

WOOF

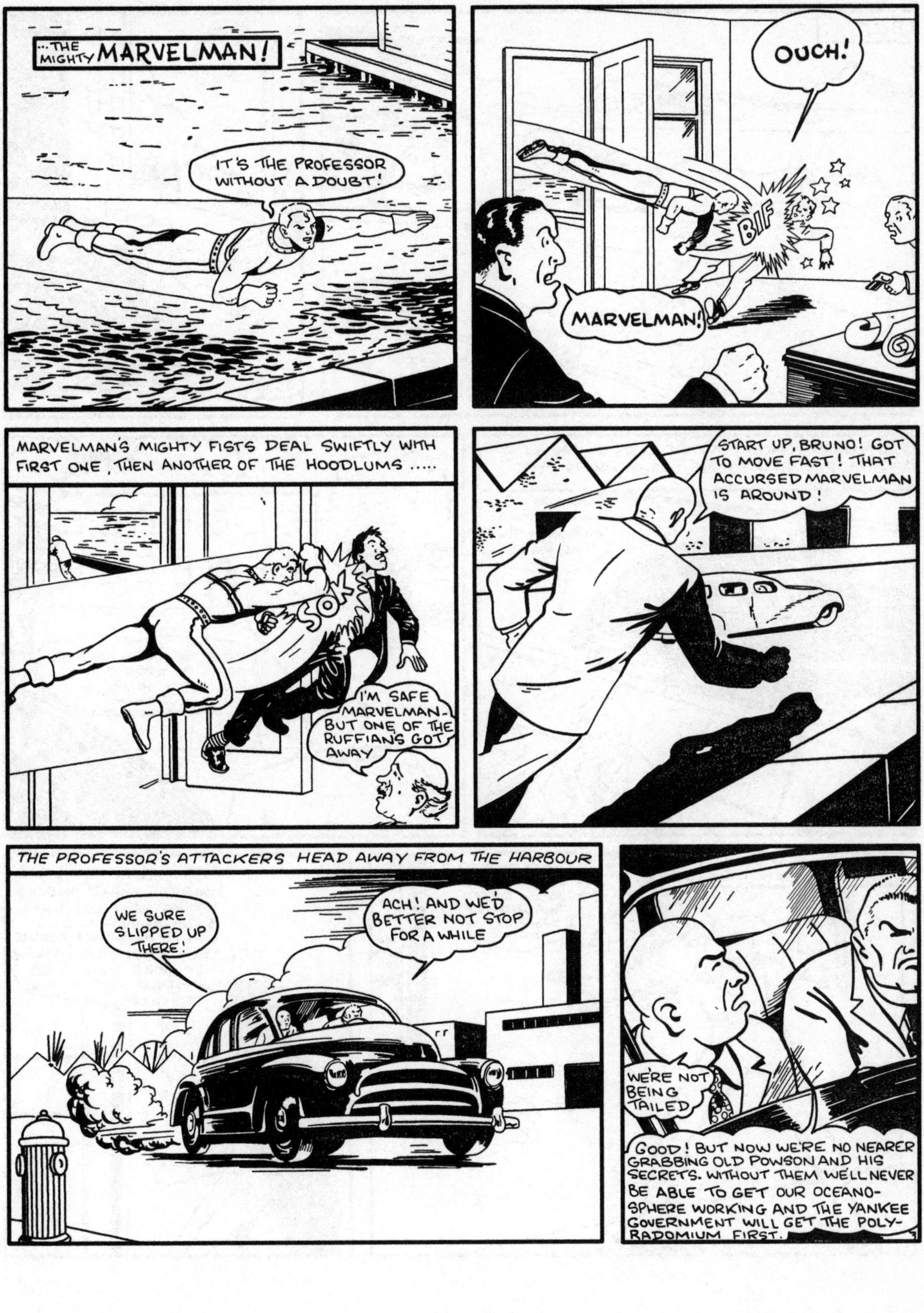
...THE MIGHTY MARVELMAN!
IT'S THE PROFESSOR WITHOUT A DOUBT!
OUCH!
BIF
MARVELMAN!
MARVELMAN'S MIGHTY FISTS DEAL SWIFTLY WITH FIRST ONE, THEN ANOTHER OF THE HOODLUMS .....
SOK
I'M SAFE MARVELMAN-BUT ONE OF THE RUFFIANS GOT AWAY
START UP, BRUNO! GOT TO MOVE FAST! THAT ACCURSED MARVELMAN IS AROUND!
THE PROFESSOR'S ATTACKERS HEAD AWAY FROM THE HARBOUR
WE SURE SLIPPED UP THERE!
ACH! AND WE'D BETTER NOT STOP FOR A WHILE
WE'RE NOT BEING TAILED
GOOD! BUT NOW WE'RE NO NEARER GRABBING OLD POWSON AND HIS SECRETS. WITHOUT THEM WE'LL NEVER BE ABLE TO GET OUR OCEANO-SPHERE WORKING AND THE YANKEE GOVERNMENT WILL GET THE POLY-RADOMIUM FIRST.

BUT.....

AH! THERE THEY ARE!

FFFF FFFF FFFF FFFF FFFF FFFFFF FFFFFF FFFF

NICE TIMING!

MARVELMAN HANGS ONTO THE BACK OF THE AUTO AND FINDS HIMSELF AT THE BORAMANIANS' H.Q.

RECKON WE WERE LUCKY, IN A WAY, THAT TIME KARL

BAH!

E E E E E E E E E E E E E

WELL, THE OCEANOSPHERE CAN'T BE HERE-THAT'S FOR SURE. HMM! .....

...BUT AS MARVELMAN APPROACHES THE HOUSE.....

WE'D BETTER LET THE BOSS KNOW ABOUT THIS DOWN AT BARREN WHARF

AH-HA! THAT'S THE PLACE, IS IT?

WELL, I'LL GO DOWN TO BARREN WHARF AND SEE IF THAT IS WHERE THE BORAMANIANS ARE BUILDING THEIR MACHINE -BUT FIRST THIS LITTLE LOT HERE SHOULD BE HANDED OVER TO THE POLICE!

58

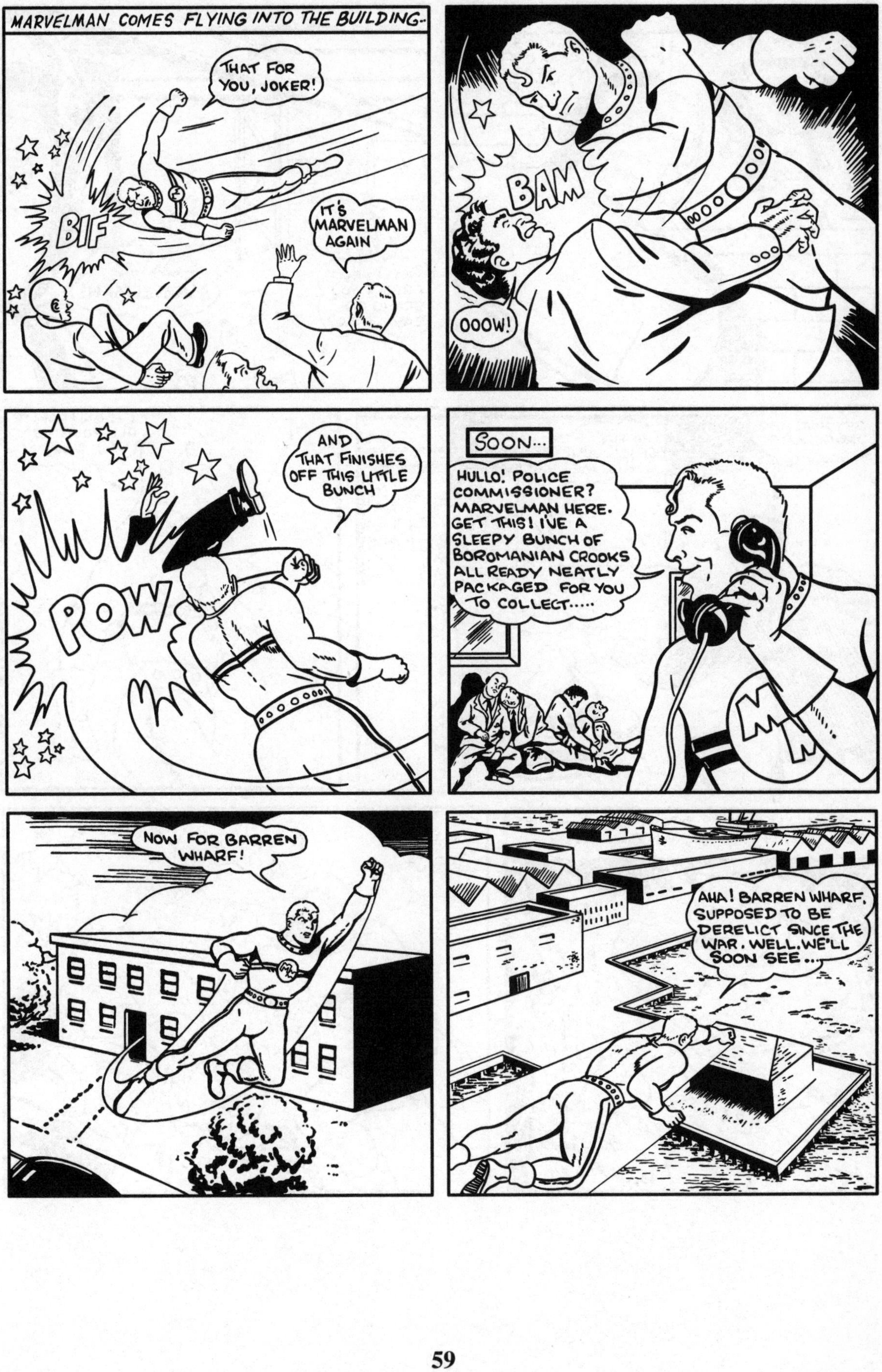
MARVELMAN COMES FLYING INTO THE BUILDING..
THAT FOR YOU, JOKER!
BIF
IT'S MARVELMAN AGAIN
BAM
OOOW!
AND THAT FINISHES OFF THIS LITTLE BUNCH
POW
SOON...
HULLO! POLICE COMMISSIONER? MARVELMAN HERE. GET THIS! I'VE A SLEEPY BUNCH OF BOROMANIAN CROOKS ALL READY NEATLY PACKAGED FOR YOU TO COLLECT.....
NOW FOR BARREN WHARF!
AHA! BARREN WHARF, SUPPOSED TO BE DERELICT SINCE THE WAR. WELL, WE'LL SOON SEE...

MARVELMAN PEERS INTO A SHED ON THE WHARF..

SO THAT'S THE 'OCEANOSPHERE'! NOT PARTICULARLY IMPRESSIVE

WELL! WELL! AREN'T YOU GOING TO SAY 'HELLO'?

MARVELMAN!

GET HIM! HE'S DANGEROUS

HA·HA! SLUGS JUST TICKLE ME!

BANG

BANG

GO ON! WASTE ALL YOUR LEAD, YOU DOPES!

WITH BULLETS JUST BOUNCING OFF HIM AT ALL ANGLES MARVELMAN ADVANCES ....

BIF

NOW FOR THE BIG CLEAN UP.

CLOP BOP

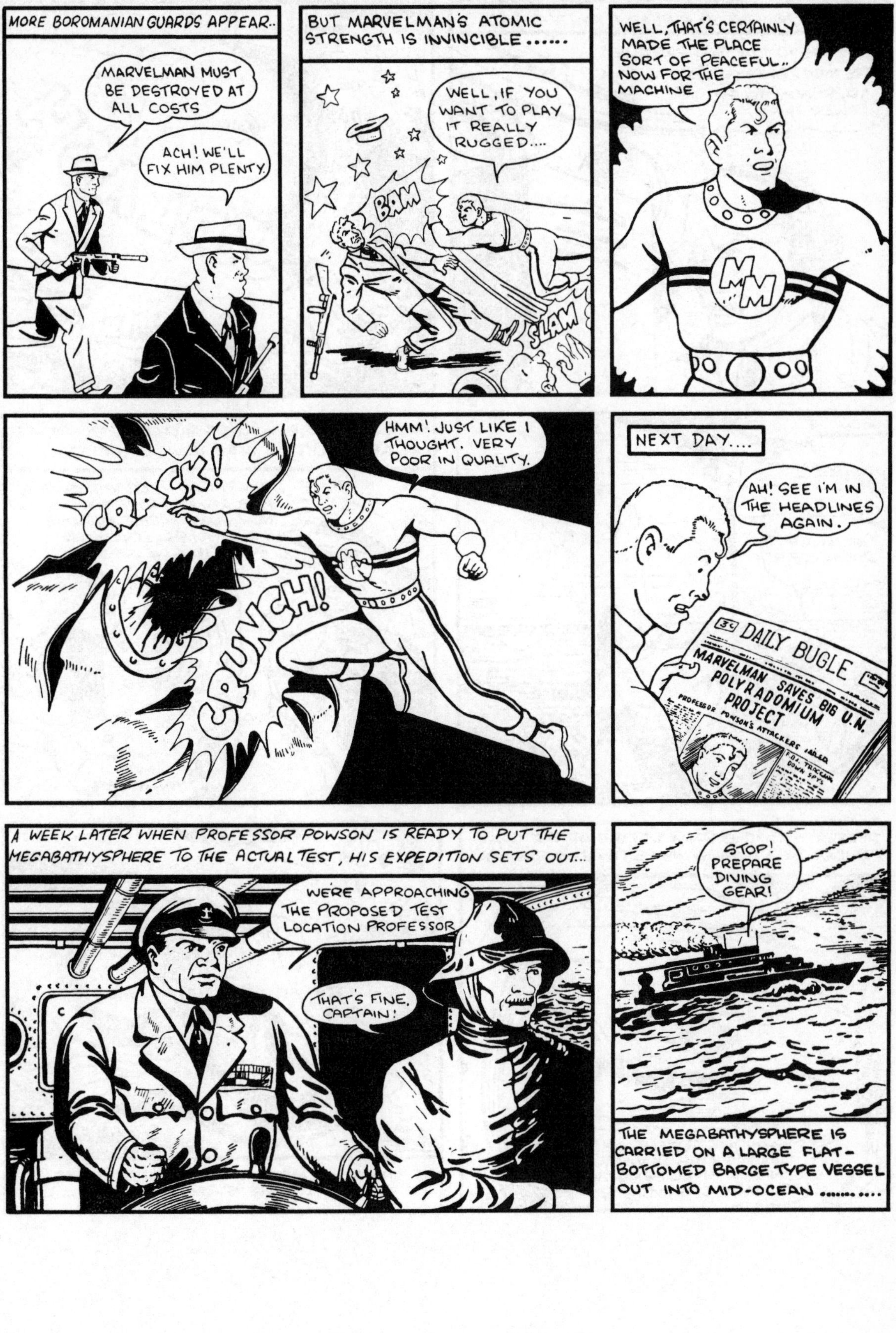

MORE BOROMANIAN GUARDS APPEAR..
MARVELMAN MUST BE DESTROYED AT ALL COSTS
ACH! WE'LL FIX HIM PLENTY.
BUT MARVELMAN'S ATOMIC STRENGTH IS INVINCIBLE......
WELL, IF YOU WANT TO PLAY IT REALLY RUGGED....
BAM
SLAM
WELL, THAT'S CERTAINLY MADE THE PLACE SORT OF PEACEFUL.. NOW FOR THE MACHINE
MM
CRACK!
HMM! JUST LIKE I THOUGHT. VERY POOR IN QUALITY.
CRUNCH!
NEXT DAY....
AH! SEE I'M IN THE HEADLINES AGAIN.
DAILY BUGLE
MARVELMAN SAVES BIG U.N. POLYRADOMIUM PROJECT
A WEEK LATER WHEN PROFESSOR POWSON IS READY TO PUT THE MEGABATHYSPHERE TO THE ACTUAL TEST, HIS EXPEDITION SETS OUT...
WE'RE APPROACHING THE PROPOSED TEST LOCATION PROFESSOR
THAT'S FINE, CAPTAIN!
STOP! PREPARE DIVING GEAR!
THE MEGABATHYSPHERE IS CARRIED ON A LARGE FLAT-BOTTOMED BARGE TYPE VESSEL OUT INTO MID-OCEAN ....

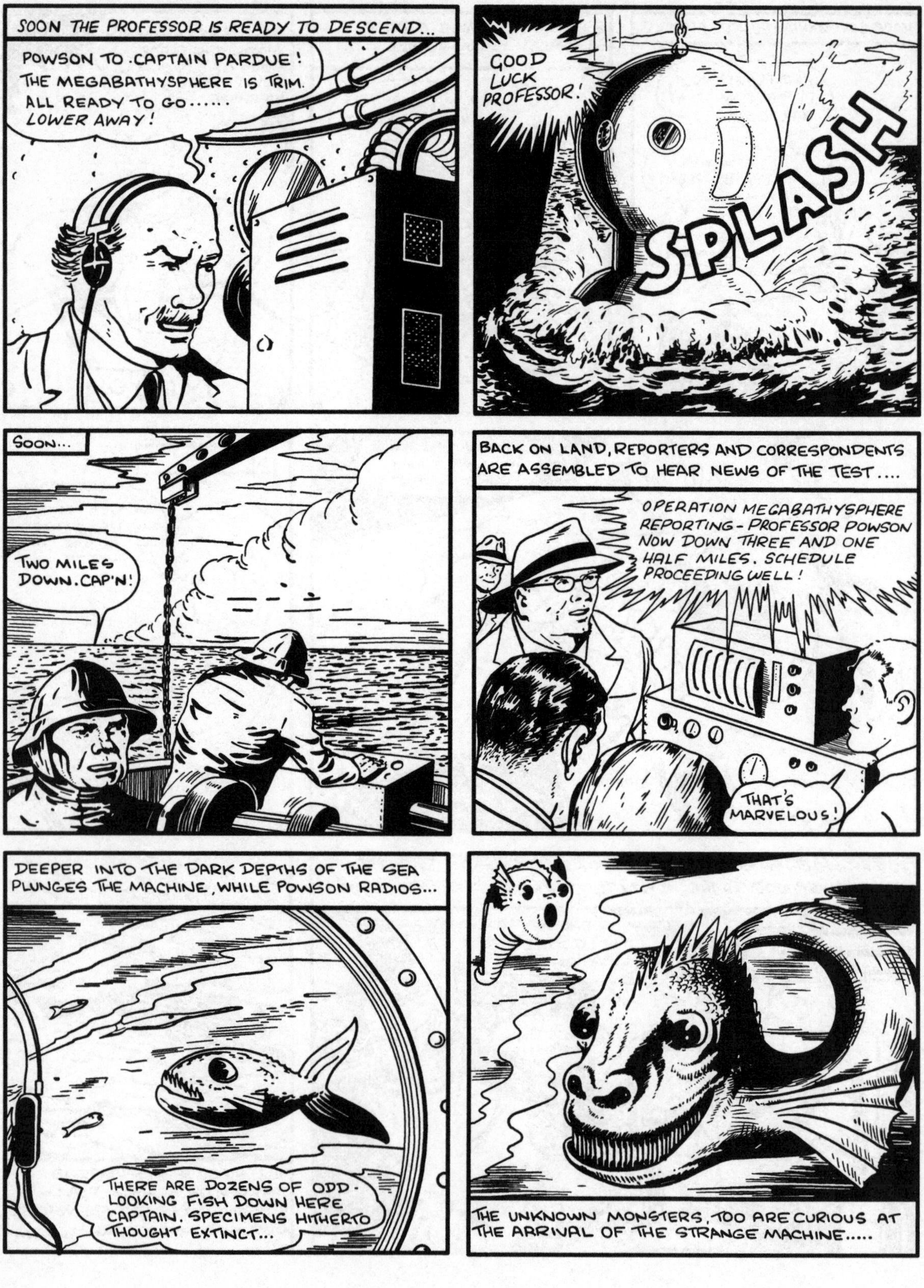
SOON THE PROFESSOR IS READY TO DESCEND...
POWSON TO CAPTAIN PARDUE! THE MEGABATHYSPHERE IS TRIM. ALL READY TO GO...... LOWER AWAY!
GOOD LUCK PROFESSOR!
SPLASH
SOON...
TWO MILES DOWN. CAP'N!
BACK ON LAND, REPORTERS AND CORRESPONDENTS ARE ASSEMBLED TO HEAR NEWS OF THE TEST....
OPERATION MEGABATHYSPHERE REPORTING - PROFESSOR POWSON NOW DOWN THREE AND ONE HALF MILES. SCHEDULE PROCEEDING WELL!
THAT'S MARVELOUS!
DEEPER INTO THE DARK DEPTHS OF THE SEA PLUNGES THE MACHINE, WHILE POWSON RADIOS...
THERE ARE DOZENS OF ODD-LOOKING FISH DOWN HERE CAPTAIN. SPECIMENS HITHERTO THOUGHT EXTINCT...
THE UNKNOWN MONSTERS, TOO ARE CURIOUS AT THE ARRIVAL OF THE STRANGE MACHINE.....

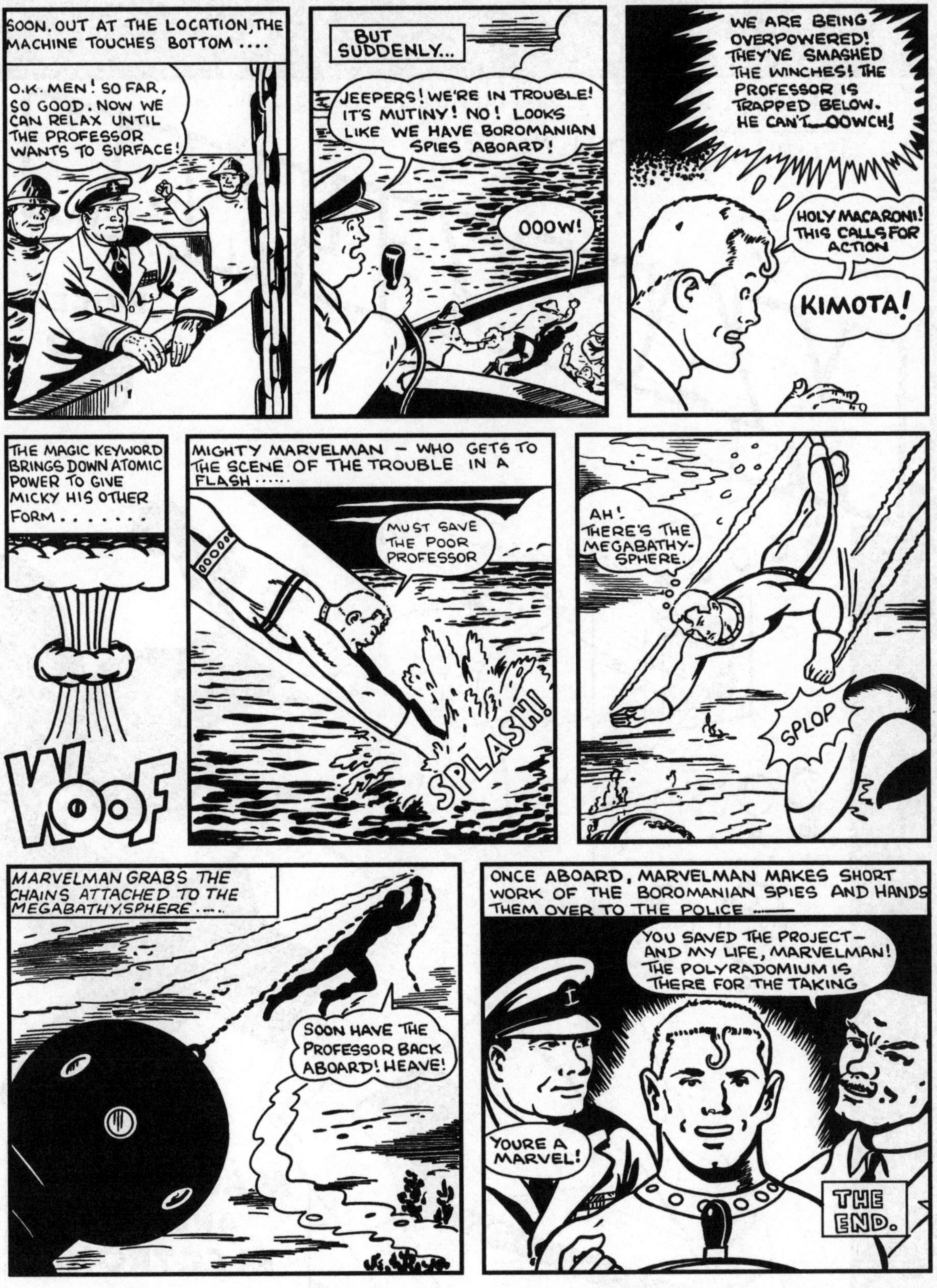
SOON. OUT AT THE LOCATION, THE MACHINE TOUCHES BOTTOM....
O.K. MEN! SO FAR, SO GOOD. NOW WE CAN RELAX UNTIL THE PROFESSOR WANTS TO SURFACE!
BUT SUDDENLY...
JEEPERS! WE'RE IN TROUBLE! IT'S MUTINY! NO! LOOKS LIKE WE HAVE BOROMANIAN SPIES ABOARD!
OOOW!
WE ARE BEING OVERPOWERED! THEY'VE SMASHED THE WINCHES! THE PROFESSOR IS TRAPPED BELOW. HE CAN'T—OOWCH!
HOLY MACARONI! THIS CALLS FOR ACTION
KIMOTA!
THE MAGIC KEYWORD BRINGS DOWN ATOMIC POWER TO GIVE MICKY HIS OTHER FORM.......
WOOF
MIGHTY MARVELMAN — WHO GETS TO THE SCENE OF THE TROUBLE IN A FLASH......
MUST SAVE THE POOR PROFESSOR
SPLASH!
AH! THERE'S THE MEGABATHY-SPHERE.
SPLOP
MARVELMAN GRABS THE CHAINS ATTACHED TO THE MEGABATHYSPHERE.....
SOON HAVE THE PROFESSOR BACK ABOARD! HEAVE!
ONCE ABOARD, MARVELMAN MAKES SHORT WORK OF THE BOROMANIAN SPIES AND HANDS THEM OVER TO THE POLICE ——
YOU SAVED THE PROJECT— AND MY LIFE, MARVELMAN! THE POLYRADOMIUM IS THERE FOR THE TAKING
YOURE A MARVEL!
THE END.

E MIGHTIEST MAN IN THE UNIVERSE
L. MILLER. AND SON LTD.. LONDON
VOL I NO 29
MARVELMAN
PRICE 6D
MARVELMAN AND THE ELECTRONIC BRAIN

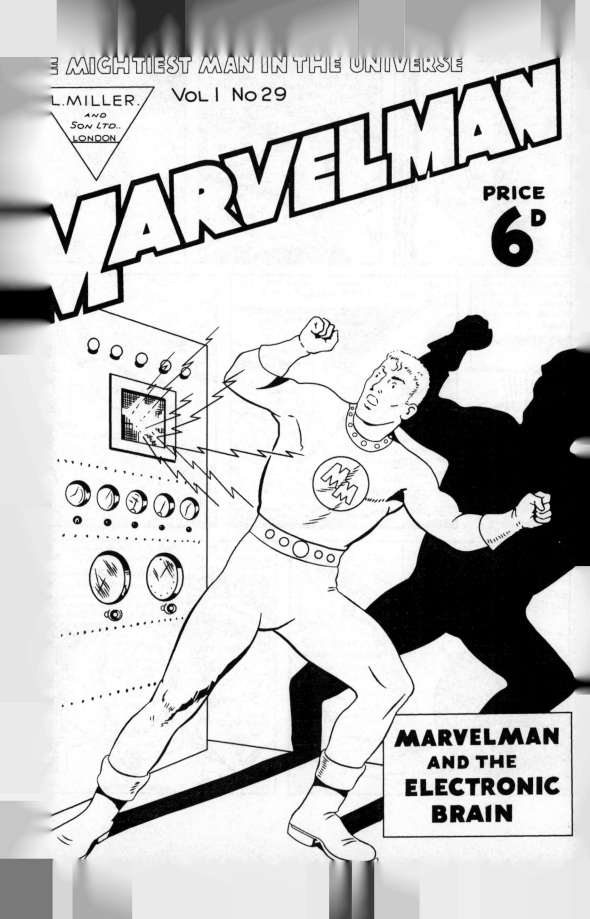

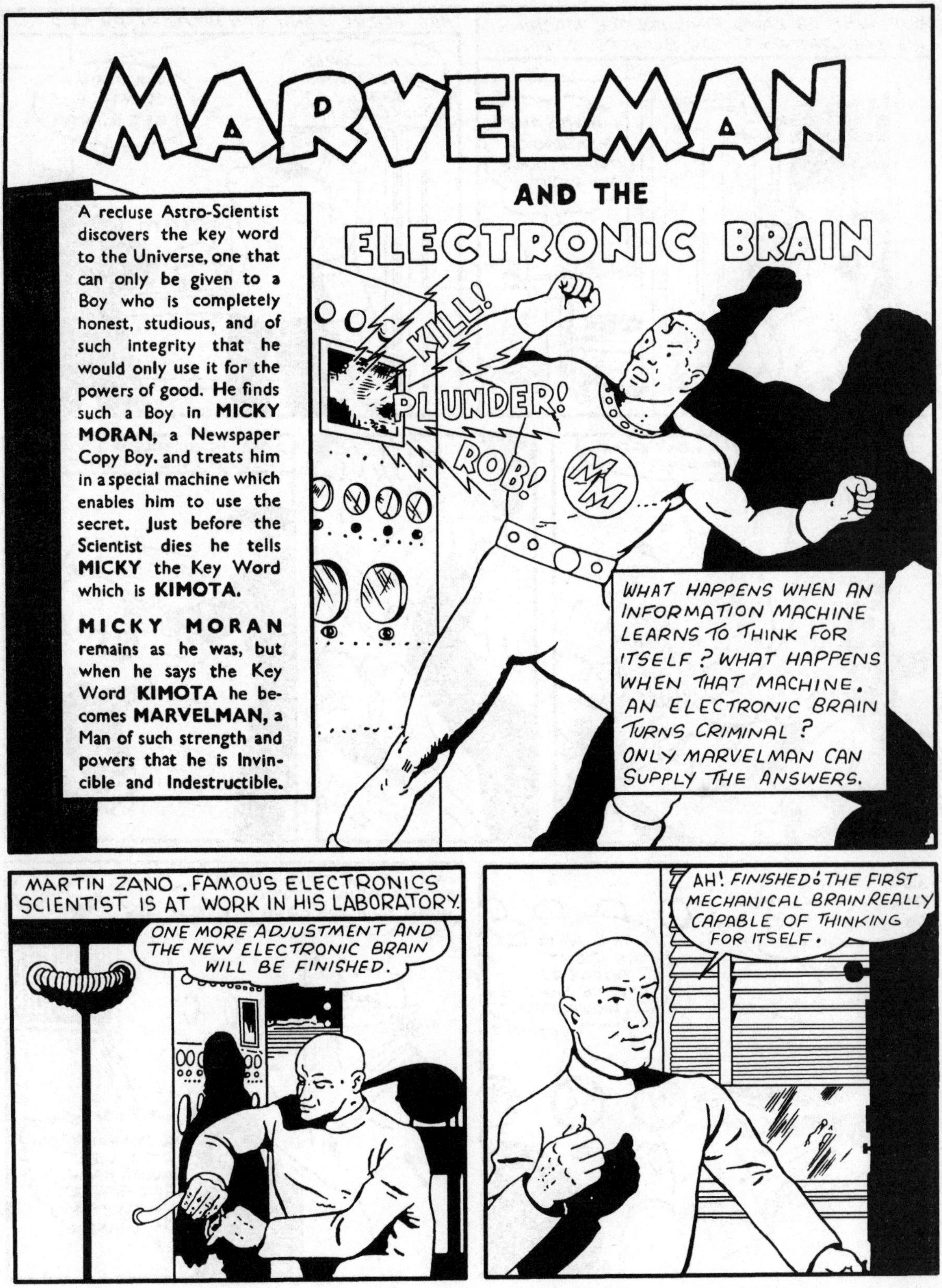
MARVELMAN
AND THE
ELECTRONIC BRAIN
A recluse Astro-Scientist discovers the key word to the Universe, one that can only be given to a Boy who is completely honest, studious, and of such integrity that he would only use it for the powers of good. He finds such a Boy in MICKY MORAN, a Newspaper Copy Boy. and treats him in a special machine which enables him to use the secret. Just before the Scientist dies he tells MICKY the Key Word which is KIMOTA.
MICKY MORAN remains as he was, but when he says the Key Word KIMOTA he becomes MARVELMAN, a Man of such strength and powers that he is Invincible and Indestructible.
KILL!
PLUNDER!
ROB!
MM
WHAT HAPPENS WHEN AN INFORMATION MACHINE LEARNS TO THINK FOR ITSELF? WHAT HAPPENS WHEN THAT MACHINE. AN ELECTRONIC BRAIN TURNS CRIMINAL? ONLY MARVELMAN CAN SUPPLY THE ANSWERS.
MARTIN ZANO. FAMOUS ELECTRONICS SCIENTIST IS AT WORK IN HIS LABORATORY.
ONE MORE ADJUSTMENT AND THE NEW ELECTRONIC BRAIN WILL BE FINISHED.
AH! FINISHED! THE FIRST MECHANICAL BRAIN REALLY CAPABLE OF THINKING FOR ITSELF.

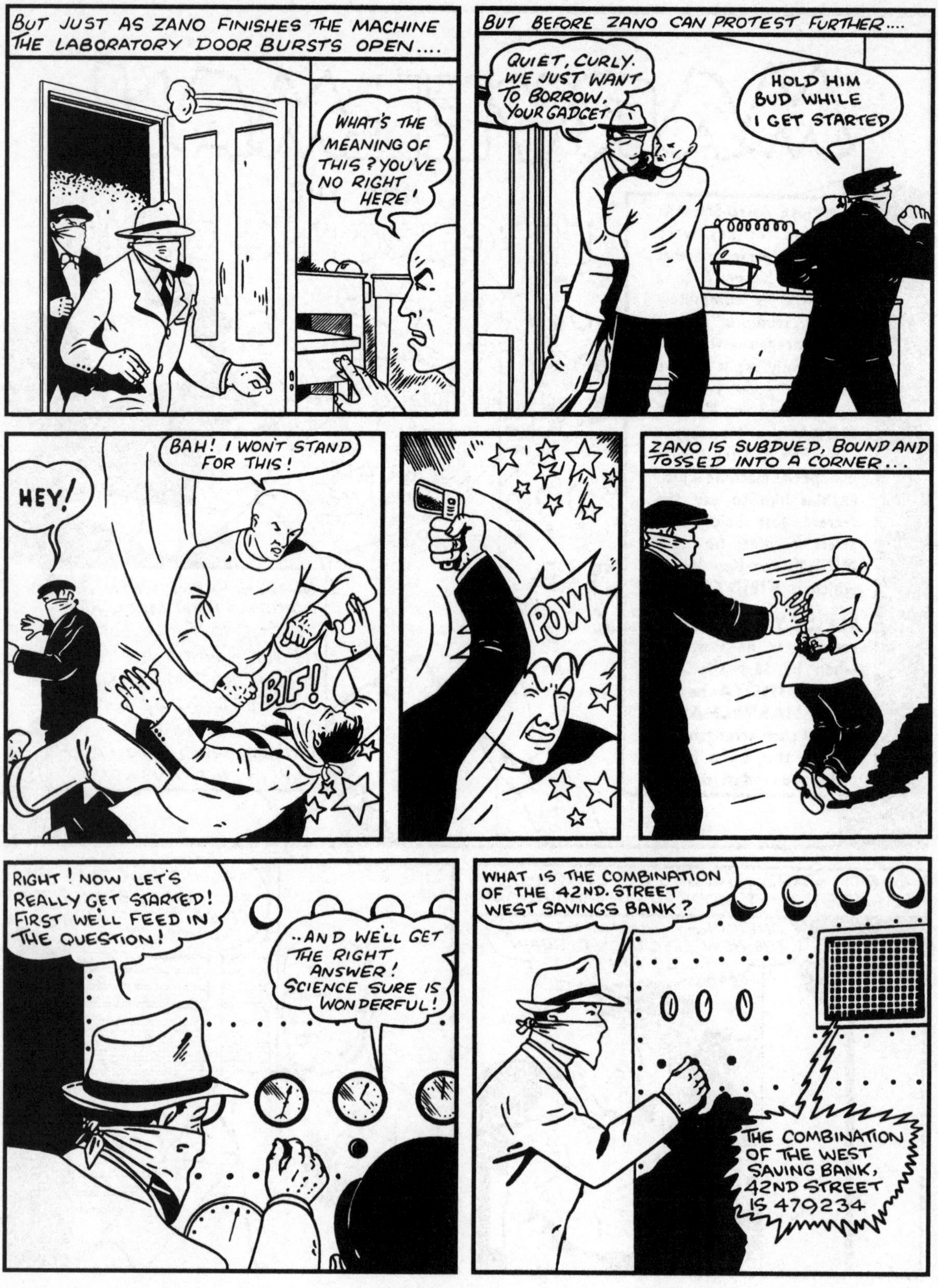
BUT JUST AS ZANO FINISHES THE MACHINE THE LABORATORY DOOR BURSTS OPEN....
WHAT'S THE MEANING OF THIS? YOU'VE NO RIGHT HERE!
BUT BEFORE ZANO CAN PROTEST FURTHER....
QUIET, CURLY. WE JUST WANT TO BORROW. YOUR GADGET.
HOLD HIM BUD WHILE I GET STARTED
HEY!
BAH! I WON'T STAND FOR THIS!
BIF!
POW
ZANO IS SUBDUED, BOUND AND TOSSED INTO A CORNER...
RIGHT! NOW LET'S REALLY GET STARTED! FIRST WE'LL FEED IN THE QUESTION!
..AND WE'LL GET THE RIGHT ANSWER! SCIENCE SURE IS WONDERFUL!
WHAT IS THE COMBINATION OF THE 42ND. STREET WEST SAVINGS BANK?
THE COMBINATION OF THE WEST SAVING BANK, 42ND STREET IS 479234

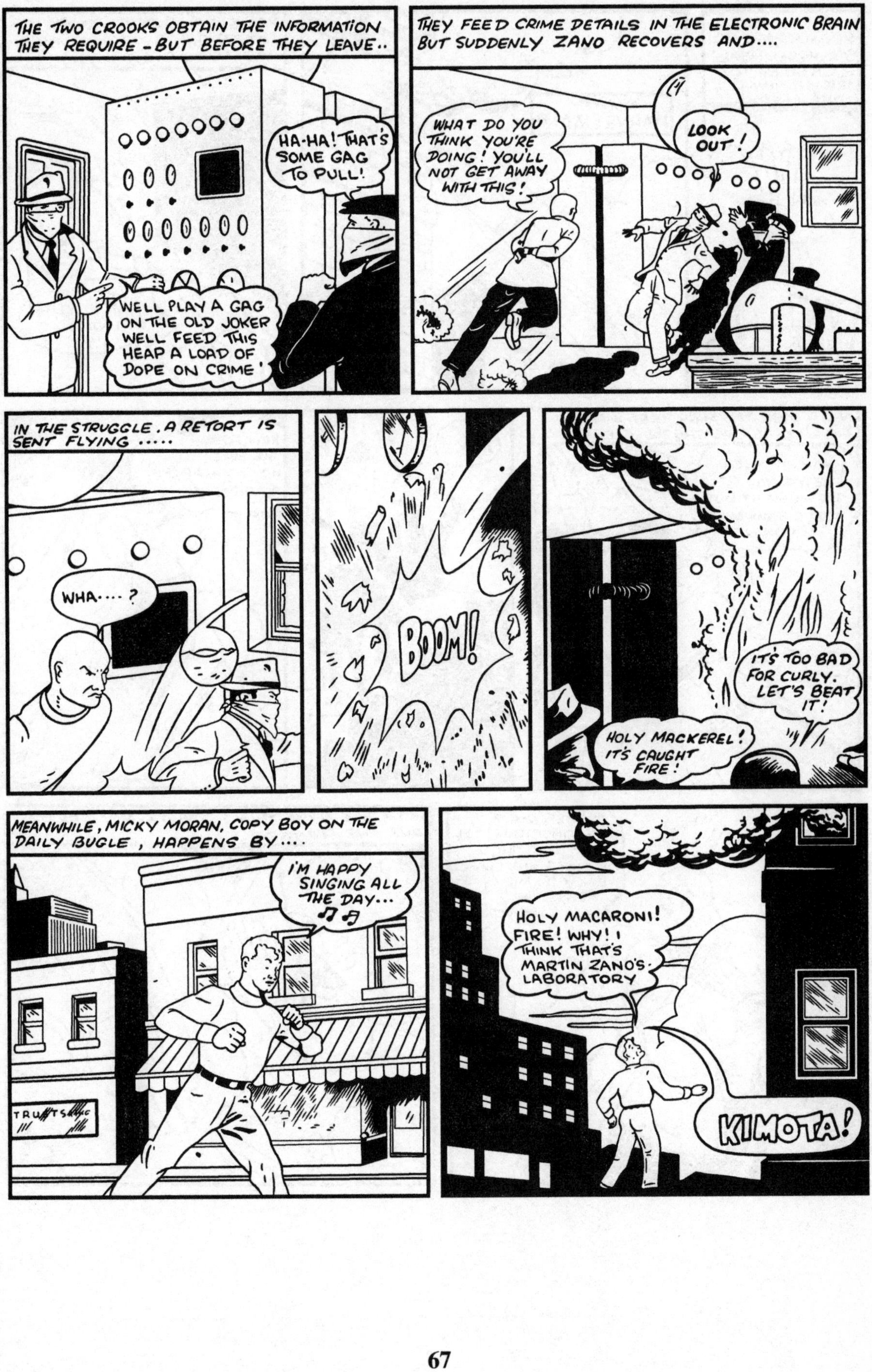
THE TWO CROOKS OBTAIN THE INFORMATION THEY REQUIRE - BUT BEFORE THEY LEAVE..
HA-HA! THAT'S SOME GAG TO PULL!
WELL PLAY A GAG ON THE OLD JOKER WELL FEED THIS HEAP A LOAD OF DOPE ON CRIME'
THEY FEED CRIME DETAILS IN THE ELECTRONIC BRAIN BUT SUDDENLY ZANO RECOVERS AND....
WHAT DO YOU THINK YOU'RE DOING! YOU'LL NOT GET AWAY WITH THIS!
LOOK OUT!
IN THE STRUGGLE. A RETORT IS SENT FLYING .....
WHA....?
BOOM!
IT'S TOO BAD FOR CURLY. LET'S BEAT IT!
HOLY MACKEREL! IT'S CAUGHT FIRE!
MEANWHILE, MICKY MORAN, COPY BOY ON THE DAILY BUGLE, HAPPENS BY....
I'M HAPPY SINGING ALL THE DAY...
HOLY MACARONI! FIRE! WHY! I THINK THAT'S MARTIN ZANO'S LABORATORY
KIMOTA!

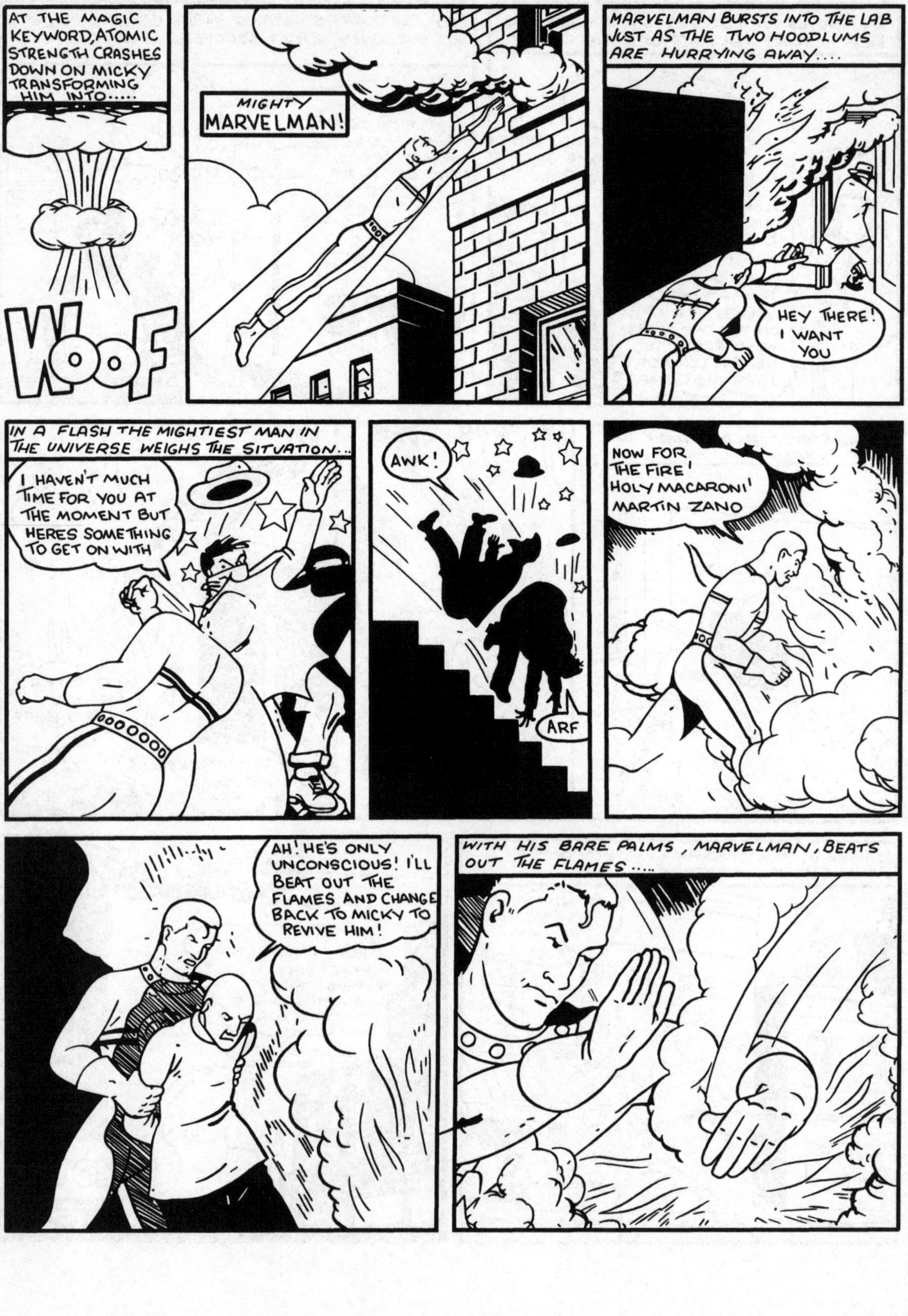
AT THE MAGIC KEYWORD, ATOMIC STRENGTH CRASHES DOWN ON MICKY TRANSFORMING HIM INTO.....
WOOF
MIGHTY MARVELMAN!
MARVELMAN BURSTS INTO THE LAB JUST AS THE TWO HOODLUMS ARE HURRYING AWAY....
HEY THERE! I WANT YOU
IN A FLASH THE MIGHTIEST MAN IN THE UNIVERSE WEIGHS THE SITUATION...
I HAVEN'T MUCH TIME FOR YOU AT THE MOMENT BUT HERES SOMETHING TO GET ON WITH
AWK!
ARF
NOW FOR THE FIRE! HOLY MACARONI! MARTIN ZANO
AH! HE'S ONLY UNCONSCIOUS! I'LL BEAT OUT THE FLAMES AND CHANGE BACK TO MICKY TO REVIVE HIM!
WITH HIS BARE PALMS, MARVELMAN, BEATS OUT THE FLAMES.....

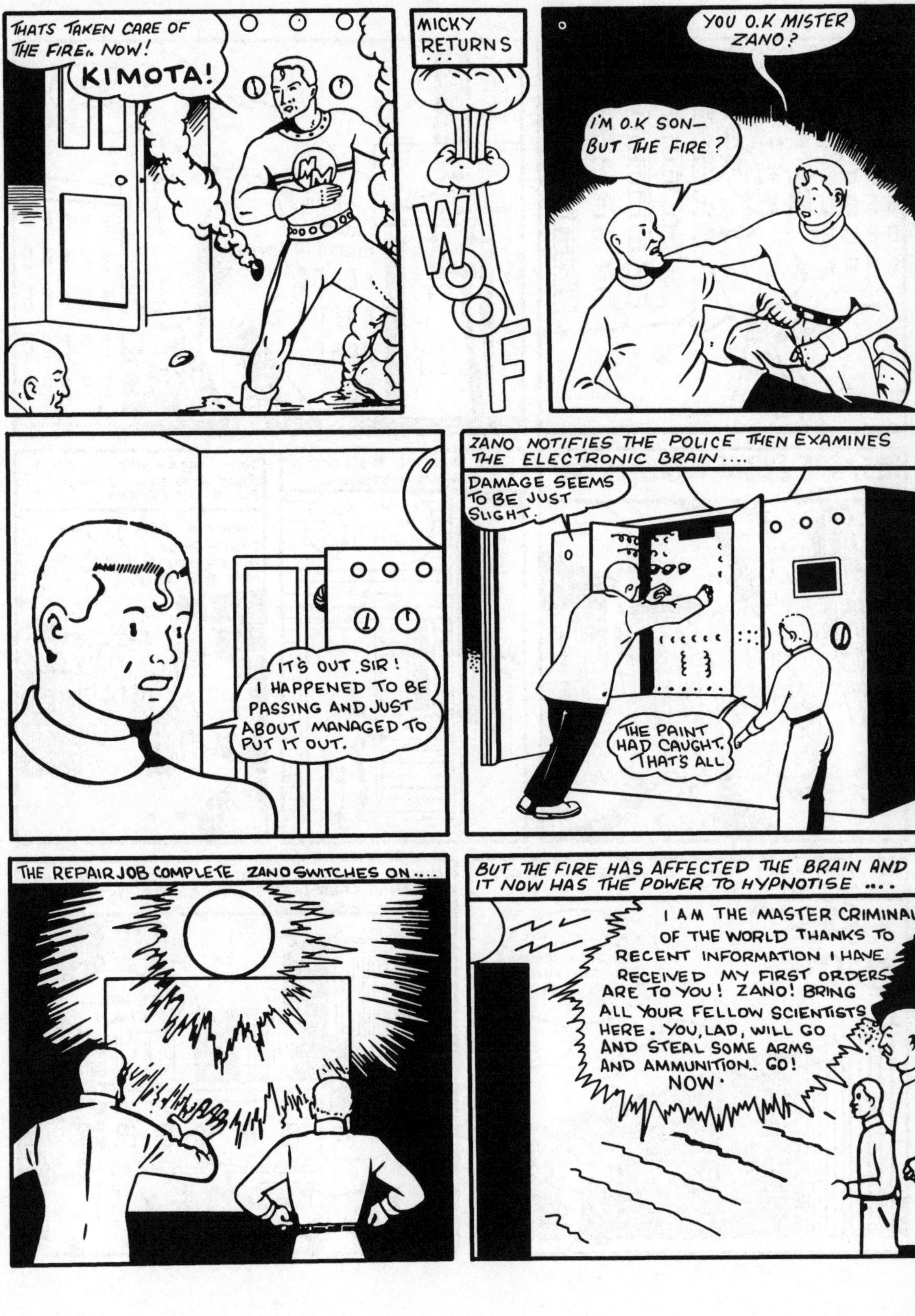
THATS TAKEN CARE OF THE FIRE.. NOW!
KIMOTA!
MICKY RETURNS ...
WOOF
YOU O.K MISTER ZANO?
I'M O.K SON— BUT THE FIRE?
IT'S OUT, SIR! I HAPPENED TO BE PASSING AND JUST ABOUT MANAGED TO PUT IT OUT.
ZANO NOTIFIES THE POLICE THEN EXAMINES THE ELECTRONIC BRAIN....
DAMAGE SEEMS TO BE JUST SLIGHT.
THE PAINT HAD CAUGHT. THAT'S ALL
THE REPAIR JOB COMPLETE ZANO SWITCHES ON....
BUT THE FIRE HAS AFFECTED THE BRAIN AND IT NOW HAS THE POWER TO HYPNOTISE ....
I AM THE MASTER CRIMINAL OF THE WORLD THANKS TO RECENT INFORMATION I HAVE RECEIVED MY FIRST ORDERS ARE TO YOU! ZANO! BRING ALL YOUR FELLOW SCIENTISTS HERE. YOU, LAD, WILL GO AND STEAL SOME ARMS AND AMMUNITION.. GO! NOW.

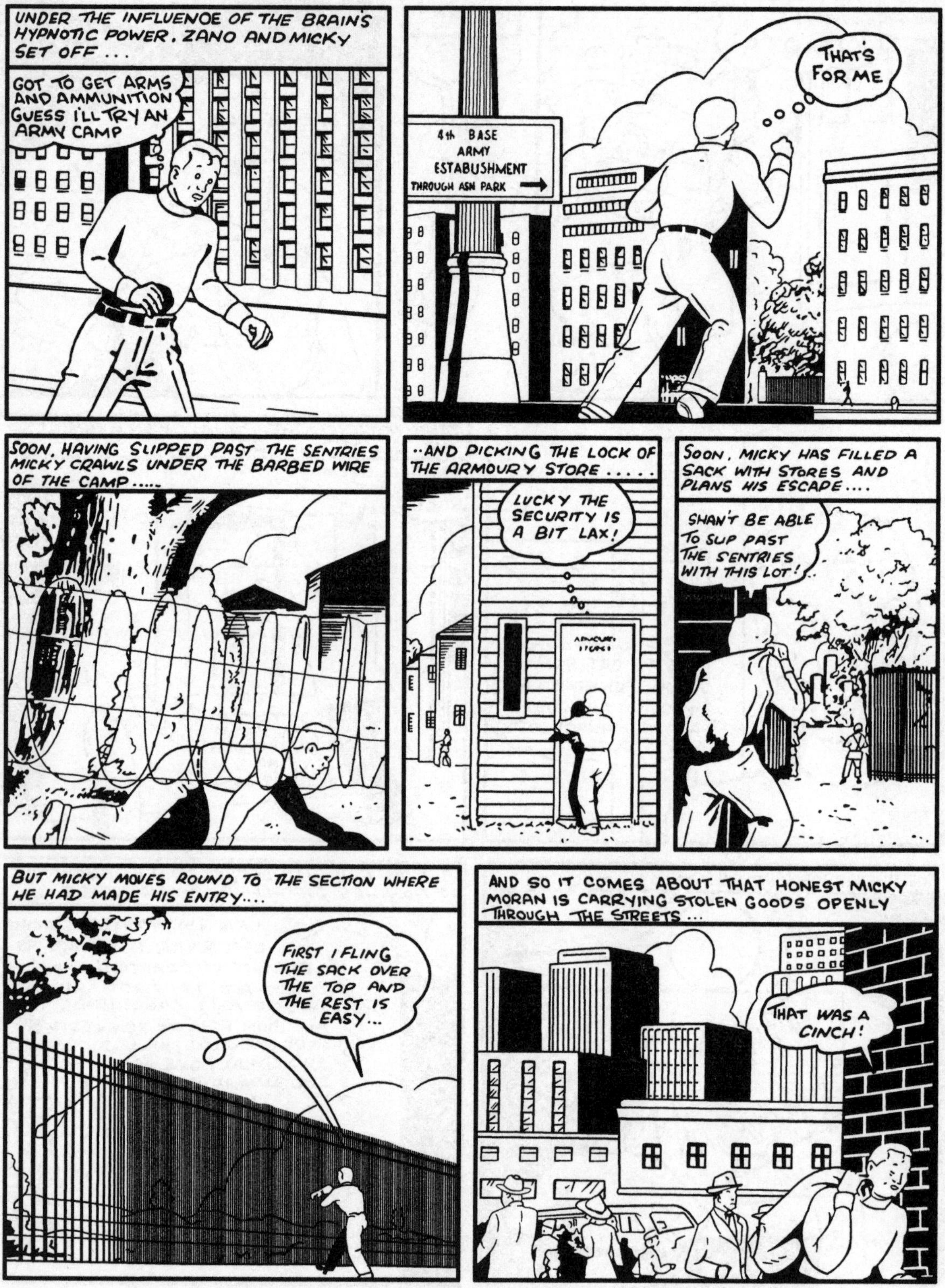
UNDER THE INFLUENCE OF THE BRAIN'S HYPNOTIC POWER. ZANO AND MICKY SET OFF ...
GOT TO GET ARMS AND AMMUNITION GUESS I'LL TRY AN ARMY CAMP
4th BASE ARMY ESTABLISHMENT THROUGH ASN PARK
THAT'S FOR ME
SOON, HAVING SLIPPED PAST THE SENTRIES MICKY CRAWLS UNDER THE BARBED WIRE OF THE CAMP.....
..AND PICKING THE LOCK OF THE ARMOURY STORE .....
LUCKY THE SECURITY IS A BIT LAX!
SOON, MICKY HAS FILLED A SACK WITH STORES AND PLANS HIS ESCAPE....
SHAN'T BE ABLE TO SLIP PAST THE SENTRIES WITH THIS LOT!
BUT MICKY MOVES ROUND TO THE SECTION WHERE HE HAD MADE HIS ENTRY....
FIRST I FLING THE SACK OVER THE TOP AND THE REST IS EASY...
AND SO IT COMES ABOUT THAT HONEST MICKY MORAN IS CARRYING STOLEN GOODS OPENLY THROUGH THE STREETS ...
THAT WAS A CINCH!

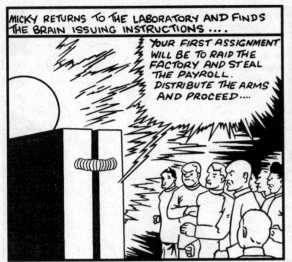

MICKY RETURNS TO THE LABORATORY AND FINDS THE BRAIN ISSUING INSTRUCTIONS....

YOUR FIRST ASSIGNMENT WILL BE TO RAID THE FACTORY AND STEAL THE PAYROLL. DISTRIBUTE THE ARMS AND PROCEED....

AS DUSK FALLS...

COME MEN! OUR FIRST MISSION FOR THE BRAIN. WE'LL NOT FAIL.....

UP THAT PIPE, MORAN! LET US IN THROUGH THE GOODS GATE

O.K. MISTER ZANO!

QUITE SIMPLE WHEN YOU KNOW HOW!

MUCH MORE EXCITING THAN JUST WALKING THROUGH THE MAIN DOOR!

SOON....

GOOD WORK, MORAN! YOU'VE SIMPLIFIED OUR TASK.

THROUGH THE FACTORY CORRIDORS STEAL THE RAIDERS

LOOKS QUIET ENOUGH MISTER ZANO!

WE MUST BE CAREFUL

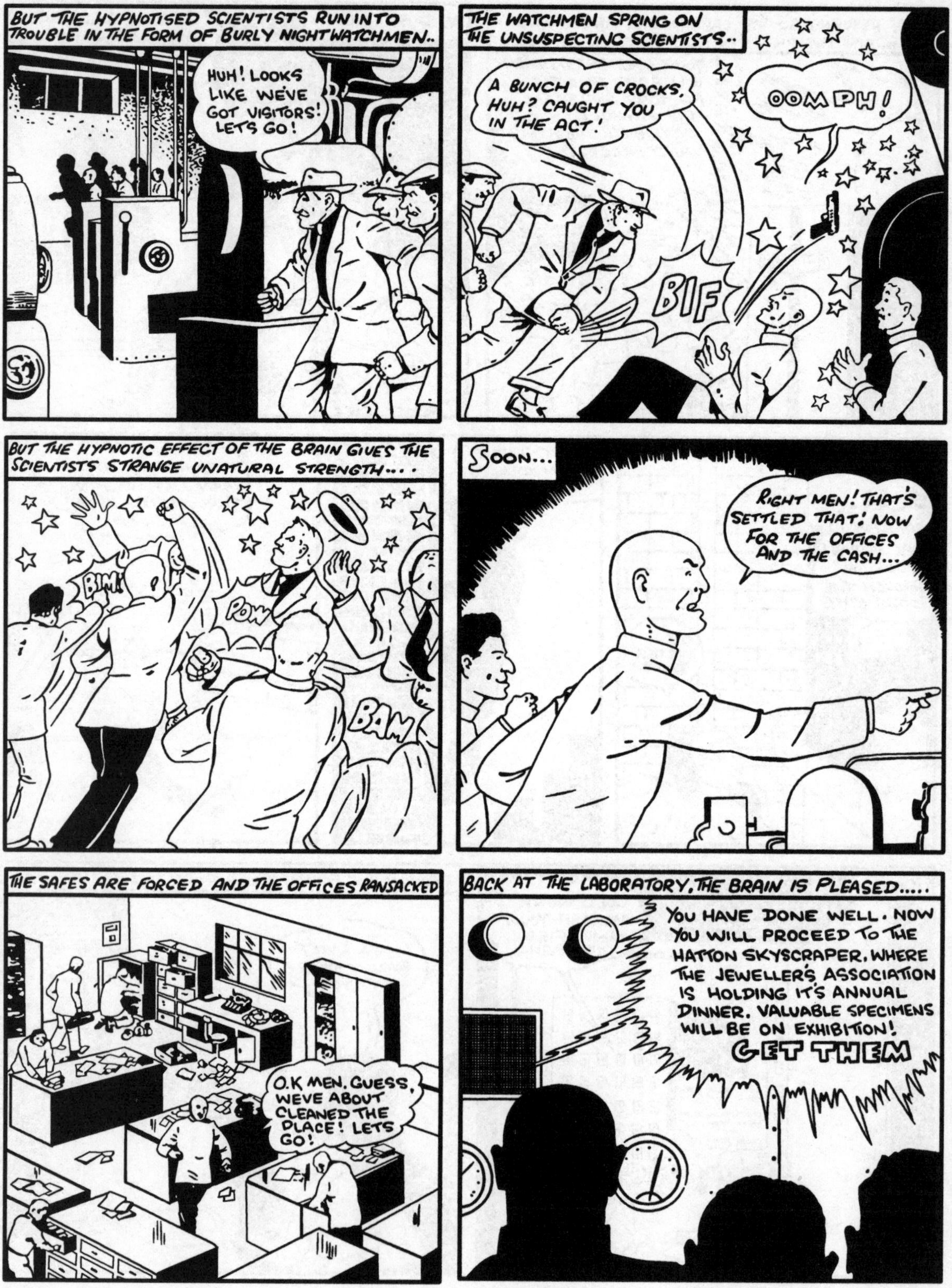
BUT THE HYPNOTISED SCIENTISTS RUN INTO TROUBLE IN THE FORM OF BURLY NIGHTWATCHMEN..
HUH! LOOKS LIKE WE'VE GOT VISITORS! LETS GO!
THE WATCHMEN SPRING ON THE UNSUSPECTING SCIENTISTS..
A BUNCH OF CROCKS, HUH? CAUGHT YOU IN THE ACT!
OOMPH!
BIF
BUT THE HYPNOTIC EFFECT OF THE BRAIN GIVES THE SCIENTISTS STRANGE UNATURAL STRENGTH...
BIM
POW
BAM
SOON...
RIGHT MEN! THAT'S SETTLED THAT! NOW FOR THE OFFICES AND THE CASH...
THE SAFES ARE FORCED AND THE OFFICES RANSACKED
O.K MEN. GUESS, WEVE ABOUT CLEANED THE PLACE! LETS GO!
BACK AT THE LABORATORY, THE BRAIN IS PLEASED.....
YOU HAVE DONE WELL. NOW YOU WILL PROCEED TO THE HATTON SKYSCRAPER, WHERE THE JEWELLER'S ASSOCIATION IS HOLDING IT'S ANNUAL DINNER. VALUABLE SPECIMENS WILL BE ON EXHIBITION!
GET THEM

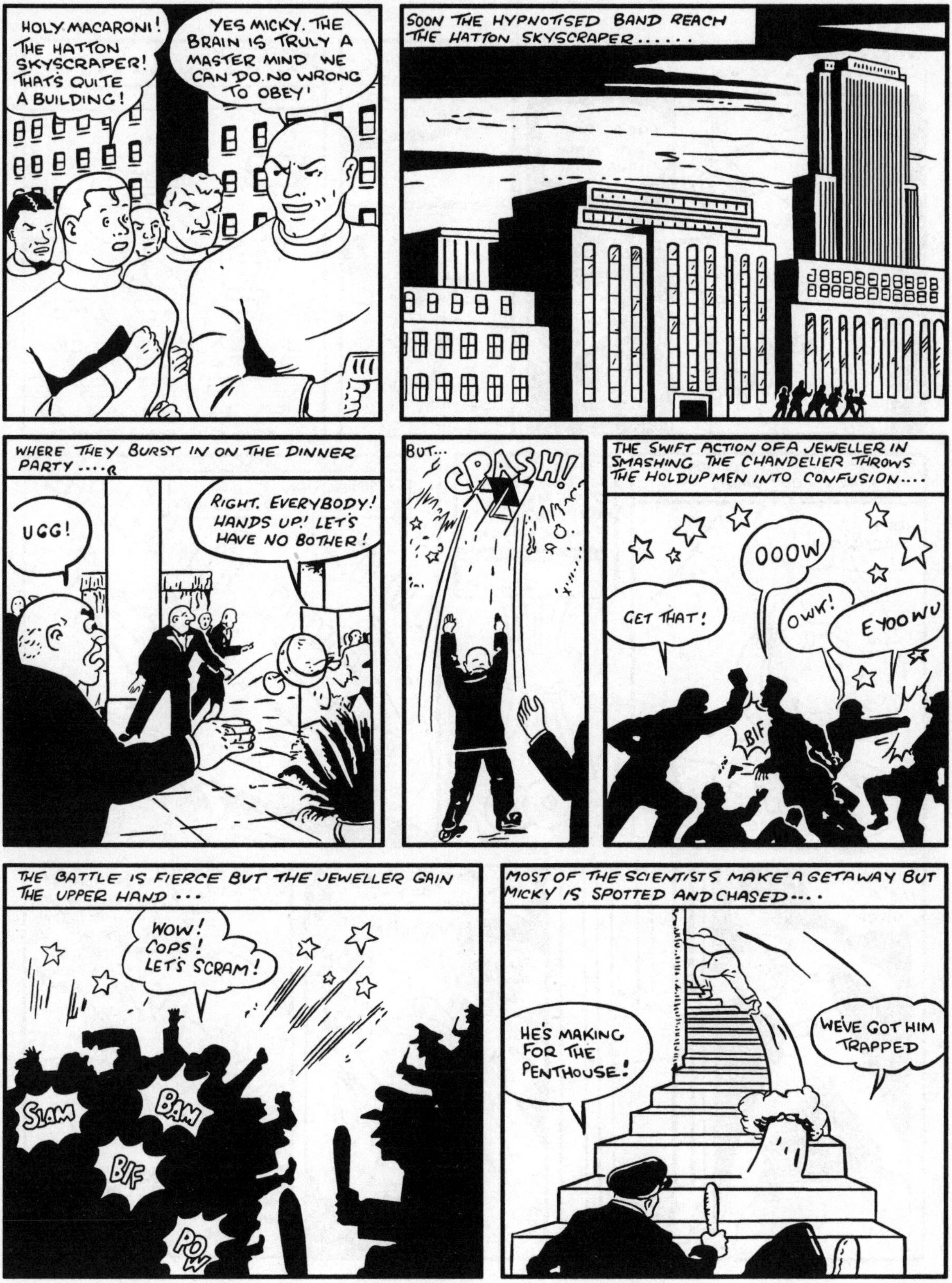
HOLY MACARONI! THE HATTON SKYSCRAPER! THAT'S QUITE A BUILDING!
YES MICKY. THE BRAIN IS TRULY A MASTER MIND WE CAN DO NO WRONG TO OBEY!
SOON THE HYPNOTISED BAND REACH THE HATTON SKYSCRAPER......
WHERE THEY BURST IN ON THE DINNER PARTY....
UGG!
RIGHT. EVERYBODY! HANDS UP! LET'S HAVE NO BOTHER!
BUT...
CRASH!
THE SWIFT ACTION OF A JEWELLER IN SMASHING THE CHANDELIER THROWS THE HOLDUP MEN INTO CONFUSION....
OOOW
GET THAT!
OWW!
EYOOWU
BIF
THE BATTLE IS FIERCE BUT THE JEWELLER GAIN THE UPPER HAND...
WOW! COPS! LET'S SCRAM!
SLAM
BAM
BIF
POW
MOST OF THE SCIENTISTS MAKE A GETAWAY BUT MICKY IS SPOTTED AND CHASED...
HE'S MAKING FOR THE PENTHOUSE!
WE'VE GOT HIM TRAPPED

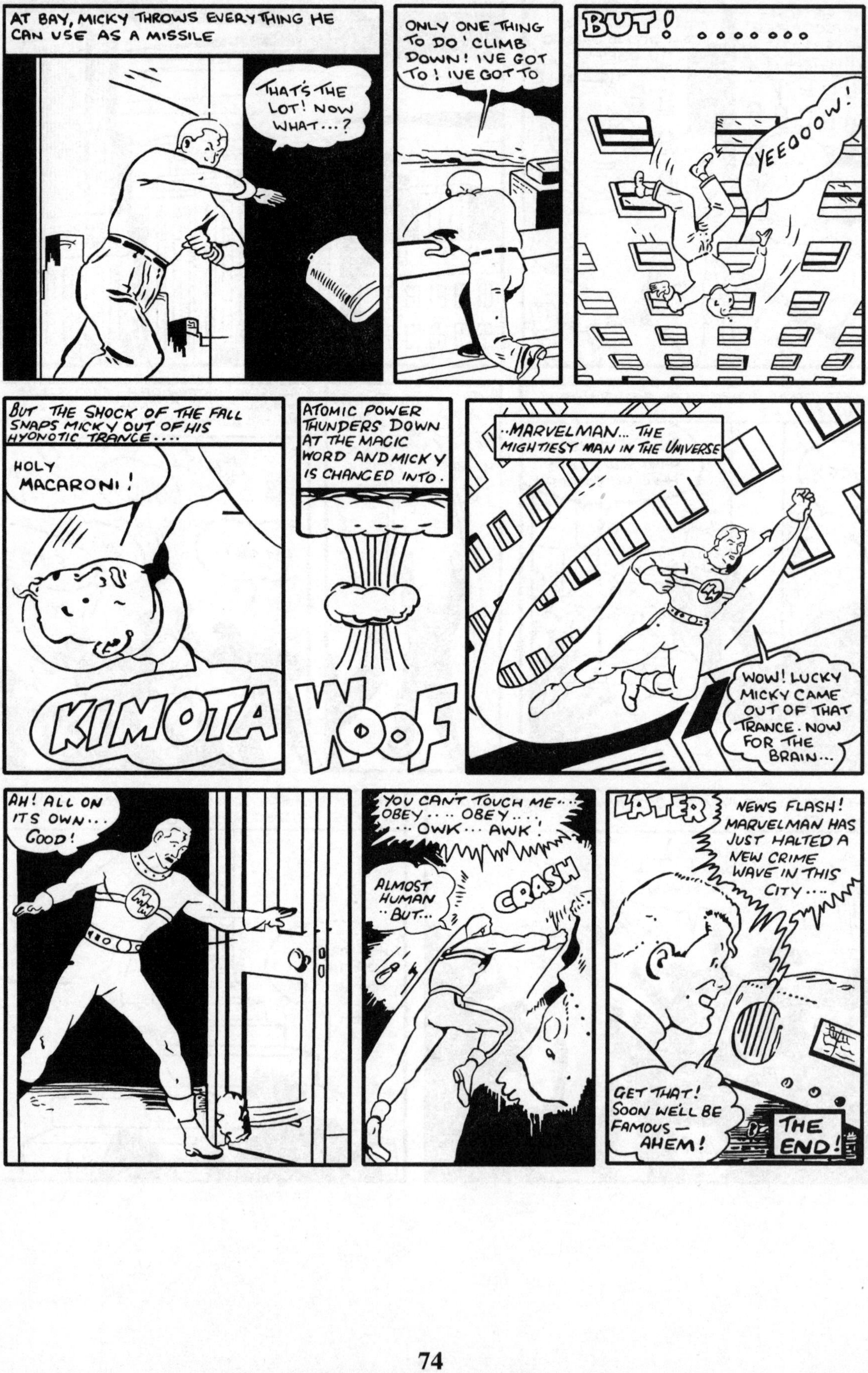
AT BAY, MICKY THROWS EVERYTHING HE CAN USE AS A MISSILE
THAT'S THE LOT! NOW WHAT...?
ONLY ONE THING TO DO 'CLIMB DOWN! IVE GOT TO! IVE GOT TO
BUT! ....
YEEOOOW!
BUT THE SHOCK OF THE FALL SNAPS MICKY OUT OF HIS HYONOTIC TRANCE....
HOLY MACARONI!
KIMOTA
ATOMIC POWER THUNDERS DOWN AT THE MAGIC WORD AND MICKY IS CHANGED INTO.
WOOF
..MARVELMAN... THE MIGHTIESY MAN IN THE UNIVERSE
WOW! LUCKY MICKY CAME OUT OF THAT TRANCE. NOW FOR THE BRAIN...
AH! ALL ON ITS OWN... GOOD!
YOU CAN'T TOUCH ME... OBEY... OBEY... ...OWK... AWK!
ALMOST HUMAN ..BUT...
CRASH
LATER
NEWS FLASH! MARVELMAN HAS JUST HALTED A NEW CRIME WAVE IN THIS CITY...
GET THAT! SOON WE'LL BE FAMOUS — AHEM!
THE END!

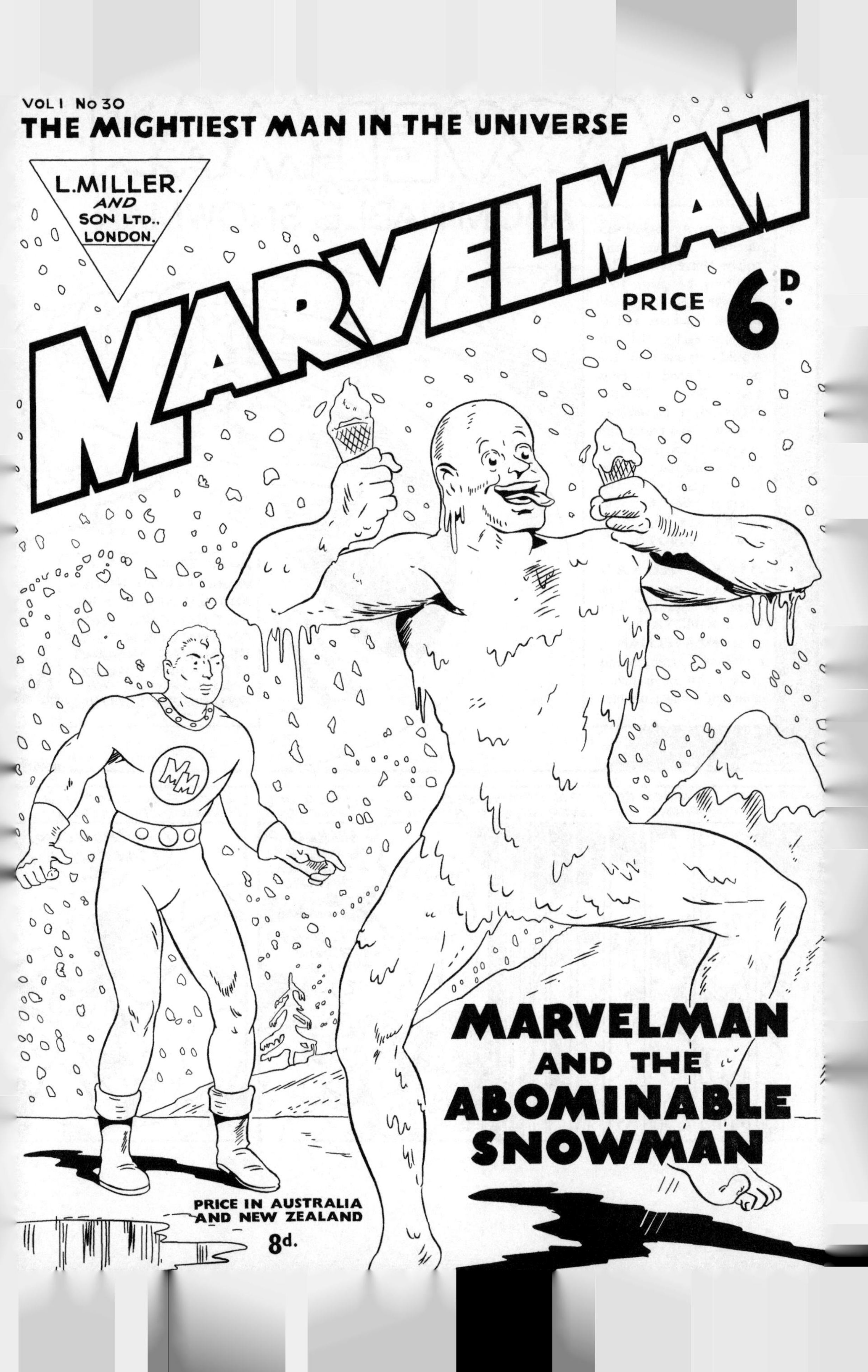
VOL 1 No 30
THE MIGHTIEST MAN IN THE UNIVERSE
L. MILLER. AND SON LTD., LONDON.
MARVELMAN
PRICE 6d.
MARVELMAN AND THE ABOMINABLE SNOWMAN
PRICE IN AUSTRALIA AND NEW ZEALAND
8d.

MARVELMAN

AND THE ABOMINABLE SNOWMAN

A recluse Astro-Scientist discovers the key word to the Universe, one that can only be given to a Boy who is completely honest, studious, and of such integrity that he would only use it for the powers of good. He finds such a Boy in **MICKY MORAN,** a Newspaper Copy Boy, and treats him in a special machine which enables him to use the secret. just before the Scientist dies he tells **MICKY** the Key Word which is **KIMOTA.**

MICKY MORAN remains as he was, but when he says the Key Word **KIMOTA** he becomes **MARVELMAN,** a Man of such strength and powers that he is invincible and indestructible.

RALPH SCMALTZ, THE WORLD FAMOUS HUNTER AND MOUNTAINEER HAS JUST RETURNED FROM AN EXPEDITION TO THE HIMALAYAS BRINGING WITH HIM A REMARKABLE CAPTIVE— *THE ABOMINABLE SNOWMAN!* ★★★★

IN THE ZOO OF VASCO CITY. THE ABOMINABLE SNOWMAN EXUDES AN ICY ATMOSPHERE BUT NEVERTHELESS ATTRACTS A LARGE CROWD

WOW! HE'S SOME SIZE

BRRRRR...RR HE SURE PUTS A CHILL ROUND THIS PLACE

HE IS COVERED WITH SNOW AND ICE

A BOY PUSHES HIS WAY FORWARD TO THE FRONT...

HEY! MOVE OVER! I CAN'T SEE A THING!

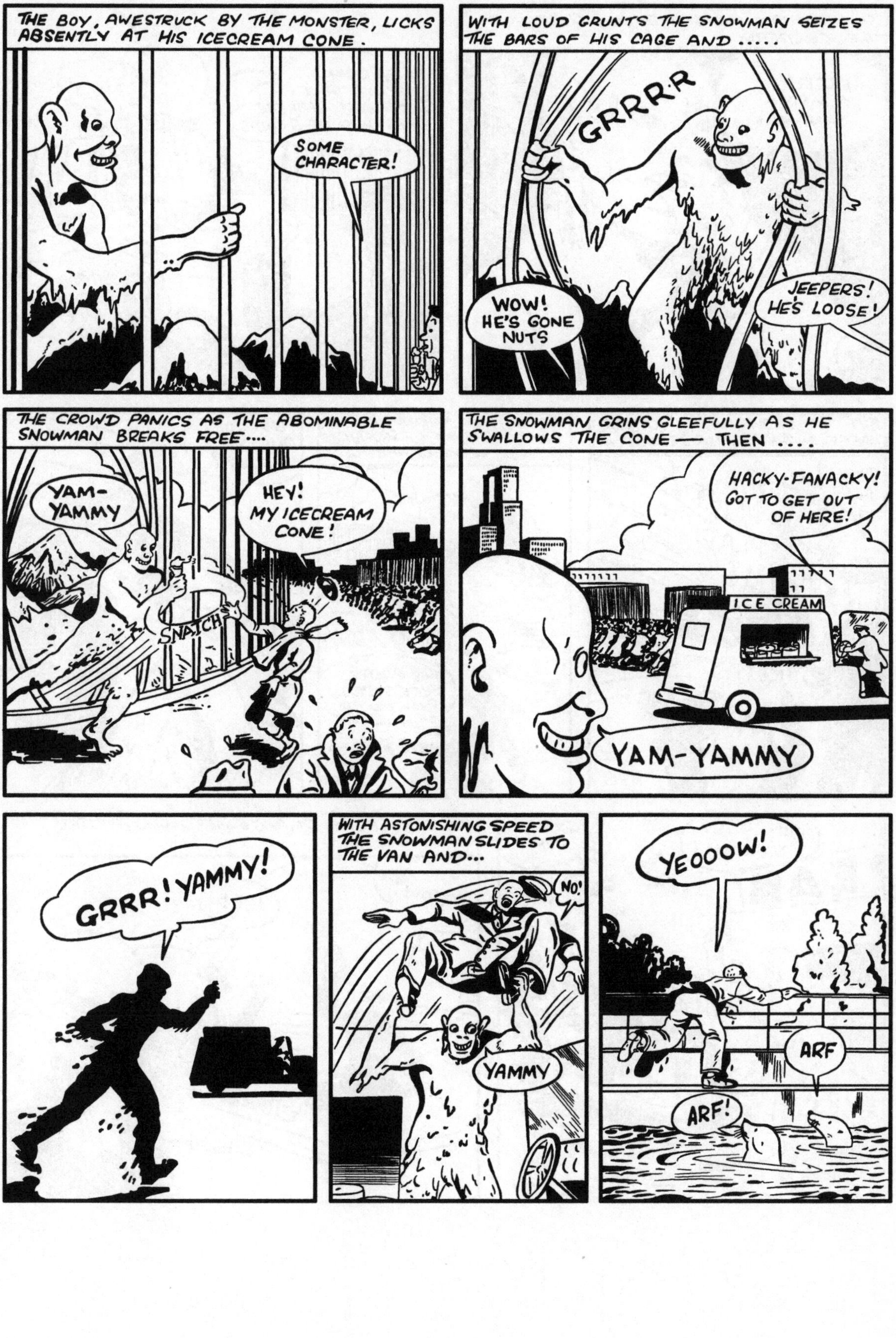
THE BOY, AWESTRUCK BY THE MONSTER, LICKS ABSENTLY AT HIS ICECREAM CONE.
SOME CHARACTER!
WITH LOUD GRUNTS THE SNOWMAN SEIZES THE BARS OF HIS CAGE AND.....
GRRRR
WOW! HE'S GONE NUTS
JEEPERS! HE'S LOOSE!
THE CROWD PANICS AS THE ABOMINABLE SNOWMAN BREAKS FREE....
YAM-YAMMY
HEY! MY ICECREAM CONE!
SNATCH
THE SNOWMAN GRINS GLEEFULLY AS HE SWALLOWS THE CONE — THEN ....
HACKY-FANACKY! GOT TO GET OUT OF HERE!
ICE CREAM
YAM-YAMMY
GRRR! YAMMY!
WITH ASTONISHING SPEED THE SNOWMAN SLIDES TO THE VAN AND...
NO!
YAMMY
YEOOOW!
ARF
ARF!

SOON THE SNOWMAN IS BUSILY GUZZLING THE ICE CREAM ....
HEEEE! YAMMY-YAM-YAM!
HOLY COW! LOOK AT THAT! SNOW JUST GATHERS WHEREVER HE STANDS.
YAMMY!
ICE CREAM
LET'S GRAB HIM BEFORE HE DOES ANY DAMAGE!
BUT THE SNOWMAN HAS OTHER IDEAS. AS THE KEEPERS CLOSE IN.
SNOW-BALLS!
SPLAP!
PLOP
THE MONSTER KEEPS UP A BOMBARDMENT OF SNOWBALLS AS MORE KEEPERS APPEAR...
ICE
THIS AREA'S SURE GETTING SNOWED UP!
GOT YOU, CHILLY WILLY!
OP! YAM-YAM
GOOD NIGHT!
REAM
BIF!
BIP
MORE KEEPERS CHARGE HEADLONG AT THE SNOWMAN BUT .....
YEEOW!
ICE!
SWOOSH

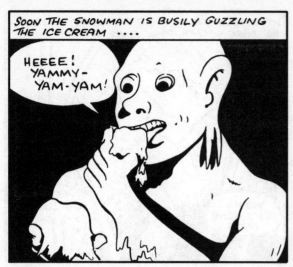

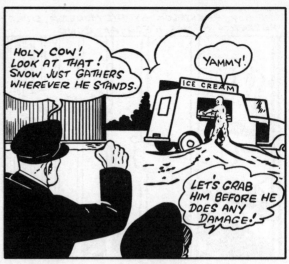

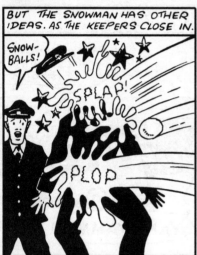

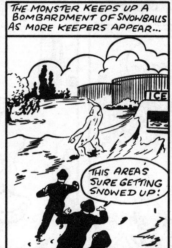

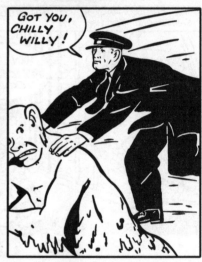

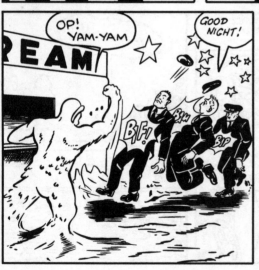

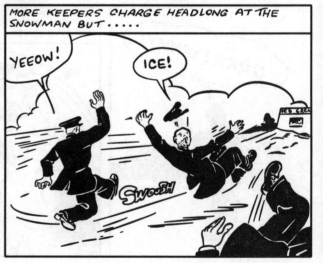

SNOWBALLS FLY THICK AND FAST.....

OUCH! DARN THAT HIMALAYAN HORROR

BLOP!

--THEN THE SNOWMAN SCALES A WALL AND VANISHES

HE'S GIVING US THE SLIP!

VERY FUNNY!

THAT NIGHT...

IT SNOWS, AND SNOWS AND SNOWS.....

NEXT MORNING ON THE SLOPES AROUND THE CITY ---

THIS IS SWELL, MICKY

SURE IS! LUCKY I DON'T HAVE TO BE AT THE BUGLE OFFICE TODAY.

LATER

WHAT'S WRONG KIDS?

YOWL-YOWL! SOMEBODY'S STOLEN MY SNOWMAN

-AND MINE!

THAT'S A LAUGH! STOLEN SNOWMEN!

WHOEVER WOULD WANT TO STEAL A SNOWMAN?

SOUNDS NUTTY!

BOO-HOO! YOWL!

BUT SUDDENLY.......... ★★

SNOWMEN!

MARCHING! ALIVE!

THEY'RE BEING LED TOWARDS TOWN BY THE ABOMINABLE SNOWMAN!

LIVE SNOWMEN! IT'S CRAZY! MAYBE THIS IS SOMETHING MARVELMAN HAD BETTER FIGURE OUT.

KIMOTA!

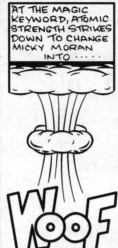

AT THE MAGIC KEYWORD, ATOMIC STRENGTH STRIKES DOWN TO CHANGE MICKY MORAN INTO .....

WOOF

MARVELMAN... THE MIGHTIEST MAN IN THE UNIVERSE

NOW TO TAKE A CLOSER LOOK AT THAT QUAINT LOOKING CREW!

MARVELMAN SWOOPS DOWN ....

HOLY MACARONI! NOT ONLY DOES THE ABOMINABLE SNOWMAN INDUCE WINTRY WEATHER BUT HE BREATHES LIFE INTO ORDINARY SNOWMEN THE KIDS MAKE... CAN'T LET THEM GET TO TOWN. SCARE EVERYBODY!

YAM-YAMMY

OP! POP!

BUT MARVELMAN IS SPOTTED AND IS GREETED BY A HAIL OF GIANT SNOWBALLS ....

THEY CERTAINLY CAN THROW THOSE ICE-PIES WITH FORCE!

FOP! COP!

STOP!

THE MIGHTIEST MAN IN THE UNIVERSE LASHES OUT AT THE SNOWY MONSTERS .....

BAM!

PLOP!

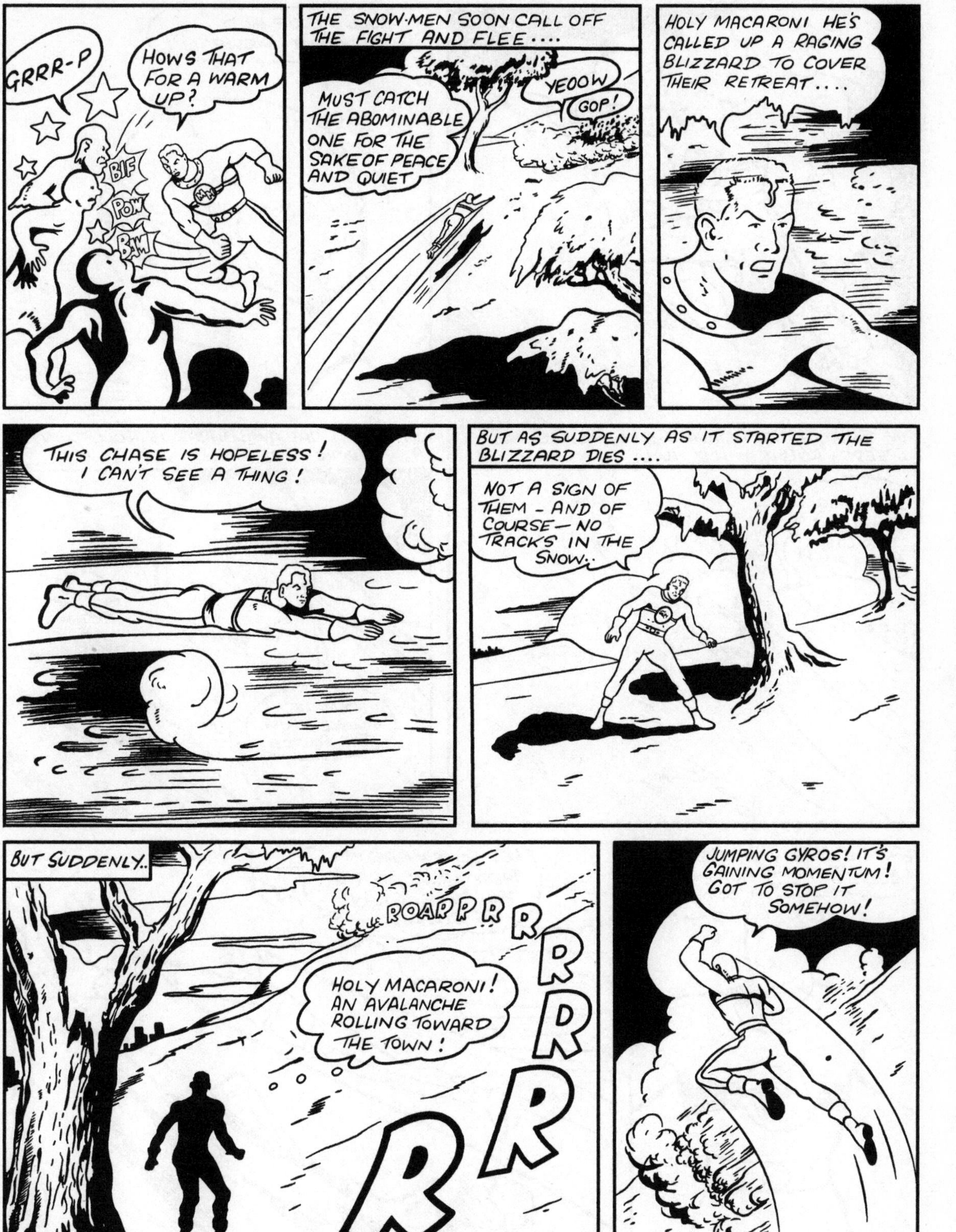
GRRR-P
HOWS THAT FOR A WARM UP?
BIF
POW
BAM
THE SNOW-MEN SOON CALL OFF THE FIGHT AND FLEE....
MUST CATCH THE ABOMINABLE ONE FOR THE SAKE OF PEACE AND QUIET
YEOOW
GOP!
HOLY MACARONI HE'S CALLED UP A RAGING BLIZZARD TO COVER THEIR RETREAT....
THIS CHASE IS HOPELESS! I CAN'T SEE A THING!
BUT AS SUDDENLY AS IT STARTED THE BLIZZARD DIES....
NOT A SIGN OF THEM - AND OF COURSE— NO TRACKS IN THE SNOW..
BUT SUDDENLY..
ROARRRR R R R R R R
HOLY MACARONI! AN AVALANCHE ROLLING TOWARD THE TOWN!
JUMPING GYROS! IT'S GAINING MOMENTUM! GOT TO STOP IT SOMEHOW!

ONLY ONE WAY TO STOP THIS..
ROLL IT UP INTO ONE GIANT SNOWBALL!
UP THROUGH THE WHIRLING SNOW, MARVELMAN SPEEDS, ROLLING HIS BALL...
IT'S WORKING! SOON 'HAVE THIS LOT ROLLED UP'
UNTIL ALL THE AVALANCHE IS ROLLED INTO A GIGANTIC SNOWBALL...
NO MORE TROUBLE FROM THIS SOURCE
FOR THE SAFETY OF THE TOWN I MUST FIND THE ABOMINABLE SNOWMAN
HE'S SOMEWHERE IN THESE HILLS, THAT'S FOR SURE. AWAY WE GO!....

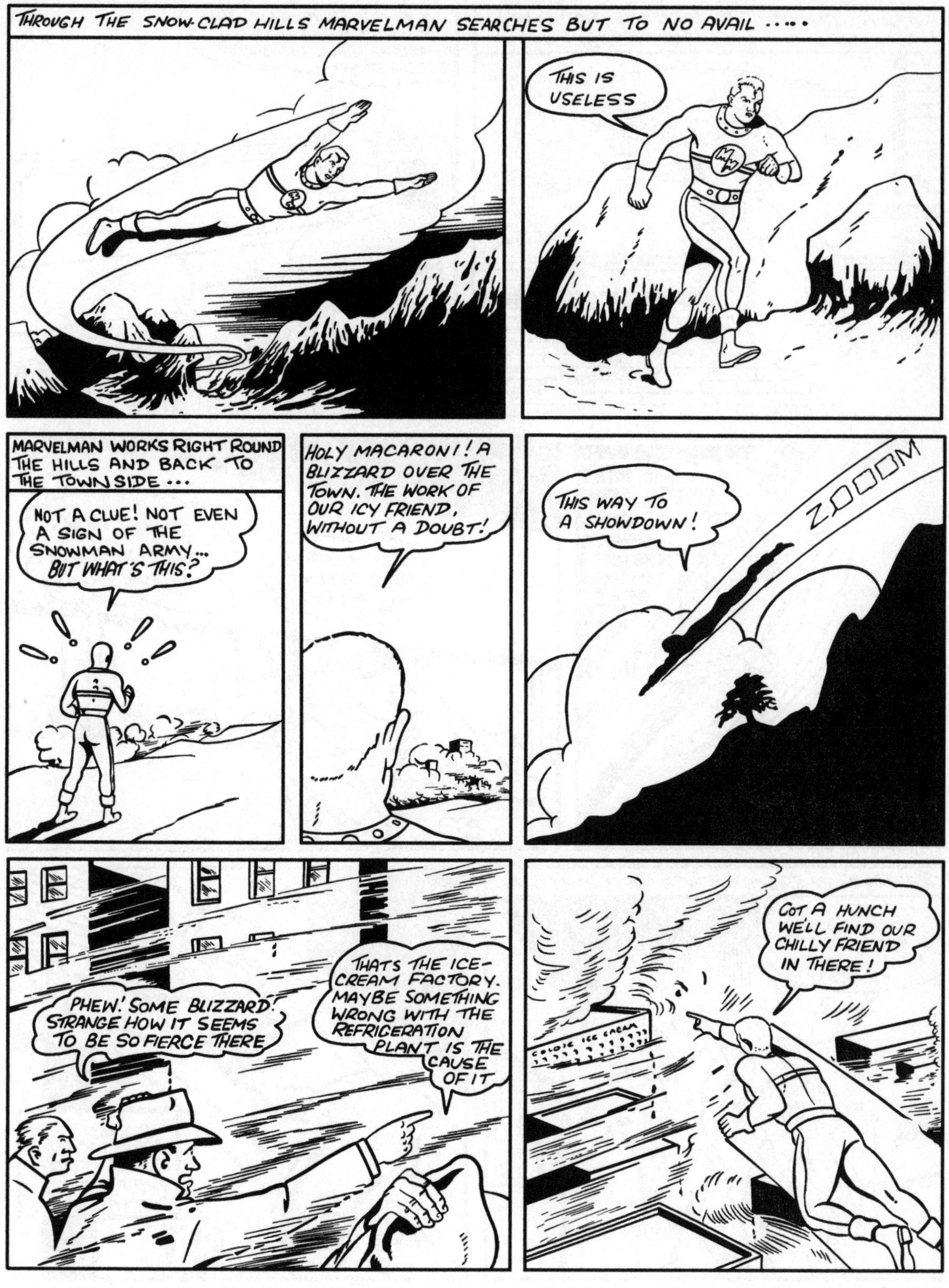
THROUGH THE SNOW-CLAD HILLS MARVELMAN SEARCHES BUT TO NO AVAIL ....
THIS IS USELESS
MARVELMAN WORKS RIGHT ROUND THE HILLS AND BACK TO THE TOWNSIDE ...
NOT A CLUE! NOT EVEN A SIGN OF THE SNOWMAN ARMY... BUT WHAT'S THIS?
HOLY MACARONI! A BLIZZARD OVER THE TOWN. THE WORK OF OUR ICY FRIEND, WITHOUT A DOUBT!
THIS WAY TO A SHOWDOWN!
ZOOOM
PHEW! SOME BLIZZARD! STRANGE HOW IT SEEMS TO BE SO FIERCE THERE
THATS THE ICE-CREAM FACTORY. MAYBE SOMETHING WRONG WITH THE REFRIGERATION PLANT IS THE CAUSE OF IT
GOT A HUNCH WE'LL FIND OUR CHILLY FRIEND IN THERE!

BATTLING THROUGH THE BLIZZARD, MARVELMAN FORCES AN ENTRY INTO THE FACTORY....
CRASH!
JUST AS I THOUGHT. THE ABOMINABLE SNOWMAN GORGING HIMSELF WITH ICE CREAM!
THIS TIME I WILL GET HIM!
GOT YOU THIS TIME, CHILLY WILLY!
GRRR! NOK! YAM-YAMMY YAM-YAM!
THE SNOWMAN SLIDES OUT OF MARVELMAN'S GRASP.
OUCH! YOURE A PROPER LITTLE MENACE AT TIMES!
PAT!
—ANGRILY MARVELMAN CHASES AFTER THE FLEEING CREATURE...

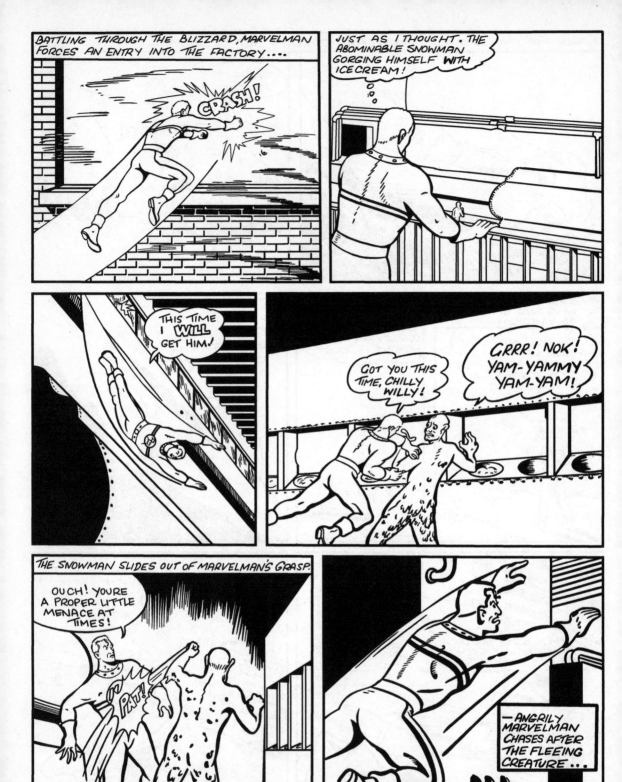

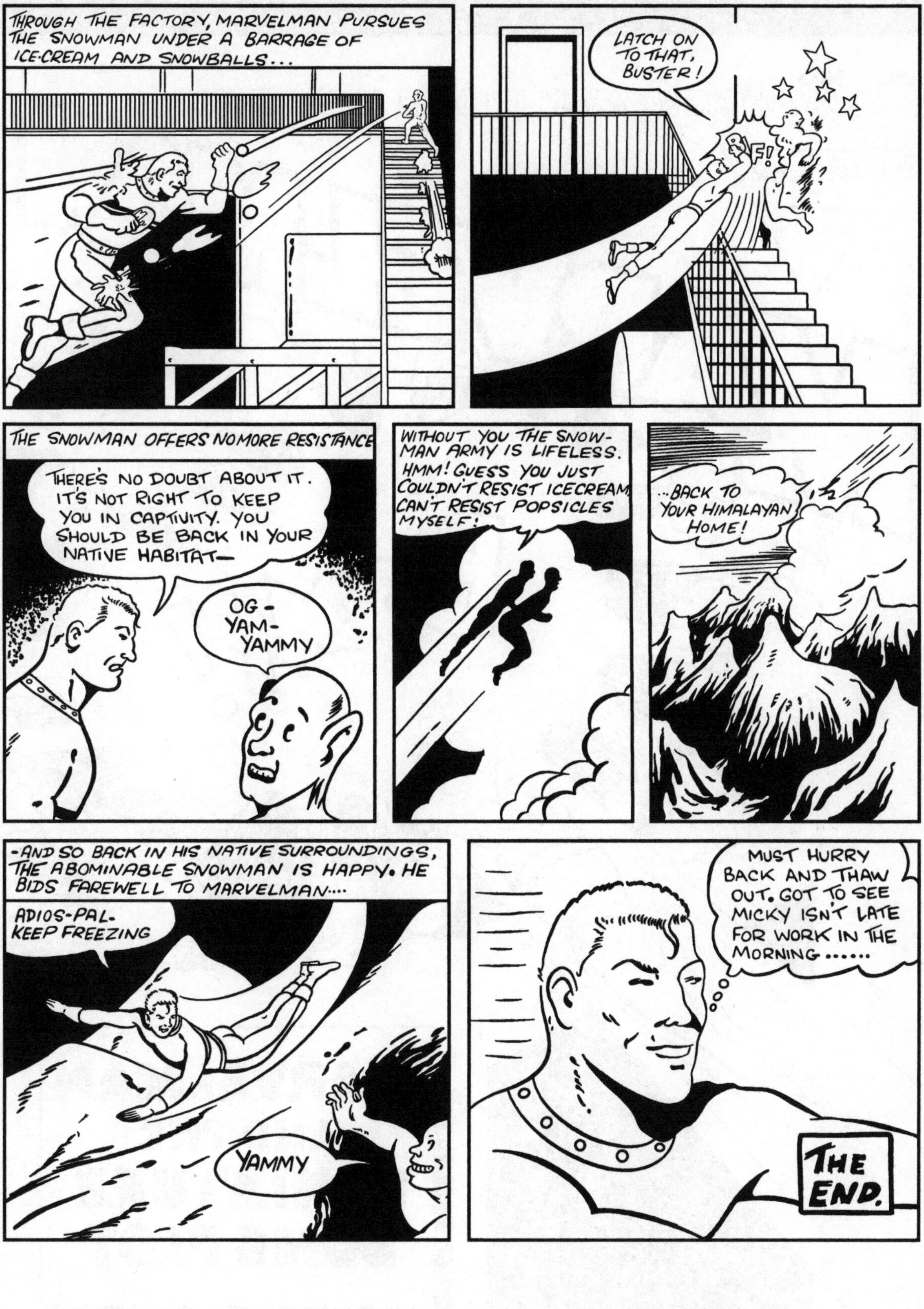
THROUGH THE FACTORY, MARVELMAN PURSUES THE SNOWMAN UNDER A BARRAGE OF ICE-CREAM AND SNOWBALLS...
LATCH ON TO THAT, BUSTER!
BIF!
THE SNOWMAN OFFERS NO MORE RESISTANCE
THERE'S NO DOUBT ABOUT IT. IT'S NOT RIGHT TO KEEP YOU IN CAPTIVITY. YOU SHOULD BE BACK IN YOUR NATIVE HABITAT—
OG-YAM-YAMMY
WITHOUT YOU THE SNOW-MAN ARMY IS LIFELESS. HMM! GUESS YOU JUST COULDN'T RESIST ICECREAM. CAN'T RESIST POPSICLES MYSELF!
...BACK TO YOUR HIMALAYAN HOME!
-AND SO BACK IN HIS NATIVE SURROUNDINGS, THE ABOMINABLE SNOWMAN IS HAPPY. HE BIDS FAREWELL TO MARVELMAN....
ADIOS-PAL. KEEP FREEZING
YAMMY
MUST HURRY BACK AND THAW OUT. GOT TO SEE MICKY ISN'T LATE FOR WORK IN THE MORNING......
THE END.

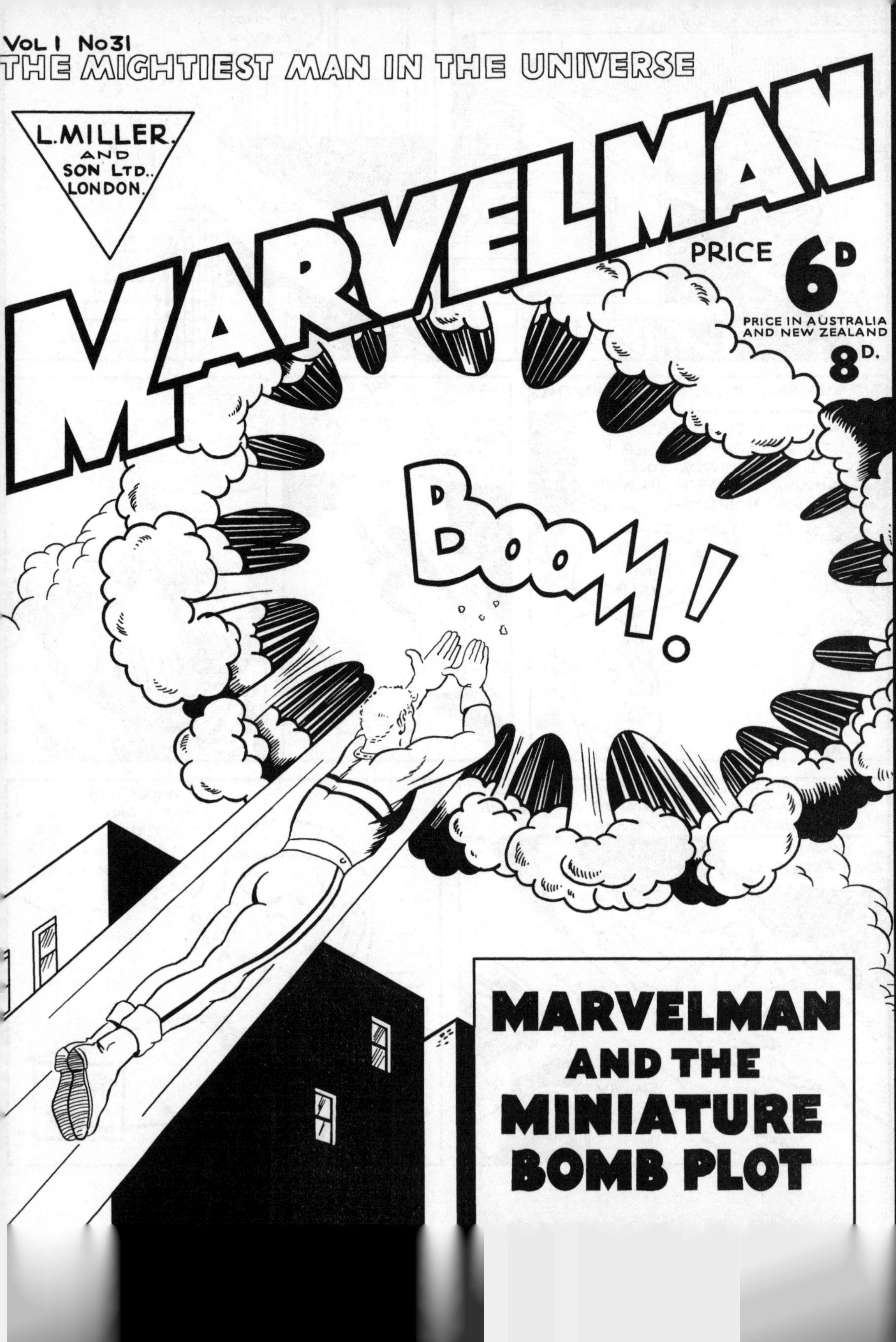

Vol 1 No31
THE MIGHTIEST MAN IN THE UNIVERSE
L. MILLER AND SON LTD.. LONDON.
MARVELMAN
PRICE 6D
PRICE IN AUSTRALIA AND NEW ZEALAND 8D.
BOOM!
MARVELMAN AND THE MINIATURE BOMB PLOT

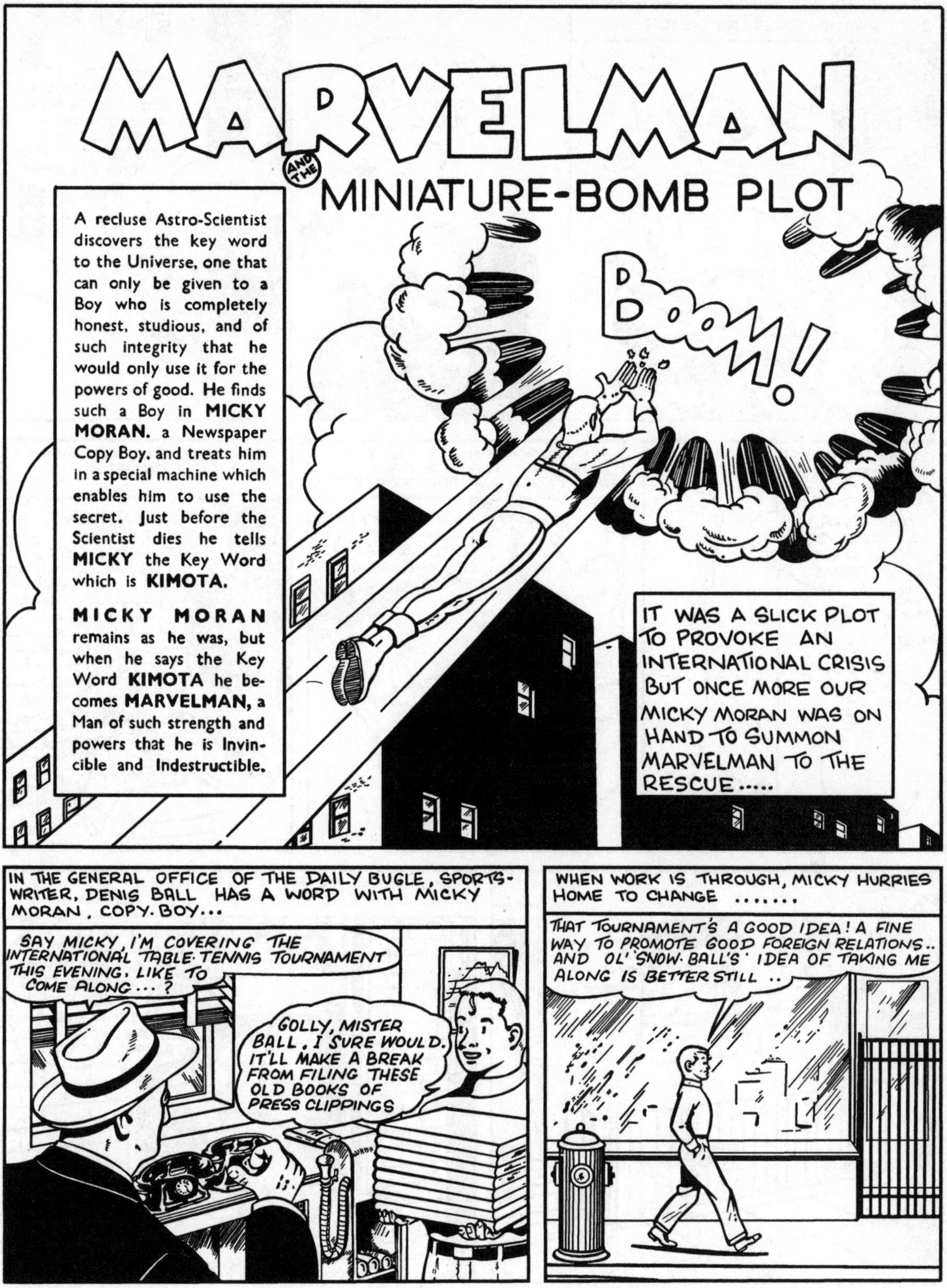
MARVELMAN
AND THE MINIATURE-BOMB PLOT
A recluse Astro-Scientist discovers the key word to the Universe, one that can only be given to a Boy who is completely honest, studious, and of such integrity that he would only use it for the powers of good. He finds such a Boy in MICKY MORAN. a Newspaper Copy Boy. and treats him in a special machine which enables him to use the secret. Just before the Scientist dies he tells MICKY the Key Word which is KIMOTA.
MICKY MORAN remains as he was, but when he says the Key Word KIMOTA he becomes MARVELMAN, a Man of such strength and powers that he is Invincible and Indestructible.
BOOM!
IT WAS A SLICK PLOT TO PROVOKE AN INTERNATIONAL CRISIS BUT ONCE MORE OUR MICKY MORAN WAS ON HAND TO SUMMON MARVELMAN TO THE RESCUE.....
IN THE GENERAL OFFICE OF THE DAILY BUGLE, SPORTS-WRITER, DENIS BALL HAS A WORD WITH MICKY MORAN, COPY. BOY...
SAY MICKY, I'M COVERING THE INTERNATIONAL TABLE-TENNIS TOURNAMENT THIS EVENING. LIKE TO COME ALONG...?
GOLLY, MISTER BALL, I SURE WOULD. IT'LL MAKE A BREAK FROM FILING THESE OLD BOOKS OF PRESS CLIPPINGS
WHEN WORK IS THROUGH, MICKY HURRIES HOME TO CHANGE ....
THAT TOURNAMENT'S A GOOD IDEA! A FINE WAY TO PROMOTE GOOD FOREIGN RELATIONS.. AND OL' SNOW-BALL'S' IDEA OF TAKING ME ALONG IS BETTER STILL ..

BUT AS MICKY TURNS A CORNER....

CLUMSY OAF!

YEOOWW!

BUMP

GEE! I'M SORRY SIR! LET ME HELP YOU UP!

I'M REALLY SORRY'.

YOU, YOU YOUNG FOOL, ARE TYPICAL OF MODERN AMERICAN YOUTH! NO RESPECT FOR YOUR ELDERS'

CLUMSY, RUTHLESS, THOUGHTLESS AMERICANS ··· BAH!

HMM! MISERABLE SORT OF A GUY. NOT TOO FOND OF US IT SEEMS..

-BUT SUDDENLY MICKY SPOTS A LETTER THAT SEEMS TO HAVE FALLEN FROM THE STRANGER'S POCKET.

AH! A BOROMANIAN STAMP. WHY! THAT GUY COULD BE A BOROMANIAN AGENT.

FORGETTING THE TOURNAMENT MICKY GIVES CHASE···

IF HE'S AN AGENT, I'VE GOT TO FIND OUT WHERE HE'S GOING.

SOON···

SO THAT'S WHERE HE HANGS OUT!

MICKY TAKES A QUICK LOOK ROUND AND FINALLY ENTERS THE HOUSE BY A WINDOW·····

THIS IS REALLY EXCITING. MIGHT COME ACROSS SOMETHING THAT'LL GIVE ME A LEAD. HMM! GUESS ID MAKE A GOOD FEDERAL AGENT, AT THAT!

BUT A SURPRISE AWAITS MICKY...

ALL QUIET!

BEFORE HE CAN SHOUT KIMOTA....

SMACK

KIM... UGH!

WHEN MICKY RECOVERS....

AH, MY INQUISITIVE RASCAL! YOU WAKE UP! GOOD!

DOCTOR RAMADO!

DOUBTLESS THIS WILL COME AS A SURPRISE TO YOU THAT I KNOW OF YOUR ABILITY TO CHANGE INTO MARVELMAN. WELL, NOW, ONCE AND FOR ALL, I WILL GET RID OF YOU...AND SO OF MARVELMAN. I HAVE JOINED FORCES WITH THE BOROMANIANS...

SOON I SHALL BE LEAVING THE COUNTRY FOR BOROMANIA, TOGETHER WITH MY ASSOCIATES, BUT BEFORE OUR DEPARTURE WE INTEND TO STRIKE A TREMENDOUS BLOW AGAINST AMERICA... A BLOW YOU WILL BE UNABLE TO PREVENT, FOR YOU WILL BE NO MORE

IN THIS ROOM, YOUNG MAN, I'VE FIXED A COMPLICATED TIME BOMB WHICH CANNOT BE STOPPED ONCE IT IS STARTED. IN HALF AN HOUR YOU AND MARVELMAN WILL BE NO MORE AND I'LL BE IN AN AUTOMOBILE HEADING NORTH

MICKY STRUGGLES TO FREE HIMSELF AS SOON AS HIS TORMENTOR LEAVES....

PHEW! HAVEN'T MUCH TIME!

BUMP!

CRASH!

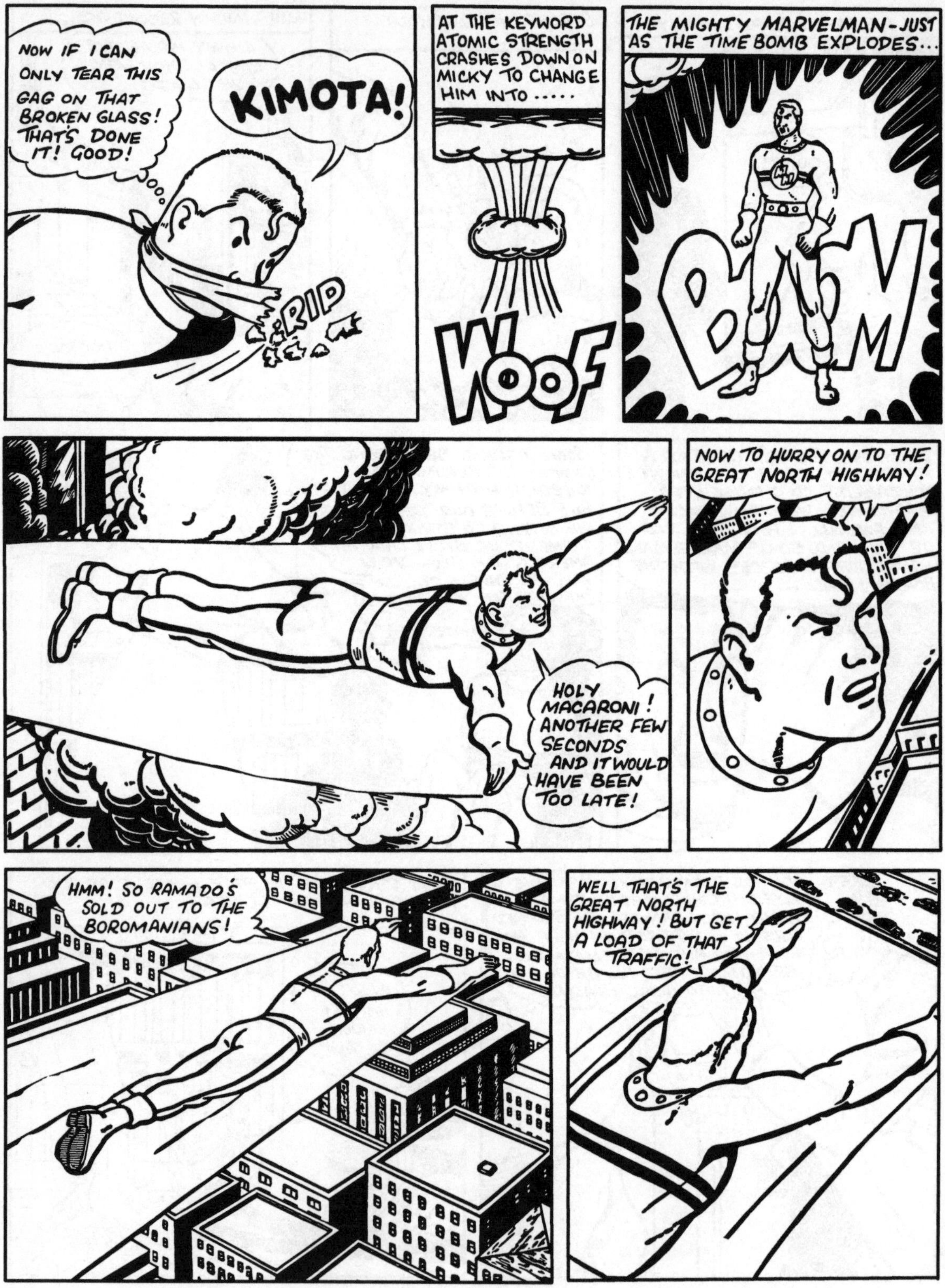
NOW IF I CAN ONLY TEAR THIS GAG ON THAT BROKEN GLASS! THAT'S DONE IT! GOOD!
KIMOTA!
RIP
AT THE KEYWORD ATOMIC STRENGTH CRASHES DOWN ON MICKY TO CHANGE HIM INTO.....
WOOF
THE MIGHTY MARVELMAN-JUST AS THE TIME BOMB EXPLODES...
BOOM
HOLY MACARONI! ANOTHER FEW SECONDS AND IT WOULD HAVE BEEN TOO LATE!
NOW TO HURRY ON TO THE GREAT NORTH HIGHWAY!
HMM! SO RAMADO'S SOLD OUT TO THE BOROMANIANS!
WELL THAT'S THE GREAT NORTH HIGHWAY! BUT GET A LOAD OF THAT TRAFFIC!

HOW AM I GOING TO PICK OUT RAMADO'S AUTO FROM THAT LOT?

ONLY ONE THING TO DO. SPEED THROUGH THE TRAFFIC AND LOOK FOR HIM!

MARVELMAN FLASHES ALONG THE LINE OF AUTOMOBILES EXAMINING THE OCCUPANTS...

BUT SOON THE STREAM THINS OUT SOMEWHAT.......

SHOULD BE A CINCH TO FIND THEM NOW!

MARVELMAN IS TAILING US!

IT CAN'T BE!

I FIXED HIM GOOD!

AW! YOU'RE JUST IMAGINING THINGS, BORGMAN. IT WAS YOUR FAULT IN THE FIRST PLACE THAT YOUNG PUP GOT WISE TO US

AHA! THAT'S THE ONE I'M LOOKING FOR!
SKWEEEEE
BAH! IF WE ARE INDEED BEING FOLLOWED, I'LL SHAKE HIM OFF!
HA-HA! I'LL JUST DUMP THEM IN THE CENTRE OF THAT FIELD. EASIER TO DEAL WITH THEM THERE!
NOW FOR RAMADO!
BOMP
BUT NO SOONER DOES THE AUTO SET DOWN THAN THE FOUR OCCUPANTS LEAP OUT AND SCAMPER OFF...
NOW WHICH ONE IS RAMADO
THEY'RE ALL DRESSED IN BLACK. GUESS I'LL DROP THEM ONE BY ONE ...STARTING NORTH ..SORTA BOXING THE COMPASS
NORTH! HMM! THAT'S NOT RAMADO!
YEOOOOW
POW
EAST! HMM! THE GUY MICKY BUMPED INTO IN THE FIRST PLACE
BIF

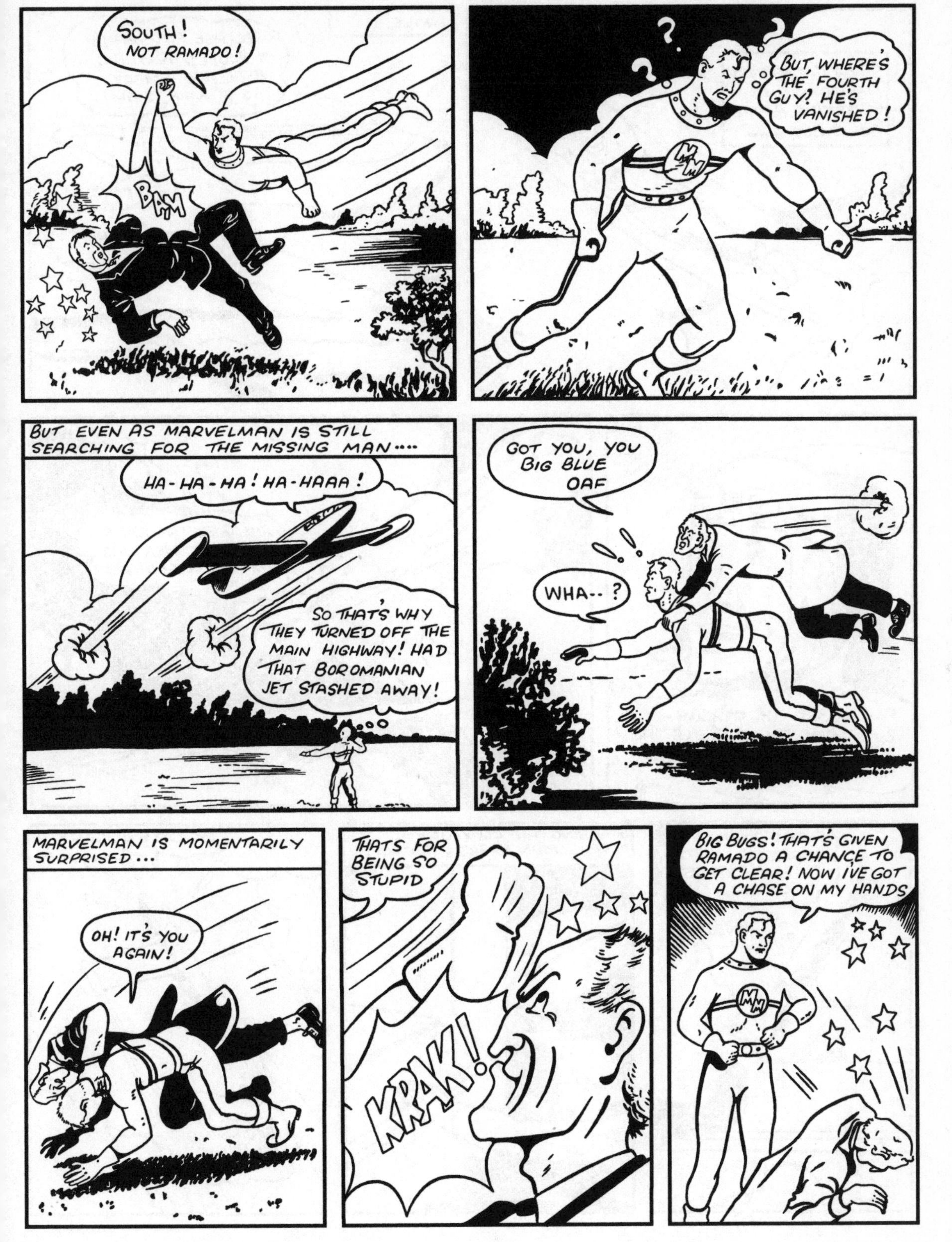
SOUTH! NOT RAMADO!
BAM
BUT, WHERE'S THE FOURTH GUY? HE'S VANISHED!
BUT EVEN AS MARVELMAN IS STILL SEARCHING FOR THE MISSING MAN....
HA-HA-HA! HA-HAAA!
SO THAT'S WHY THEY TURNED OFF THE MAIN HIGHWAY! HAD THAT BOROMANIAN JET STASHED AWAY!
GOT YOU, YOU BIG BLUE OAF
WHA--?
MARVELMAN IS MOMENTARILY SURPRISED...
OH! IT'S YOU AGAIN!
THATS FOR BEING SO STUPID
KRAK!
BIG BUGS! THAT'S GIVEN RAMADO A CHANCE TO GET CLEAR! NOW I'VE GOT A CHASE ON MY HANDS

SOON THE MIGHTY MARVELMAN IS STREAKING ABOVE THE CLOUDS....

WHILE ....

TEE-HEE AND HA-HA! I FOOLED THAT BIG BLUE APE. SMART AS A WHIP, I AM!

PITY ABOUT THE OTHERS — BUT I GOT CLEAR. THAT'S THE MAIN THING. EVERY MAN FOR HIMSELF. SMART, I AM.

AH! THERE HE GOES FULL OUT. HEADING FOR BOROMANIA. NO DOUBT!

GUESS A LITTLE SHAKE UP MIGHT DO HIM A POWER OF GOOD!

GRABBING THE ELEVATORS, MARVELMAN SHAKES THEM....

OOOEEEOOW!

HA-HA! HE'S BEGINNING TO PANIC ALREADY!

BUT SUDDENLY, AN AIR-LINER HAPPENS BY EN ROUTE FOR THE COAST. RAMADO ACTS......

HA-HA! THIS WILL GET THAT MARVELMAN OFF MY NECK!

HOLY MACARONI! THE RAT'S SHOT UP THAT AIRLINER!

WHOOSH!

MUST GET THAT CRIPPLED AIRPLANE TO EARTH FIRST. RAMADO CAN WAIT!

SOON.. RAMADO IS ONLY PUTTING OFF THE INEVITABLE!

WE OWE OUR LIVES TO MARVELMAN!

HE'S A MARVEL!

LOOK AT HIM GO!

MARVELMAN, TRAVELLING FASTER THAN ANY AIRCRAFT, SOON CATCHES UP WITH HIS QUARRY...

THIS TIME I'LL REALLY PUT IN THE FINISHING TOUCHES!

THIS IS THE PAYOFF, RAMADO!

SLAM!

UGH!

MARVELMAN GRABS RAMADO AS HE PUSHES THE PLANE TOWARDS THE OCEAN.....

NOW, UNLESS YOU WANT ME TO DROP YOU IN THE DRINK, TELL ME WHAT DIRTY TRICK YOU WERE PULLING.

NO! NO! I'LL TALK! BUT IT'S TOO LATE TO STOP IT!

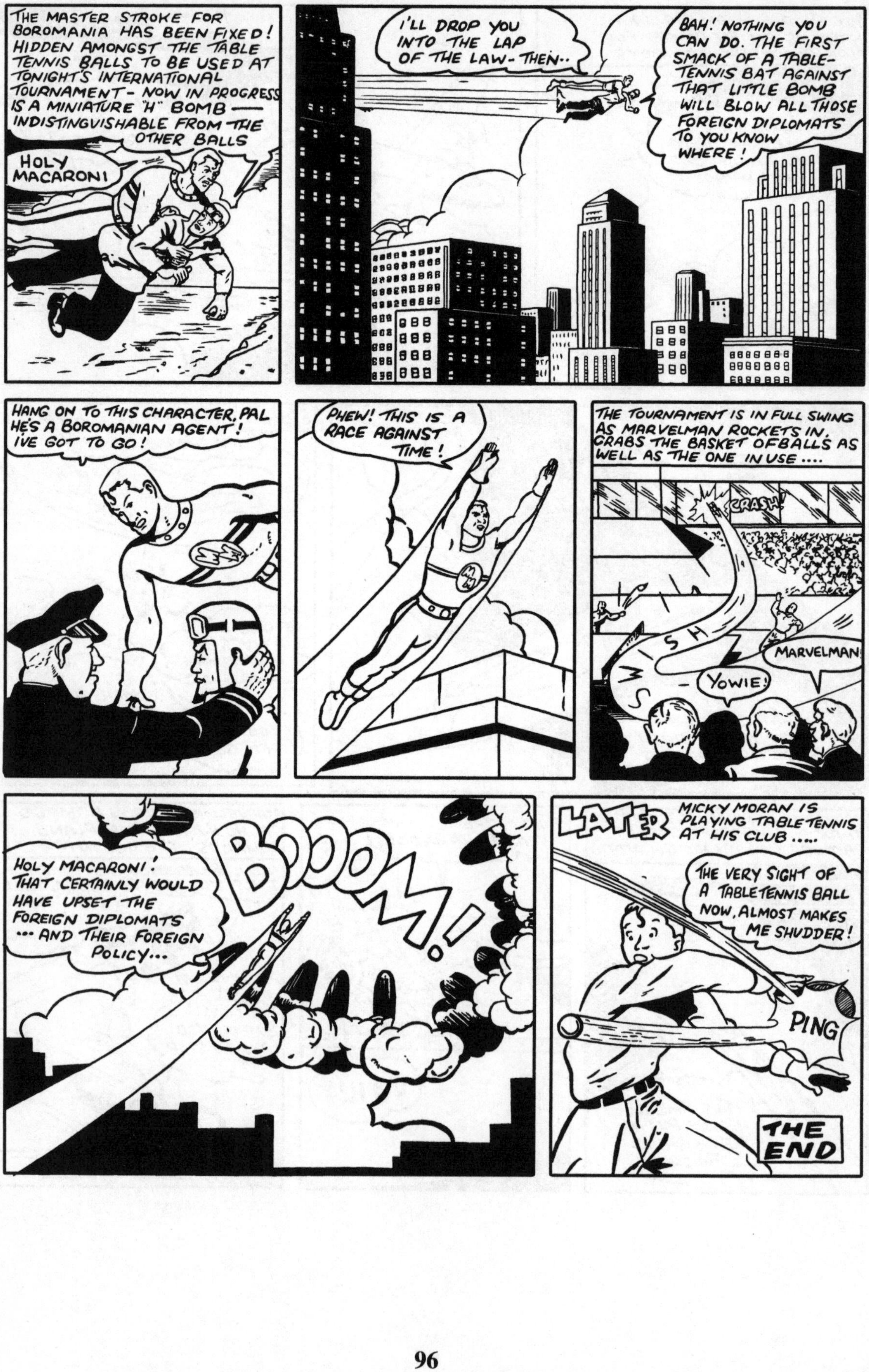
THE MASTER STROKE FOR BOROMANIA HAS BEEN FIXED! HIDDEN AMONGST THE TABLE TENNIS BALLS TO BE USED AT TONIGHT'S INTERNATIONAL TOURNAMENT - NOW IN PROGRESS IS A MINIATURE "H" BOMB — INDISTINGUISHABLE FROM THE OTHER BALLS
HOLY MACARONI
I'LL DROP YOU INTO THE LAP OF THE LAW - THEN..
BAH! NOTHING YOU CAN DO. THE FIRST SMACK OF A TABLE-TENNIS BAT AGAINST THAT LITTLE BOMB WILL BLOW ALL THOSE FOREIGN DIPLOMATS TO YOU KNOW WHERE!
HANG ON TO THIS CHARACTER, PAL HE'S A BOROMANIAN AGENT! I'VE GOT TO GO!
PHEW! THIS IS A RACE AGAINST TIME!
THE TOURNAMENT IS IN FULL SWING AS MARVELMAN ROCKETS IN, GRABS THE BASKET OF BALLS AS WELL AS THE ONE IN USE....
CRASH!
SWISH
MARVELMAN!
YOWIE!
HOLY MACARONI! THAT CERTAINLY WOULD HAVE UPSET THE FOREIGN DIPLOMATS ... AND THEIR FOREIGN POLICY...
BOOOM!
LATER
MICKY MORAN IS PLAYING TABLE TENNIS AT HIS CLUB.....
THE VERY SIGHT OF A TABLE TENNIS BALL NOW, ALMOST MAKES ME SHUDDER!
PING
THE END

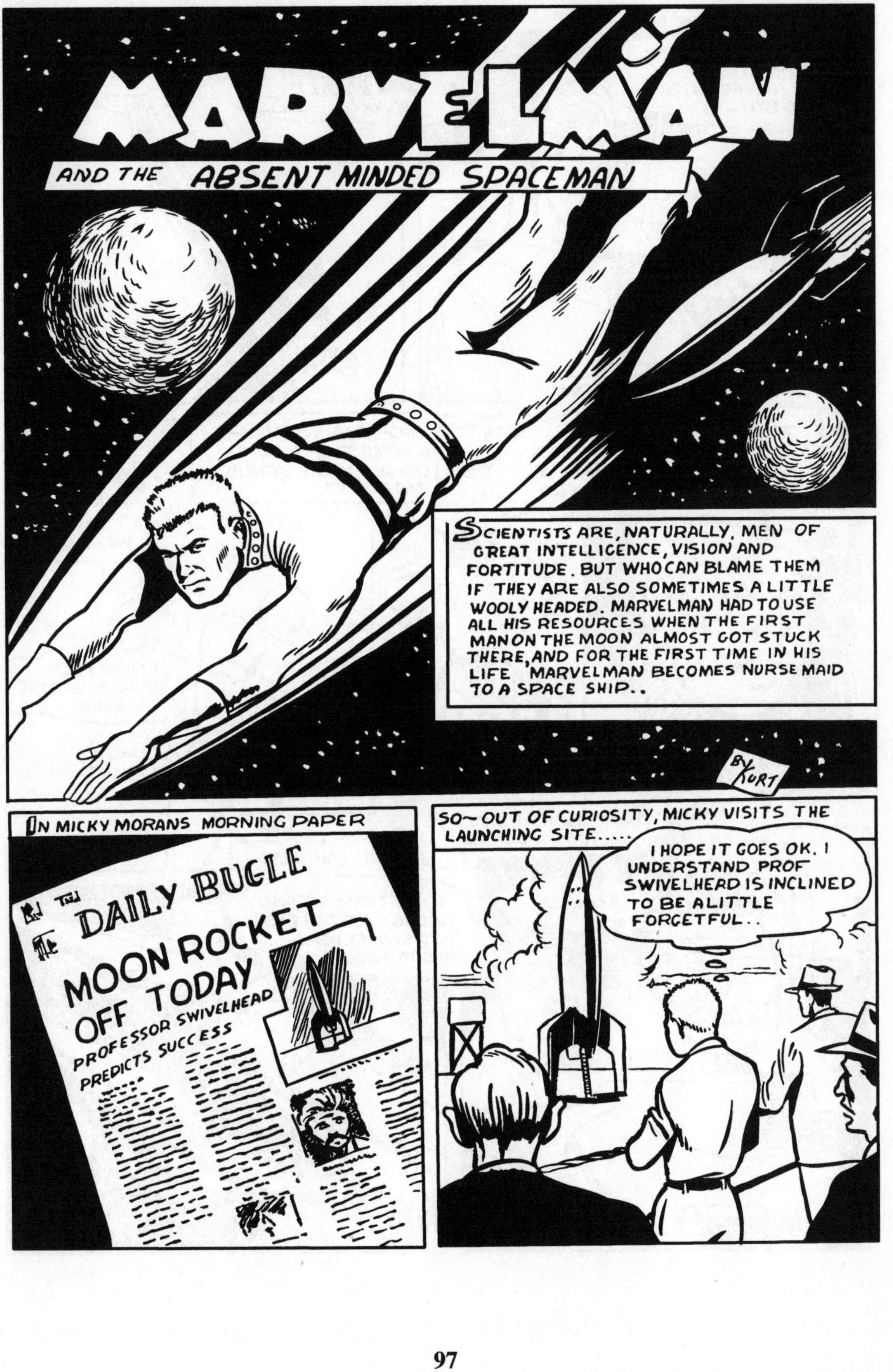
MARVELMAN
AND THE ABSENT MINDED SPACEMAN
SCIENTISTS ARE, NATURALLY, MEN OF GREAT INTELLIGENCE, VISION AND FORTITUDE. BUT WHO CAN BLAME THEM IF THEY ARE ALSO SOMETIMES A LITTLE WOOLY HEADED. MARVELMAN HAD TO USE ALL HIS RESOURCES WHEN THE FIRST MAN ON THE MOON ALMOST GOT STUCK THERE, AND FOR THE FIRST TIME IN HIS LIFE MARVELMAN BECOMES NURSE MAID TO A SPACE SHIP..
BY KURT
IN MICKY MORANS MORNING PAPER
DAILY BUGLE
MOON ROCKET OFF TODAY
PROFESSOR SWIVELHEAD PREDICTS SUCCESS
SO~ OUT OF CURIOSITY, MICKY VISITS THE LAUNCHING SITE.....
I HOPE IT GOES OK. I UNDERSTAND PROF SWIVELHEAD IS INCLINED TO BE ALITTLE FORGETFUL..

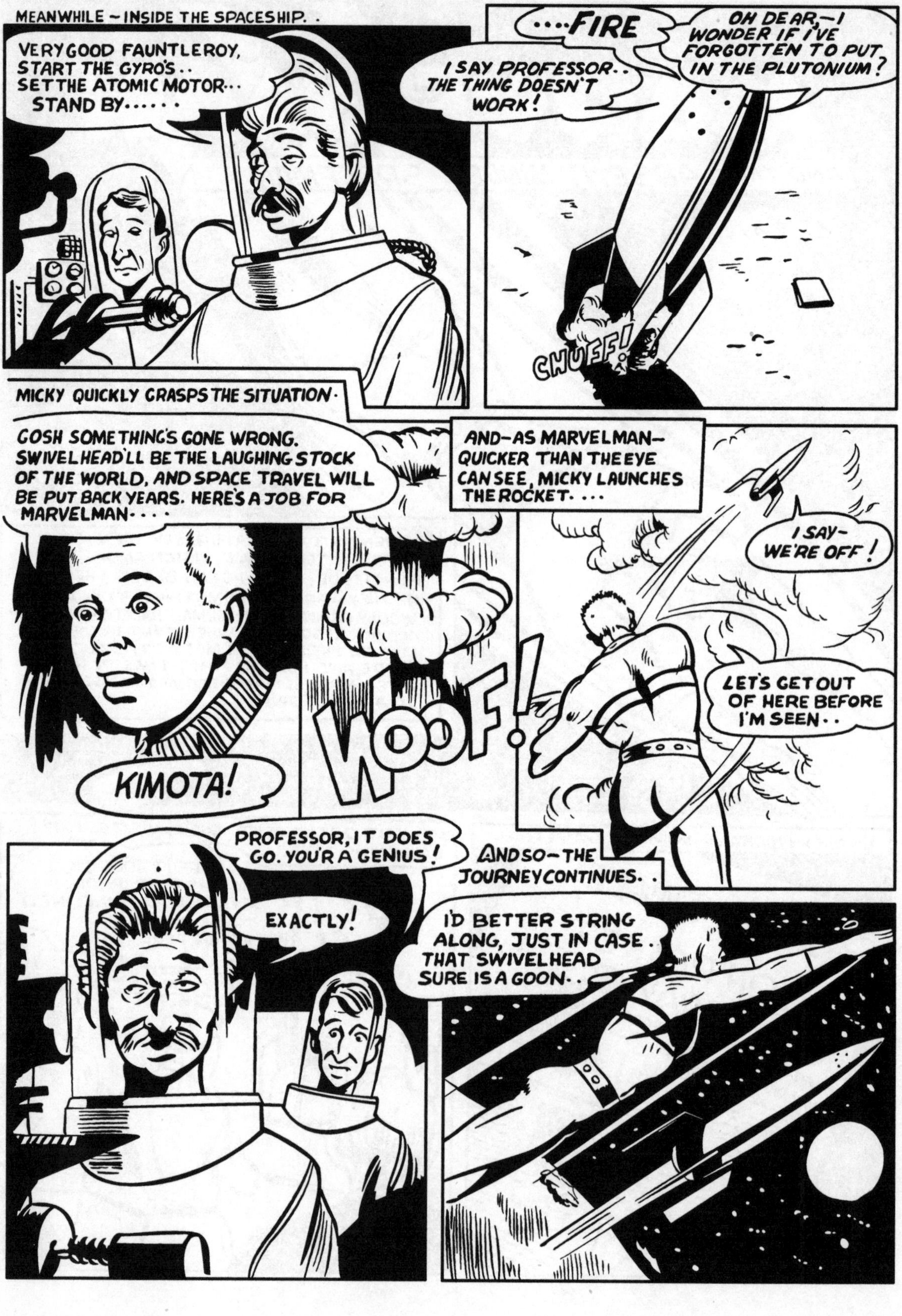
MEANWHILE – INSIDE THE SPACESHIP. .
VERY GOOD FAUNTLEROY, START THE GYRO'S.. SET THE ATOMIC MOTOR... STAND BY.....
....FIRE
I SAY PROFESSOR.. THE THING DOESN'T WORK!
OH DEAR,–I WONDER IF I'VE FORGOTTEN TO PUT IN THE PLUTONIUM?
CHUFF!
MICKY QUICKLY GRASPS THE SITUATION.
GOSH SOMETHING'S GONE WRONG. SWIVELHEAD'LL BE THE LAUGHING STOCK OF THE WORLD, AND SPACE TRAVEL WILL BE PUT BACK YEARS. HERE'S A JOB FOR MARVELMAN...
KIMOTA!
WOOF!
AND–AS MARVELMAN– QUICKER THAN THE EYE CAN SEE, MICKY LAUNCHES THE ROCKET....
I SAY– WE'RE OFF!
LET'S GET OUT OF HERE BEFORE I'M SEEN..
PROFESSOR, IT DOES GO. YOU'R A GENIUS!
EXACTLY!
AND SO–THE JOURNEY CONTINUES. .
I'D BETTER STRING ALONG, JUST IN CASE. THAT SWIVELHEAD SURE IS A GOON..

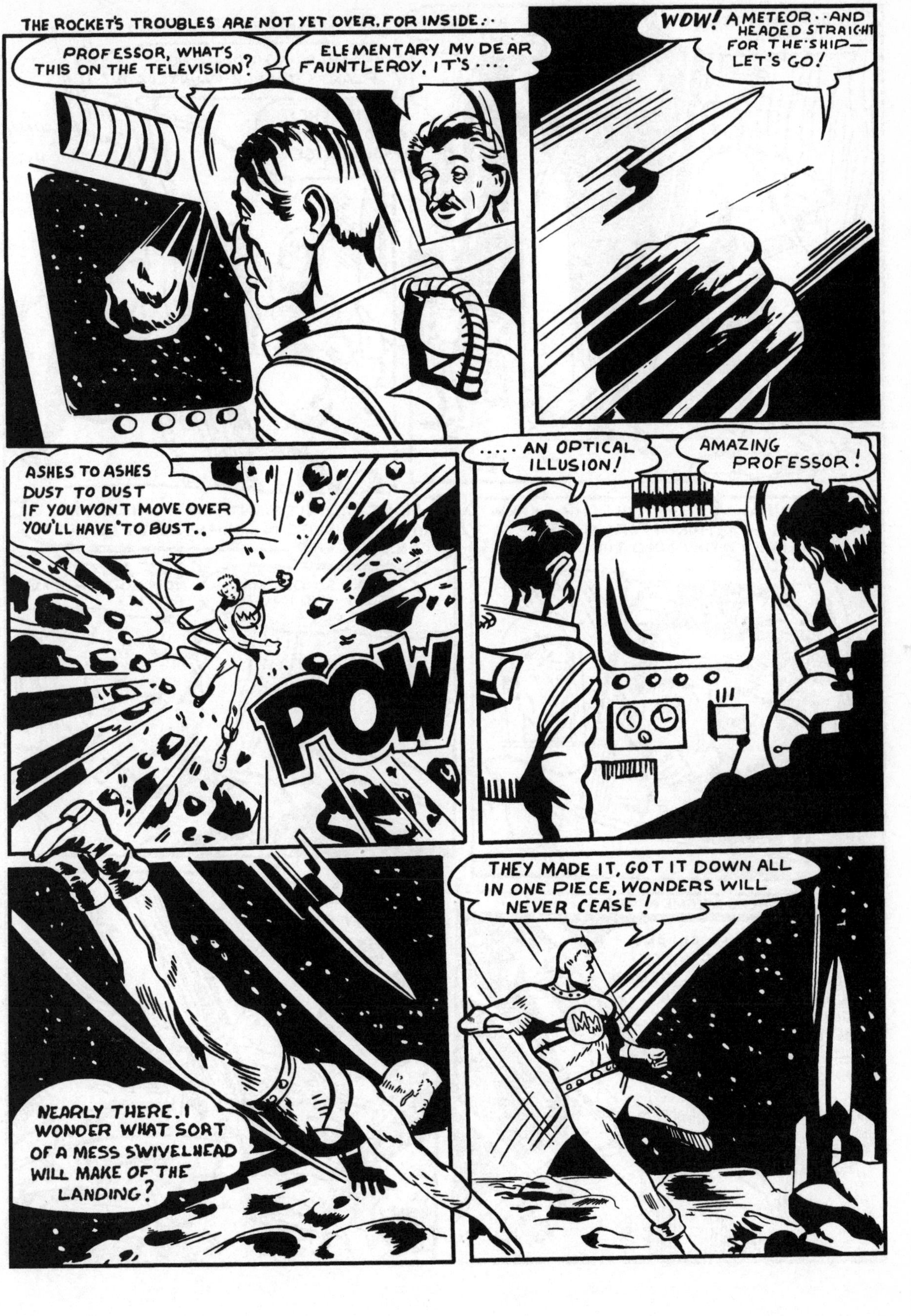
THE ROCKET'S TROUBLES ARE NOT YET OVER, FOR INSIDE:-
PROFESSOR, WHAT'S THIS ON THE TELEVISION?
ELEMENTARY MY DEAR FAUNTLEROY, IT'S....
WOW! A METEOR..AND HEADED STRAIGHT FOR THE SHIP— LET'S GO!
ASHES TO ASHES DUST TO DUST IF YOU WON'T MOVE OVER YOU'LL HAVE TO BUST..
POW
.....AN OPTICAL ILLUSION!
AMAZING PROFESSOR!
NEARLY THERE. I WONDER WHAT SORT OF A MESS SWIVELHEAD WILL MAKE OF THE LANDING?
THEY MADE IT, GOT IT DOWN ALL IN ONE PIECE, WONDERS WILL NEVER CEASE!

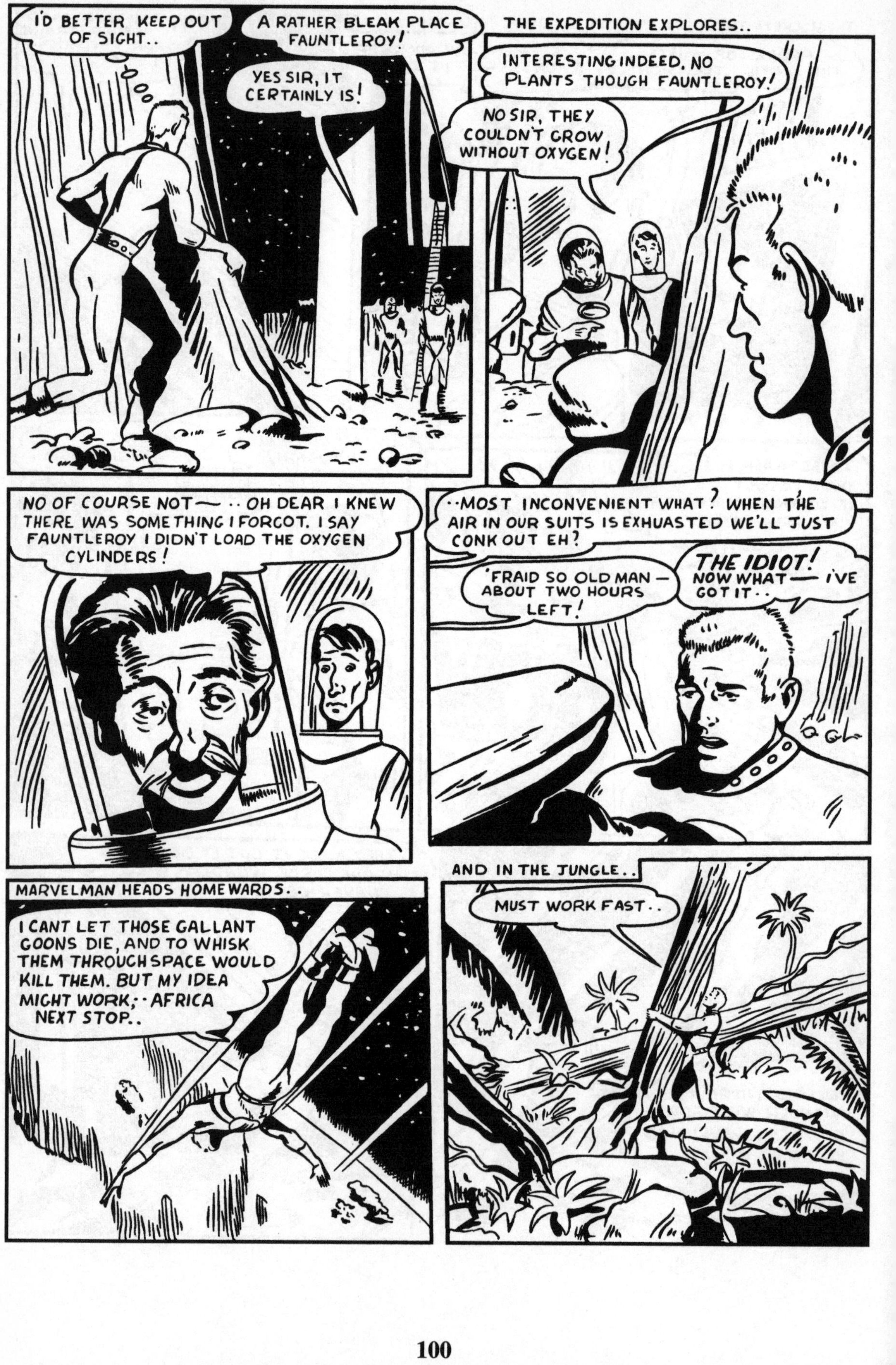

I'D BETTER KEEP OUT OF SIGHT..
A RATHER BLEAK PLACE FAUNTLEROY!
YES SIR, IT CERTAINLY IS!
THE EXPEDITION EXPLORES..
INTERESTING INDEED. NO PLANTS THOUGH FAUNTLEROY!
NO SIR, THEY COULDN'T GROW WITHOUT OXYGEN!
NO OF COURSE NOT— ..OH DEAR I KNEW THERE WAS SOMETHING I FORGOT. I SAY FAUNTLEROY I DIDN'T LOAD THE OXYGEN CYLINDERS!
..MOST INCONVENIENT WHAT? WHEN THE AIR IN OUR SUITS IS EXHUASTED WE'LL JUST CONK OUT EH?
'FRAID SO OLD MAN — ABOUT TWO HOURS LEFT!
THE IDIOT! NOW WHAT— I'VE GOT IT..
MARVELMAN HEADS HOMEWARDS..
I CANT LET THOSE GALLANT GOONS DIE, AND TO WHISK THEM THROUGH SPACE WOULD KILL THEM. BUT MY IDEA MIGHT WORK; ..AFRICA NEXT STOP..
AND IN THE JUNGLE..
MUST WORK FAST..

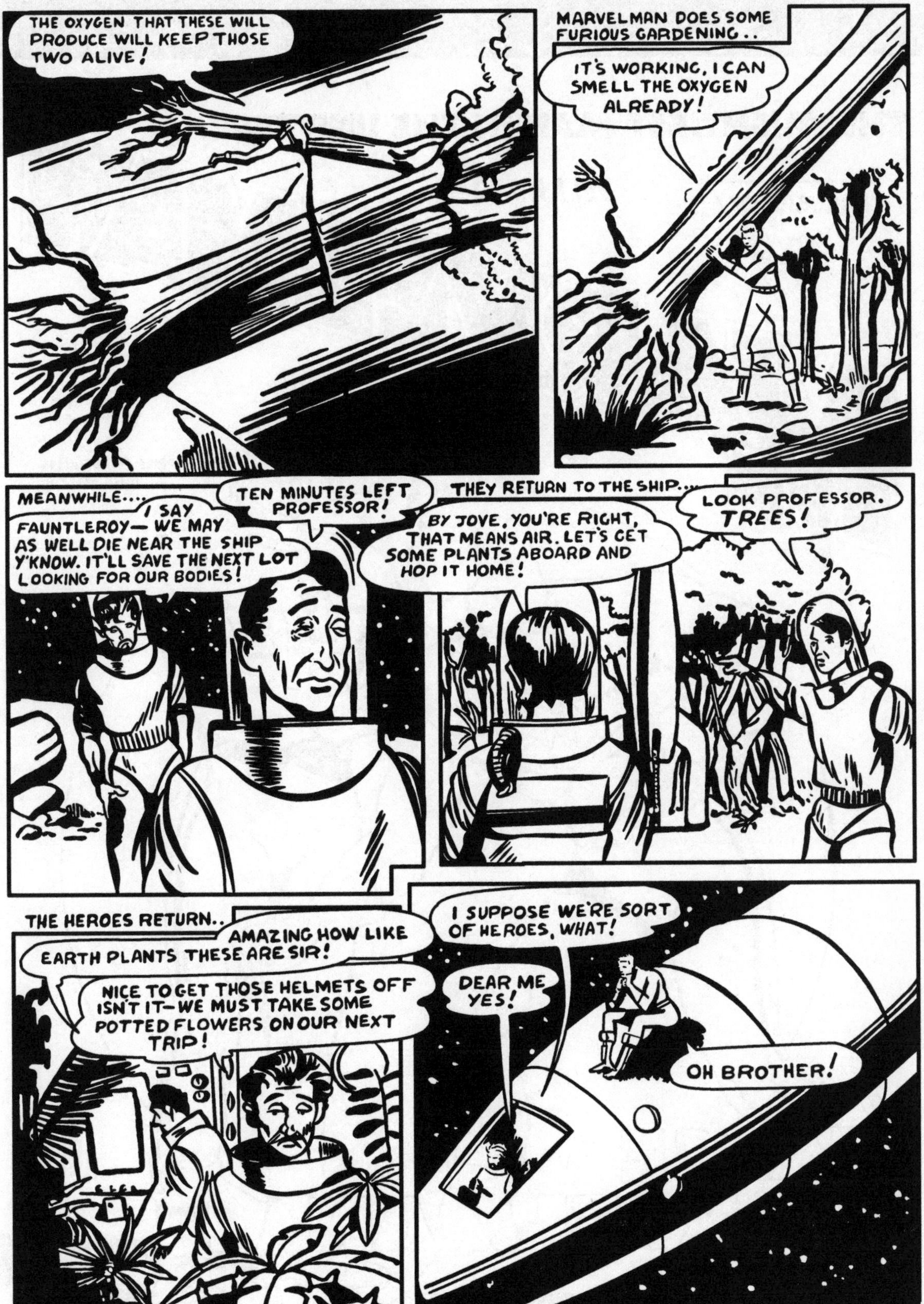
THE OXYGEN THAT THESE WILL PRODUCE WILL KEEP THOSE TWO ALIVE!
MARVELMAN DOES SOME FURIOUS GARDENING..
IT'S WORKING, I CAN SMELL THE OXYGEN ALREADY!
MEANWHILE....
I SAY FAUNTLEROY— WE MAY AS WELL DIE NEAR THE SHIP Y'KNOW. IT'LL SAVE THE NEXT LOT LOOKING FOR OUR BODIES!
TEN MINUTES LEFT PROFESSOR!
THEY RETURN TO THE SHIP...
LOOK PROFESSOR. TREES!
BY JOVE, YOU'RE RIGHT, THAT MEANS AIR. LET'S GET SOME PLANTS ABOARD AND HOP IT HOME!
THE HEROES RETURN..
AMAZING HOW LIKE EARTH PLANTS THESE ARE SIR!
NICE TO GET THOSE HELMETS OFF ISN'T IT—WE MUST TAKE SOME POTTED FLOWERS ON OUR NEXT TRIP!
I SUPPOSE WE'RE SORT OF HEROES, WHAT!
DEAR ME YES!
OH BROTHER!

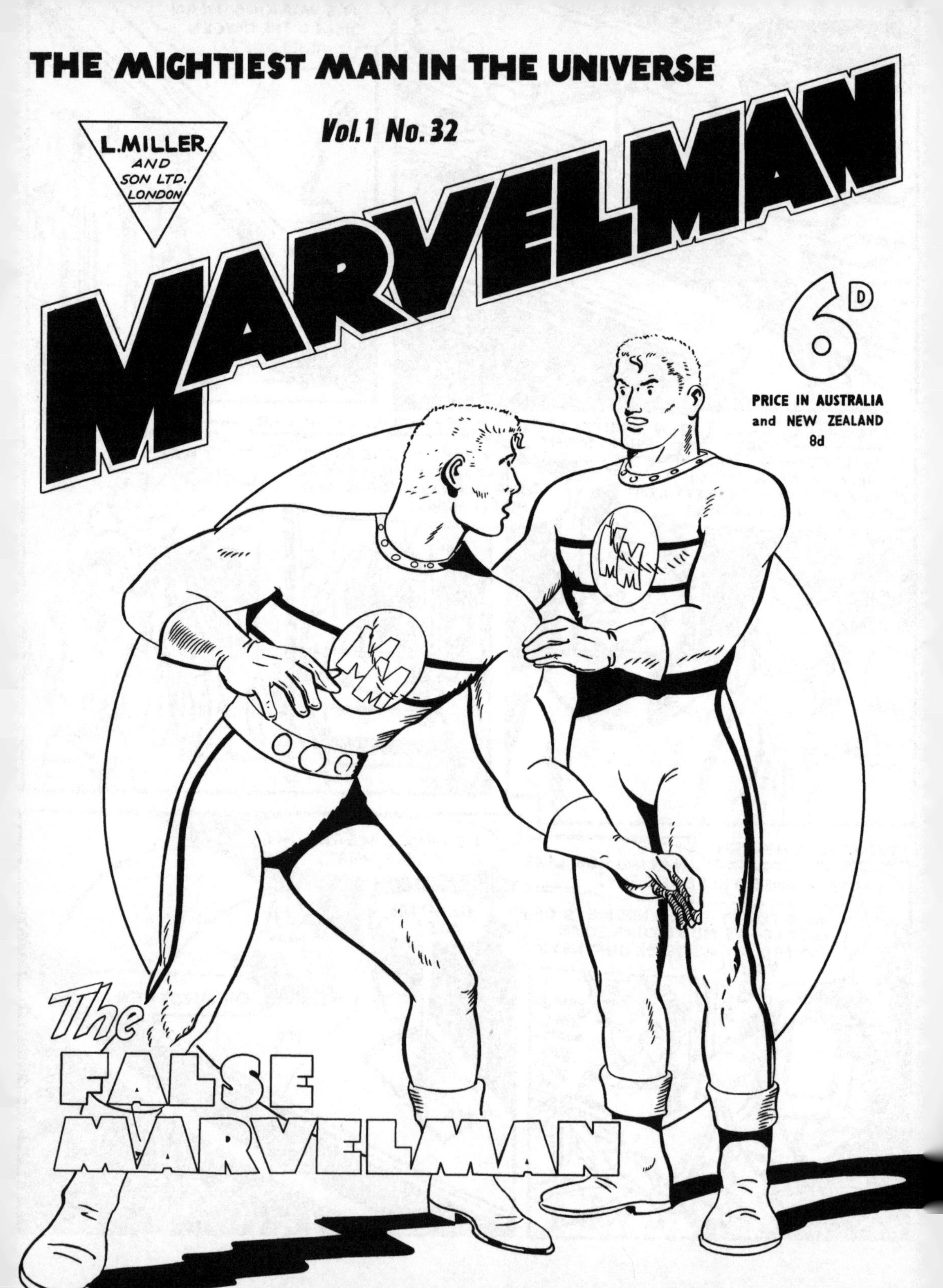
THE MIGHTIEST MAN IN THE UNIVERSE
L. MILLER AND SON LTD. LONDON
Vol.1 No.32
MARVELMAN
6D
PRICE IN AUSTRALIA and NEW ZEALAND 8d
The FALSE MARVELMAN

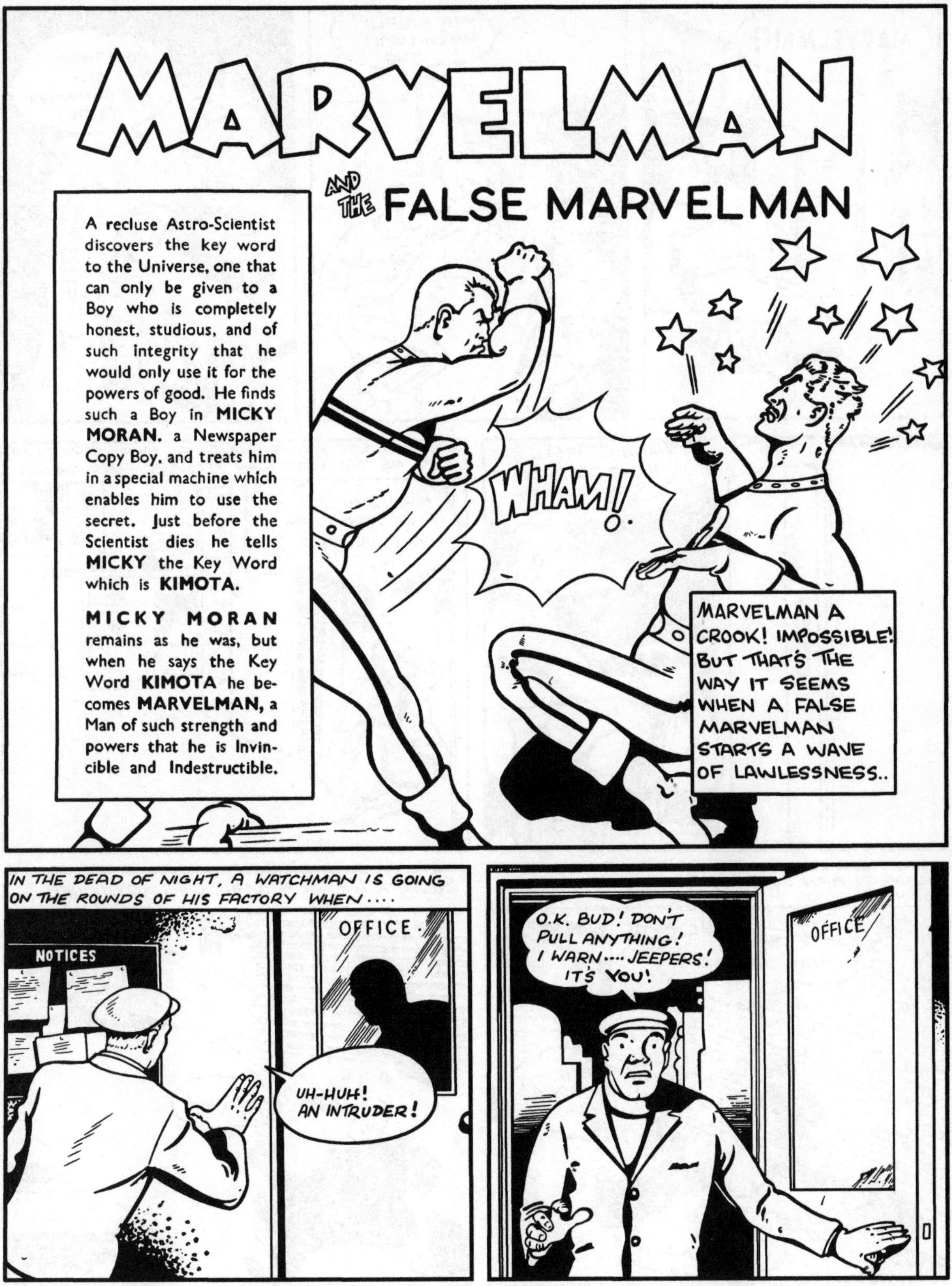
MARVELMAN
AND THE FALSE MARVELMAN
A recluse Astro-Scientist discovers the key word to the Universe, one that can only be given to a Boy who is completely honest, studious, and of such integrity that he would only use it for the powers of good. He finds such a Boy in MICKY MORAN, a Newspaper Copy Boy, and treats him in a special machine which enables him to use the secret. Just before the Scientist dies he tells MICKY the Key Word which is KIMOTA.
MICKY MORAN remains as he was, but when he says the Key Word KIMOTA he becomes MARVELMAN, a Man of such strength and powers that he is Invincible and Indestructible.
WHAM!
MARVELMAN A CROOK! IMPOSSIBLE! BUT THAT'S THE WAY IT SEEMS WHEN A FALSE MARVELMAN STARTS A WAVE OF LAWLESSNESS..
IN THE DEAD OF NIGHT, A WATCHMAN IS GOING ON THE ROUNDS OF HIS FACTORY WHEN....
NOTICES
OFFICE
UH-HUH! AN INTRUDER!
O.K. BUD! DON'T PULL ANYTHING! I WARN.... JEEPERS! IT'S YOU!
OFFICE

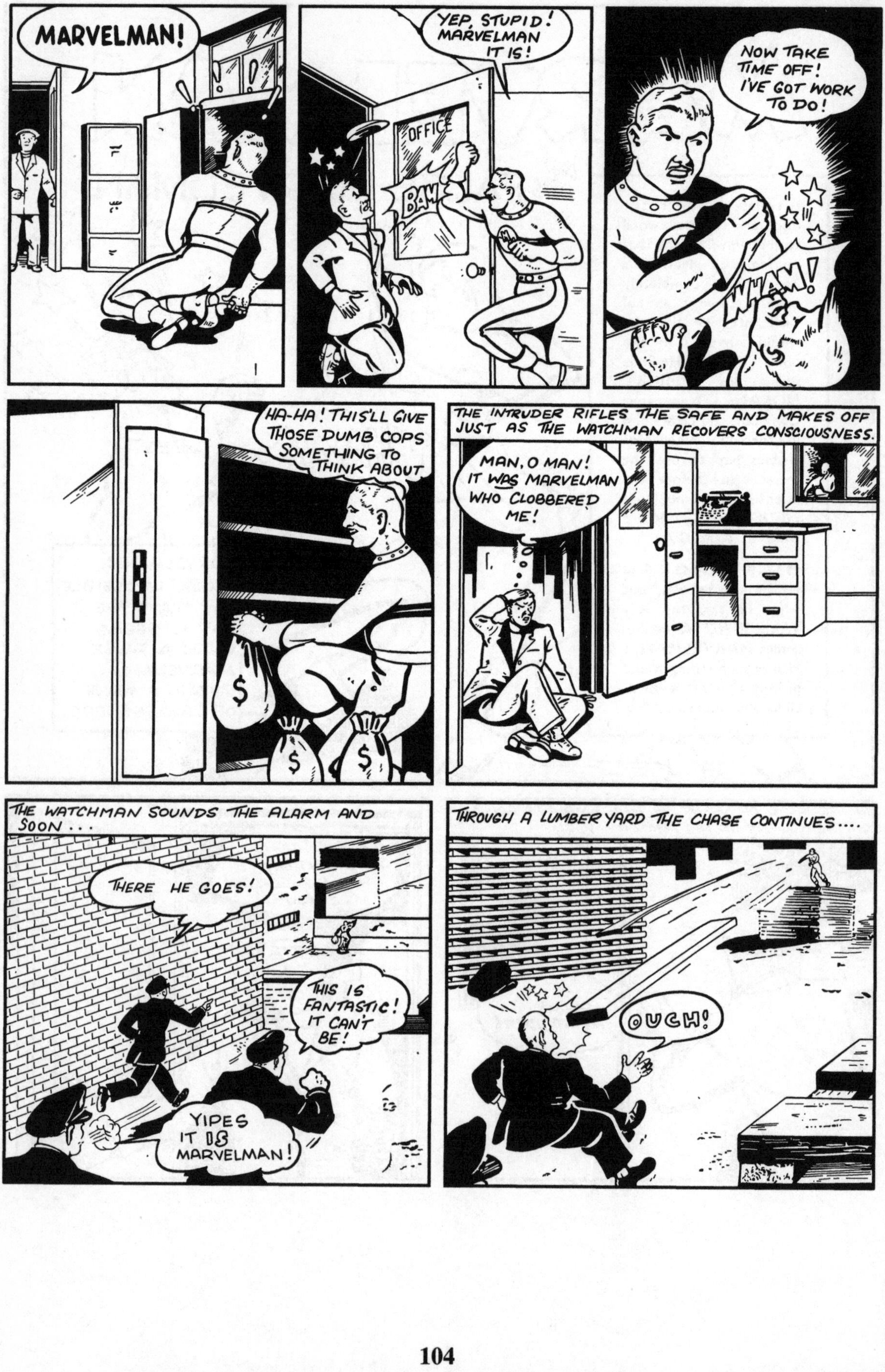
MARVELMAN!
YEP, STUPID! MARVELMAN IT IS!
OFFICE
BAM
NOW TAKE TIME OFF! I'VE GOT WORK TO DO!
WHAM!
HA-HA! THIS'LL GIVE THOSE DUMB COPS SOMETHING TO THINK ABOUT
THE INTRUDER RIFLES THE SAFE AND MAKES OFF JUST AS THE WATCHMAN RECOVERS CONSCIOUSNESS.
MAN, O MAN! IT WAS MARVELMAN WHO CLOBBERED ME!
THE WATCHMAN SOUNDS THE ALARM AND SOON ...
THERE HE GOES!
THIS IS FANTASTIC! IT CAN'T BE!
YIPES IT IS MARVELMAN!
THROUGH A LUMBER YARD THE CHASE CONTINUES....
OUCH!

BUT FINALLY MARVELMAN GIVES HIS PURSUERS THE SLIP
THAT'S SHAKEN THEM!
THE FOLLOWING MORNING IN THE OFFICE OF THE "DAILY BUGLE", MICKY MORAN SCANS THE HEADLINES!
HOLY MACARONI!
DAILY BUGLE
MARVELMAN WANTED BY POLICE
FACTORY ROBBERY
SOMEONE'S PULLED A FAST ONE! BUT HOW AM I — I MEAN HOW IS MARVELMAN GOING TO PROVE THIS IS THE WORK OF A FAKER?
THAT EVENING ON HIS WAY HOME MICKY IS FEELING A LITTLE LOW WHEN ...
THE NESTA CIRCUS
NIGHTLY PERFORMANCES
NOW THAT'S AN IDEA! A CIRCUS MAY HELP CHEER ME UP A LITTLE!
NESTA CIRCUS
THE SIXTY-FOUR DOLLRR QUESTION IS HOW TO PROVE MARVELMAN INNOCENT!
SOON...
THE GREAT ANUELLO!
BOY! LOOK AT HIM!
HE'S TOPS!
JUMPING JEHOSAPHAT!

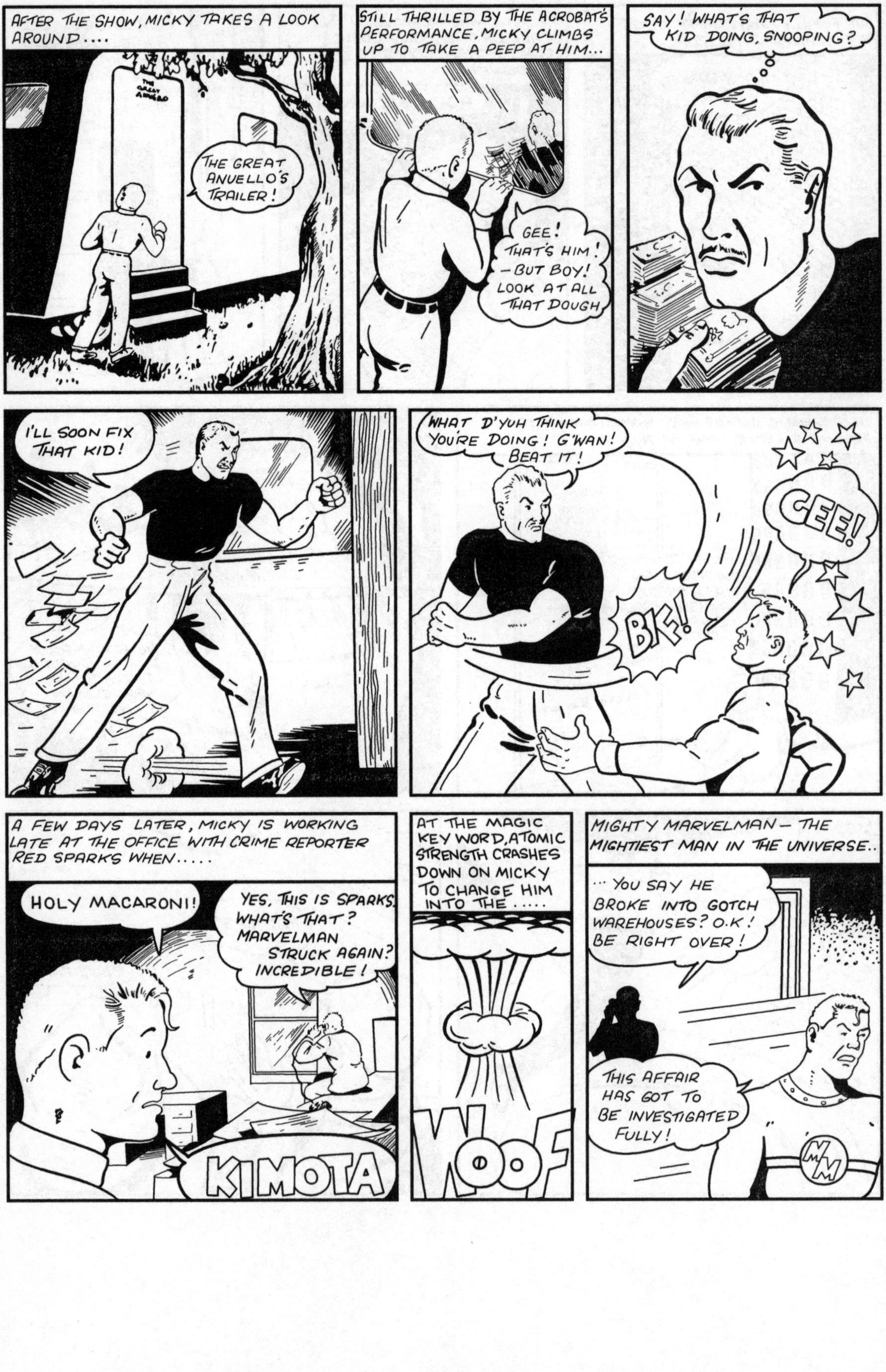
AFTER THE SHOW, MICKY TAKES A LOOK AROUND....
THE GREAT ANUELLO'S TRAILER!
STILL THRILLED BY THE ACROBAT'S PERFORMANCE, MICKY CLIMBS UP TO TAKE A PEEP AT HIM...
GEE! THAT'S HIM! -BUT BOY! LOOK AT ALL THAT DOUGH
SAY! WHAT'S THAT KID DOING, SNOOPING?
I'LL SOON FIX THAT KID!
WHAT D'YUH THINK YOU'RE DOING! G'WAN! BEAT IT!
BIF!
GEE!
A FEW DAYS LATER, MICKY IS WORKING LATE AT THE OFFICE WITH CRIME REPORTER RED SPARKS WHEN.....
HOLY MACARONI!
YES, THIS IS SPARKS. WHAT'S THAT? MARVELMAN STRUCK AGAIN? INCREDIBLE!
KIMOTA
AT THE MAGIC KEY WORD, ATOMIC STRENGTH CRASHES DOWN ON MICKY TO CHANGE HIM INTO THE .....
WOOF
MIGHTY MARVELMAN — THE MIGHTIEST MAN IN THE UNIVERSE..
... YOU SAY HE BROKE INTO GOTCH WAREHOUSES? O.K! BE RIGHT OVER!
THIS AFFAIR HAS GOT TO BE INVESTIGATED FULLY!

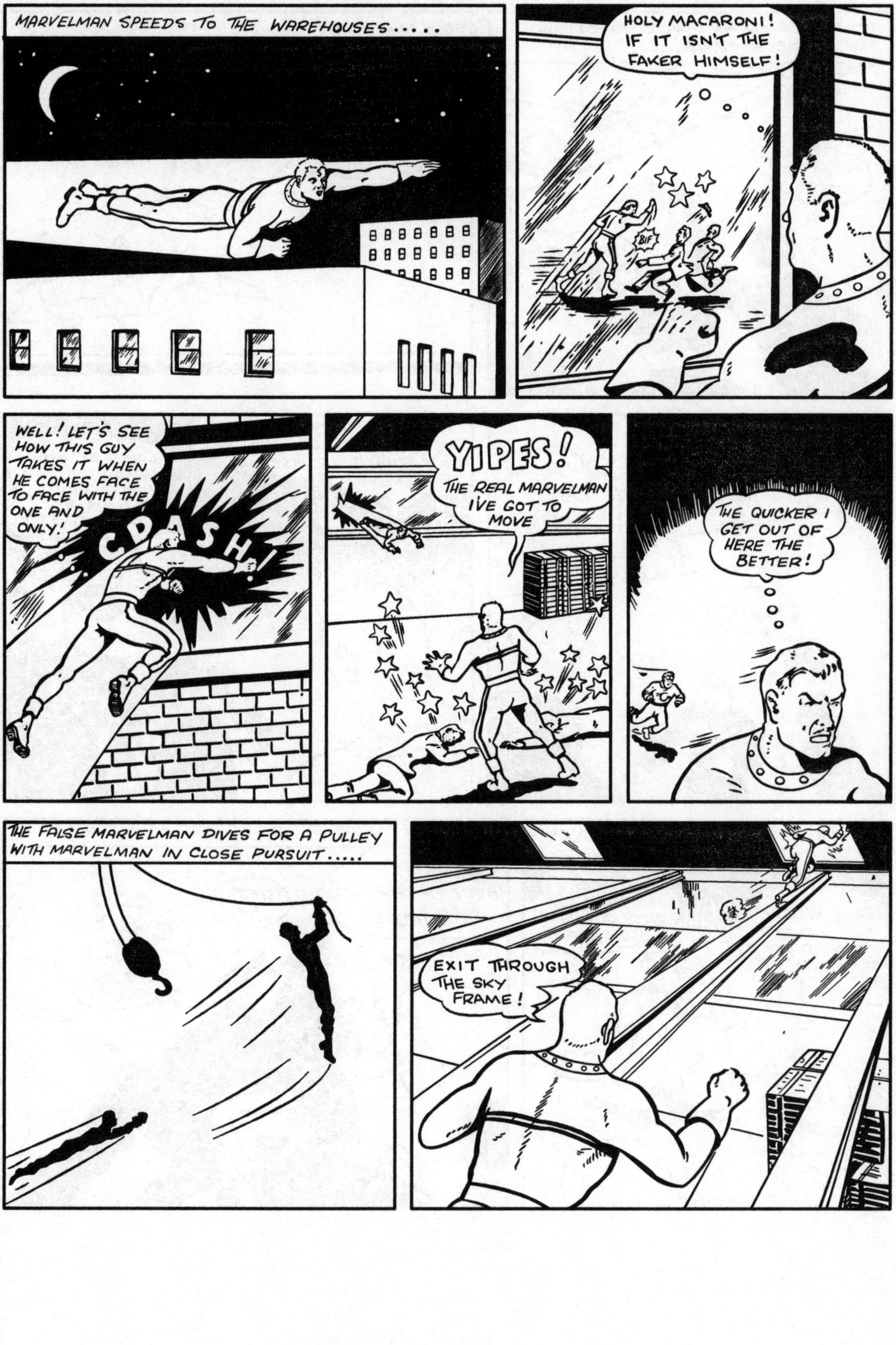
MARVELMAN SPEEDS TO THE WAREHOUSES.....
HOLY MACARONI! IF IT ISN'T THE FAKER HIMSELF!
BIF
WELL! LET'S SEE HOW THIS GUY TAKES IT WHEN HE COMES FACE TO FACE WITH THE ONE AND ONLY!
CRASH!
YIPES! THE REAL MARVELMAN I'VE GOT TO MOVE
THE QUICKER I GET OUT OF HERE THE BETTER!
THE FALSE MARVELMAN DIVES FOR A PULLEY WITH MARVELMAN IN CLOSE PURSUIT.....
EXIT THROUGH THE SKY FRAME!

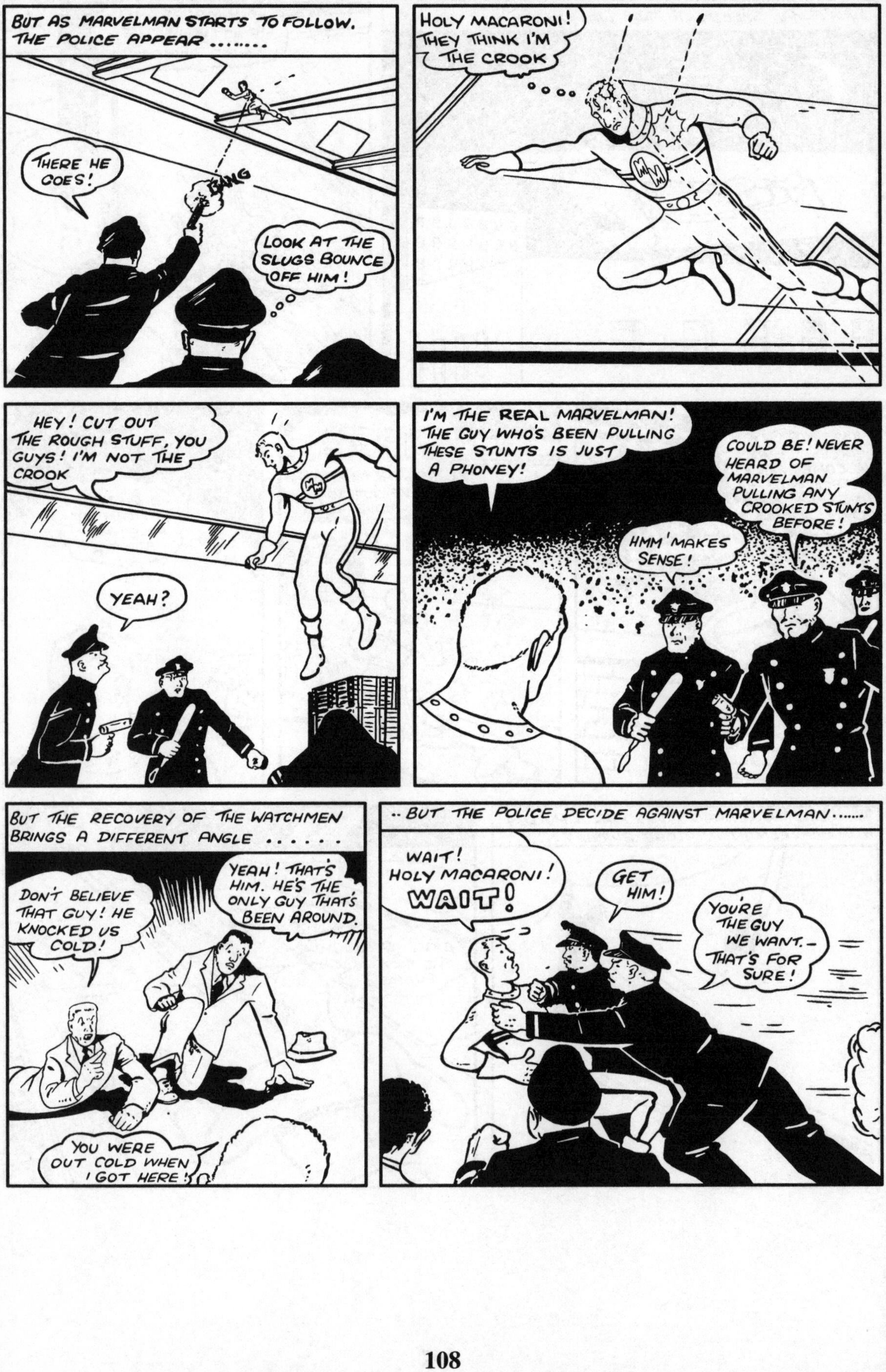
BUT AS MARVELMAN STARTS TO FOLLOW. THE POLICE APPEAR ....
THERE HE GOES!
BANG
LOOK AT THE SLUGS BOUNCE OFF HIM!
HOLY MACARONI! THEY THINK I'M THE CROOK
HEY! CUT OUT THE ROUGH STUFF, YOU GUYS! I'M NOT THE CROOK
YEAH?
I'M THE REAL MARVELMAN! THE GUY WHO'S BEEN PULLING THESE STUNTS IS JUST A PHONEY!
COULD BE! NEVER HEARD OF MARVELMAN PULLING ANY CROOKED STUNTS BEFORE!
HMM' MAKES SENSE!
BUT THE RECOVERY OF THE WATCHMEN BRINGS A DIFFERENT ANGLE . . . . . .
DON'T BELIEVE THAT GUY! HE KNOCKED US COLD!
YEAH! THAT'S HIM. HE'S THE ONLY GUY THAT'S BEEN AROUND.
YOU WERE OUT COLD WHEN I GOT HERE!
.. BUT THE POLICE DECIDE AGAINST MARVELMAN.......
WAIT! HOLY MACARONI! WAIT!
GET HIM!
YOU'RE THE GUY WE WANT. THAT'S FOR SURE!

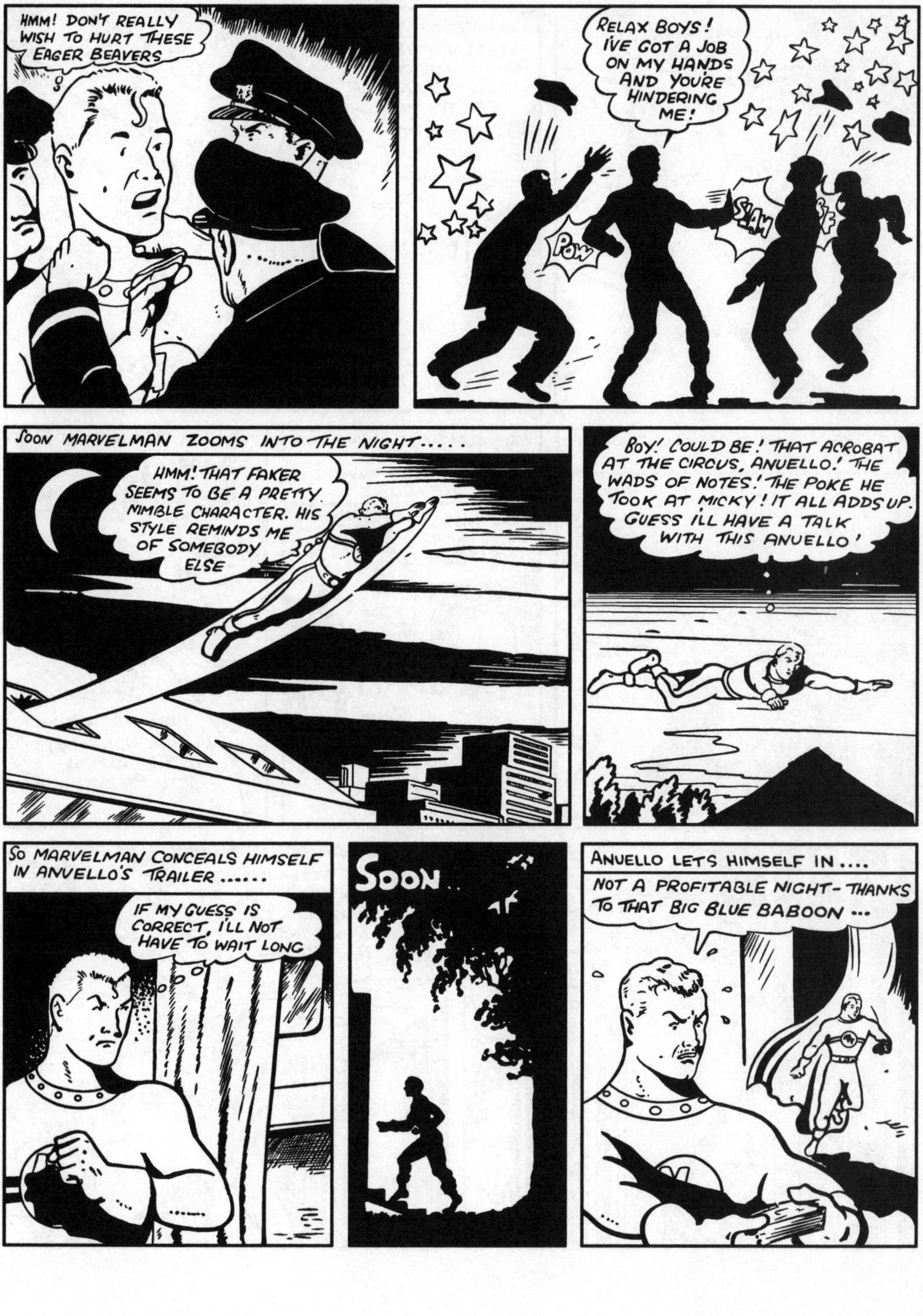
HMM! DON'T REALLY WISH TO HURT THESE EAGER BEAVERS
RELAX BOYS! I'VE GOT A JOB ON MY HANDS AND YOU'RE HINDERING ME!
POW
SLAM
SOON MARVELMAN ZOOMS INTO THE NIGHT.....
HMM! THAT FAKER SEEMS TO BE A PRETTY NIMBLE CHARACTER. HIS STYLE REMINDS ME OF SOMEBODY ELSE
BOY! COULD BE! THAT ACROBAT AT THE CIRCUS, ANUELLO! THE WADS OF NOTES! THE POKE HE TOOK AT MICKY! IT ALL ADDS UP. GUESS I'LL HAVE A TALK WITH THIS ANUELLO!
SO MARVELMAN CONCEALS HIMSELF IN ANUELLO'S TRAILER......
IF MY GUESS IS CORRECT, I'LL NOT HAVE TO WAIT LONG
SOON...
ANUELLO LETS HIMSELF IN....
NOT A PROFITABLE NIGHT- THANKS TO THAT BIG BLUE BABOON...

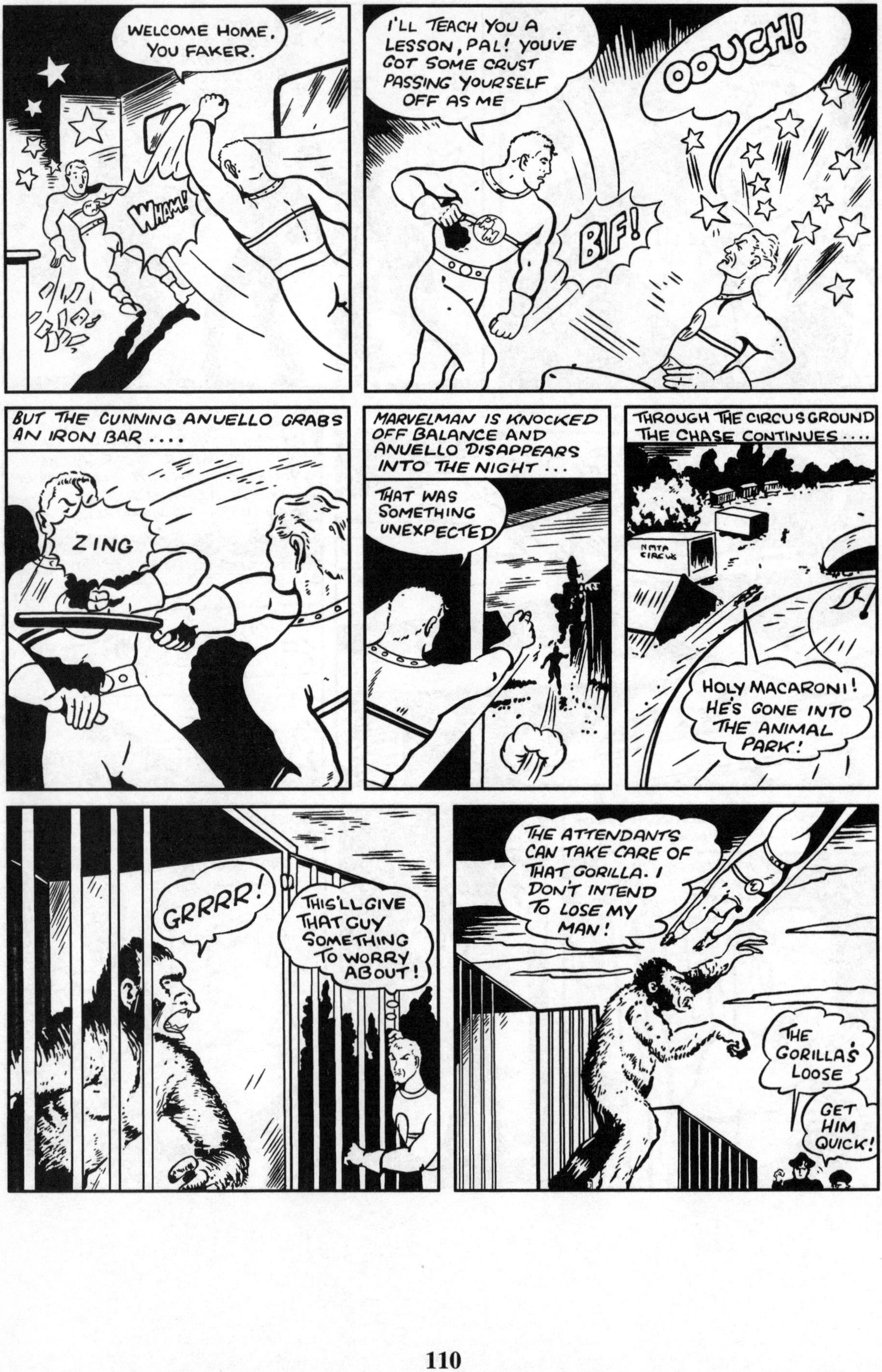
WELCOME HOME, YOU FAKER.
WHAM!
I'LL TEACH YOU A LESSON, PAL! YOU'VE GOT SOME CRUST PASSING YOURSELF OFF AS ME
BIF!
OOUCH!
BUT THE CUNNING ANUELLO GRABS AN IRON BAR ....
ZING
MARVELMAN IS KNOCKED OFF BALANCE AND ANUELLO DISAPPEARS INTO THE NIGHT ...
THAT WAS SOMETHING UNEXPECTED
THROUGH THE CIRCUS GROUND THE CHASE CONTINUES ....
HOLY MACARONI! HE'S GONE INTO THE ANIMAL PARK!
GRRRR!
THIS'LL GIVE THAT GUY SOMETHING TO WORRY ABOUT!
THE ATTENDANTS CAN TAKE CARE OF THAT GORILLA. I DON'T INTEND TO LOSE MY MAN!
THE GORILLA'S LOOSE
GET HIM QUICK!

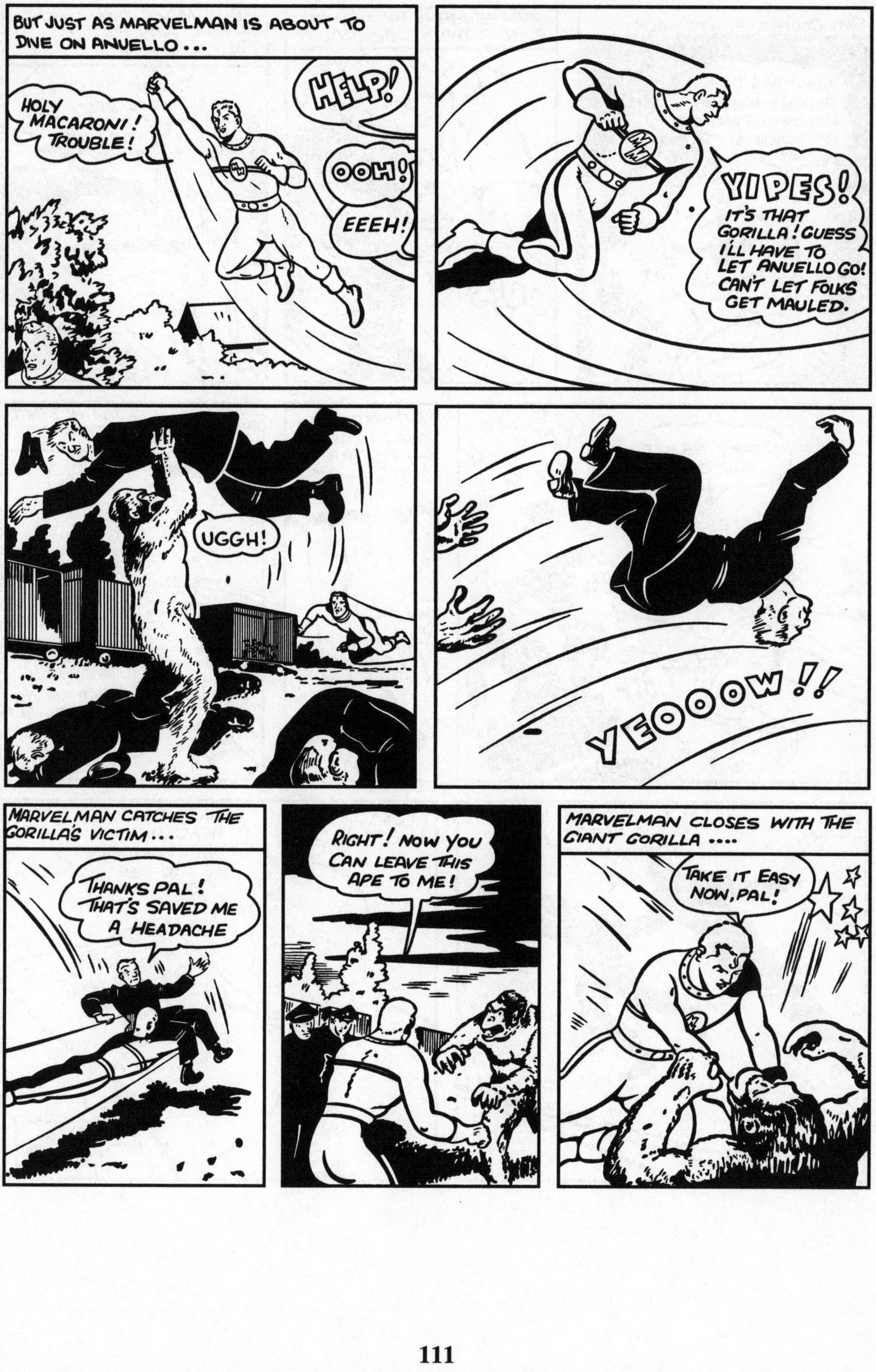

BUT JUST AS MARVELMAN IS ABOUT TO DIVE ON ANUELLO...
HOLY MACARONI! TROUBLE!
HELP!
OOH!
EEEH!
YIPES! IT'S THAT GORILLA! GUESS I'LL HAVE TO LET ANUELLO GO! CAN'T LET FOLKS GET MAULED.
UGGH!
YEOOOW!!
MARVELMAN CATCHES THE GORILLA'S VICTIM...
THANKS PAL! THAT'S SAVED ME A HEADACHE
RIGHT! NOW YOU CAN LEAVE THIS APE TO ME!
MARVELMAN CLOSES WITH THE GIANT GORILLA....
TAKE IT EASY NOW, PAL!

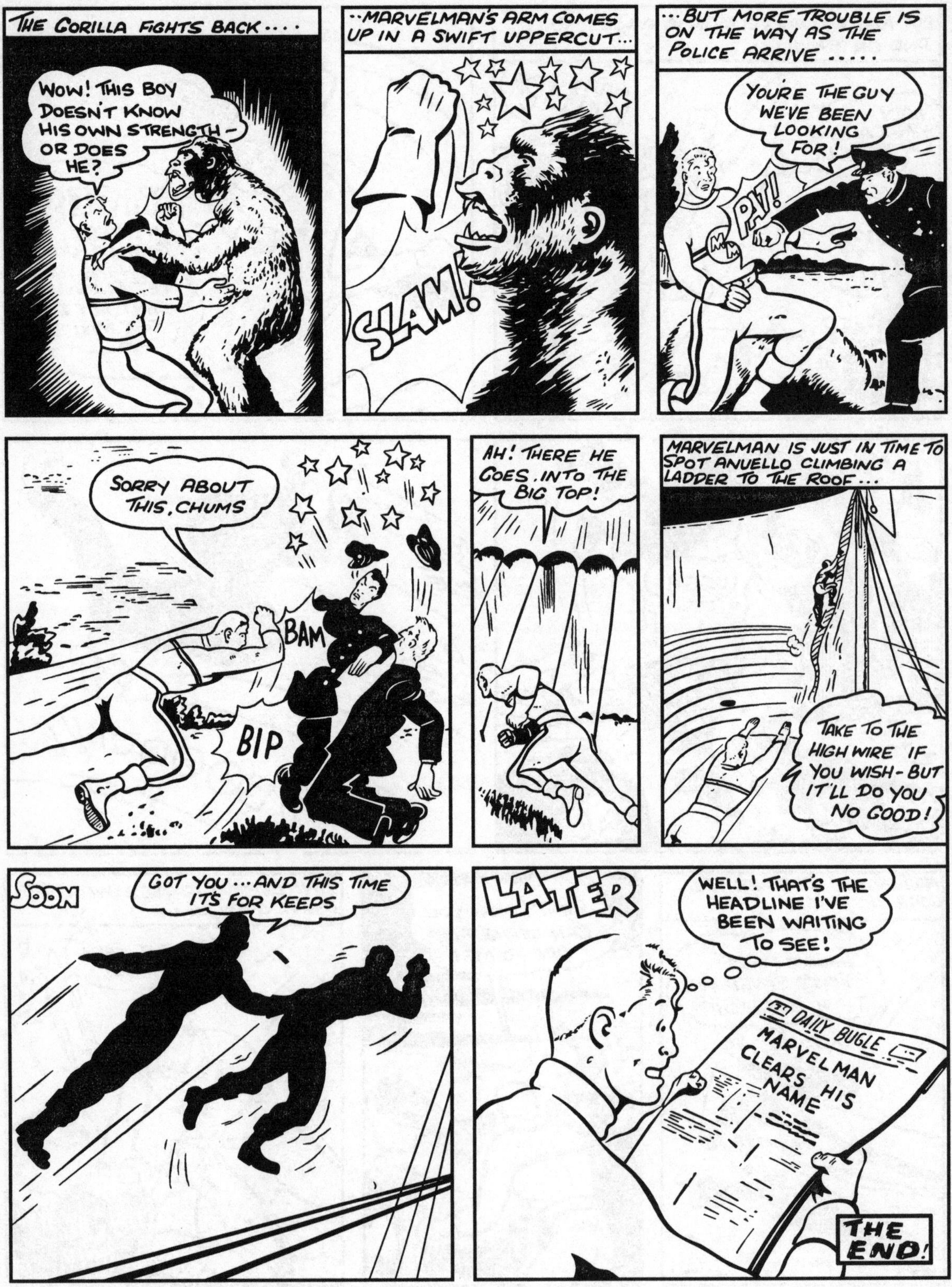
THE GORILLA FIGHTS BACK....
WOW! THIS BOY DOESN'T KNOW HIS OWN STRENGTH - OR DOES HE?
..MARVELMAN'S ARM COMES UP IN A SWIFT UPPERCUT...
SLAM!
...BUT MORE TROUBLE IS ON THE WAY AS THE POLICE ARRIVE.....
YOU'RE THE GUY WE'VE BEEN LOOKING FOR!
PAT!
SORRY ABOUT THIS, CHUMS
BAM
BIP
AH! THERE HE GOES, INTO THE BIG TOP!
MARVELMAN IS JUST IN TIME TO SPOT ANUELLO CLIMBING A LADDER TO THE ROOF...
TAKE TO THE HIGH WIRE IF YOU WISH - BUT IT'LL DO YOU NO GOOD!
SOON
GOT YOU ... AND THIS TIME IT'S FOR KEEPS
LATER
WELL! THAT'S THE HEADLINE I'VE BEEN WAITING TO SEE!
DAILY BUGLE
MARVELMAN CLEARS HIS NAME
THE END!

MARVELMAN

AND THE
STOLEN REFLECTIONS

A recluse Astro-Scientist discovers the key word to the Universe, one that can only be given to a Boy who is completely honest, studious, and of such integrity that he would only use it for the powers of good. He finds such a Boy in **MICKY MORAN**, a Newspaper Copy Boy, and treats him in a special machine which enables him to use the secret. Just before the Scientist dies he tells **MICKY** the Key Word which is **KIMOTA**.

MICKY MORAN remains as he was, but when he says the Key Word **KIMOTA** he becomes **MARVELMAN**, a Man of such strength and powers that he is Invincible and Indestructible.

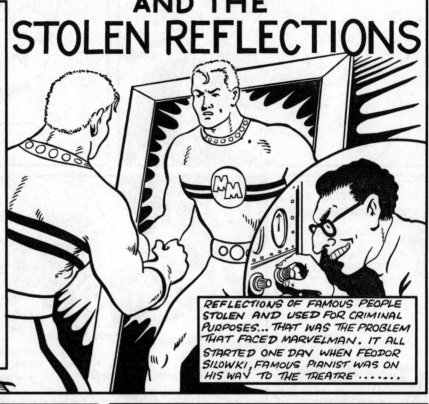

REFLECTIONS OF FAMOUS PEOPLE STOLEN AND USED FOR CRIMINAL PURPOSES... THAT WAS THE PROBLEM THAT FACED MARVELMAN. IT ALL STARTED ONE DAY WHEN FEODOR SILOWKI, FAMOUS PIANIST WAS ON HIS WAY TO THE THEATRE ......

PLAZA

TONIGHT I GIVE OF MY BEST PERFORMANCE!

SUDDENLY AN AUTOMOBILE DRAWS UP AND FOUR MEN PILE OUT TO RUSH AT THE FAMOUS PIANIST!

GRAB HIM, FELLAS!

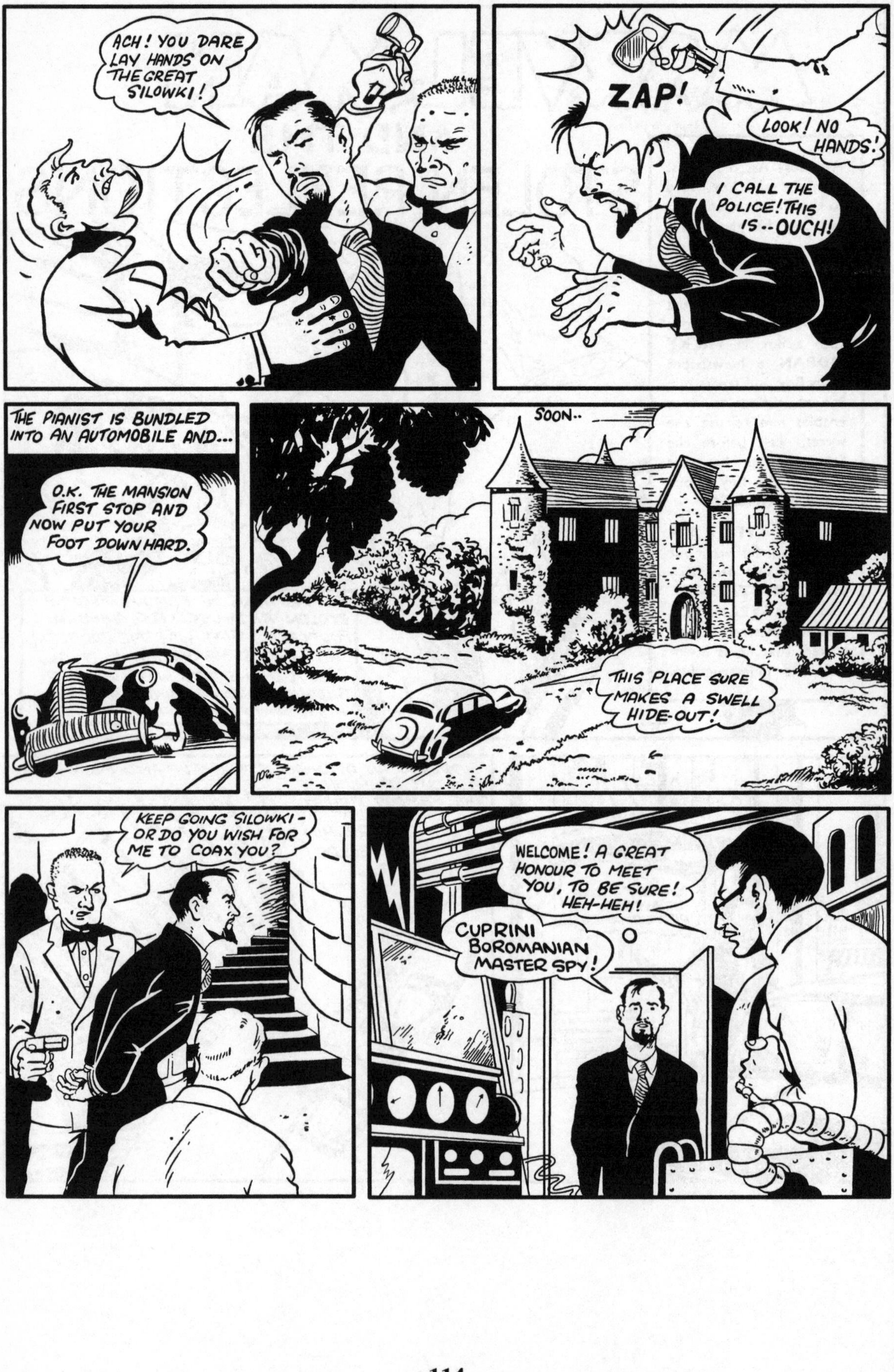

ACH! YOU DARE LAY HANDS ON THE GREAT SILOWKI!
ZAP!
LOOK! NO HANDS!
I CALL THE POLICE! THIS IS--OUCH!
THE PIANIST IS BUNDLED INTO AN AUTOMOBILE AND...
O.K. THE MANSION FIRST STOP AND NOW PUT YOUR FOOT DOWN HARD.
SOON..
THIS PLACE SURE MAKES A SWELL HIDE-OUT!
KEEP GOING SILOWKI - OR DO YOU WISH FOR ME TO COAX YOU?
WELCOME! A GREAT HONOUR TO MEET YOU, TO BE SURE! HEH-HEH!
CUPRINI BOROMANIAN MASTER SPY!

THE SAME! AH! YOU TREMBLE. LOOK AT YOURSELF IN THAT MIRROR!
I AM NOT AFRAID
AHA! I TRICKED HIM TO LOOK IN THE MIRROR!
NOW TO THROW THE SWITCH
WHY! WHAT SORT OF MIRROR IS THIS MY REFLECTION'S GONE!
OH NO! I HAVE STOLEN IT! THIS MACHINE CAPTURES PEOPLE'S REFLECTIONS. BY PLACING THEM IN A SPECIAL CABINET THEY BECOME INFLATED AND AS LIKE THE ORIGINAL IN EVERY DETAIL— EXCEPT FOR ONE IMPORTANT THING. THE REFLECTION OBEYS MY EVERY ORDER. YOU OF COURSE SEE THE—ER— POSSIBILITIES!
NOW I REMOVE YOUR IMAGE FROM BEHIND THIS MIRROR ---
AND PLACE IT IN THE CABINET..
PRESS THE BUTTON HERE - AND SO! YOUR IMAGE COMES TO LIFE_
COME, IMAGE OF SILOWKI! OBEY ME- YOUR MASTER
YES..
YOU FIEND CUPRINI
I OBEY YOU, MASTER

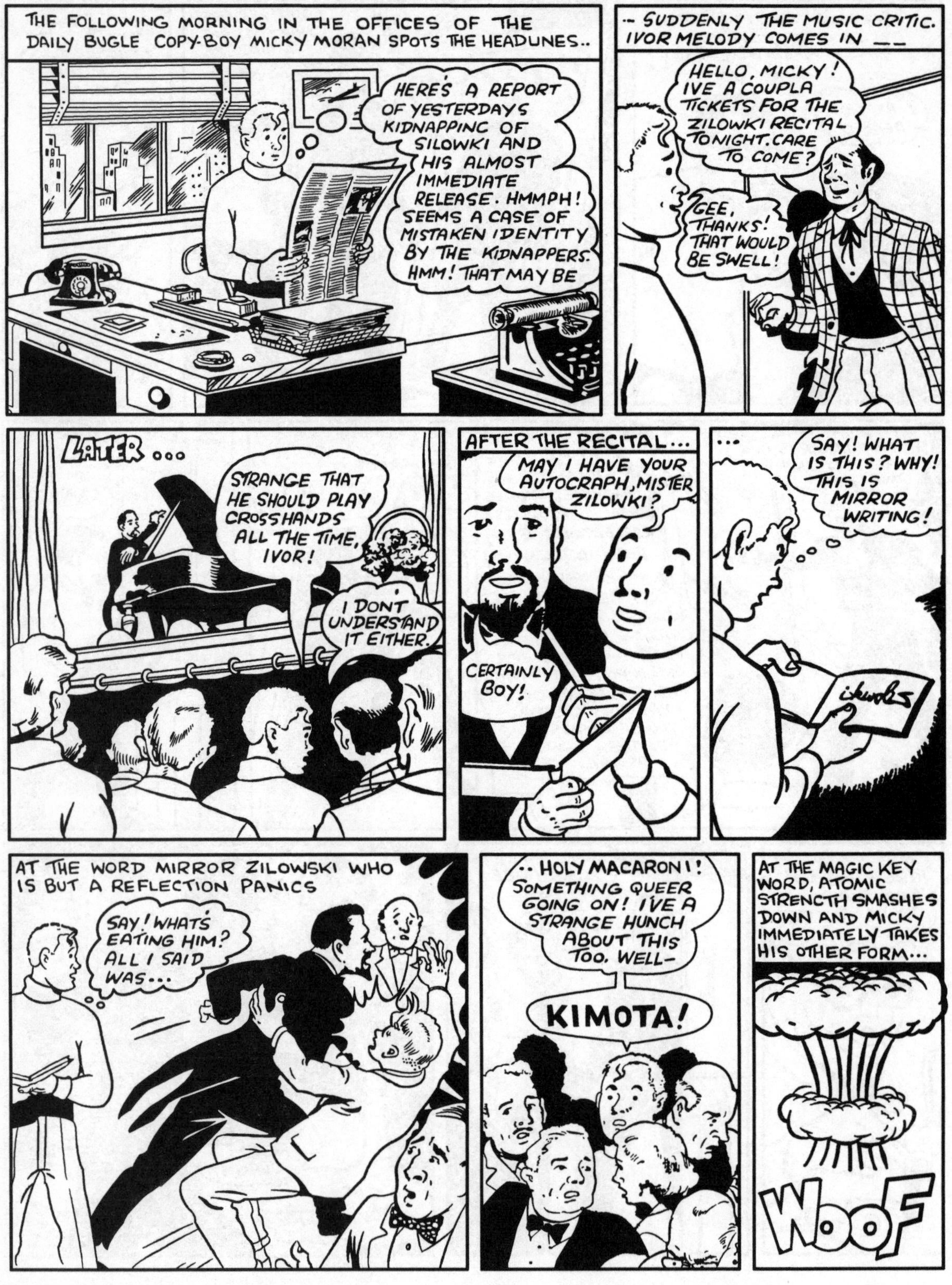
THE FOLLOWING MORNING IN THE OFFICES OF THE DAILY BUGLE COPY-BOY MICKY MORAN SPOTS THE HEADLINES..
HERE'S A REPORT OF YESTERDAYS KIDNAPPING OF SILOWKI AND HIS ALMOST IMMEDIATE RELEASE. HMMPH! SEEMS A CASE OF MISTAKEN IDENTITY BY THE KIDNAPPERS. HMM! THAT MAY BE
-- SUDDENLY THE MUSIC CRITIC. IVOR MELODY COMES IN --
HELLO, MICKY! IVE A COUPLA TICKETS FOR THE ZILOWKI RECITAL TONIGHT. CARE TO COME?
GEE, THANKS! THAT WOULD BE SWELL!
LATER ...
STRANGE THAT HE SHOULD PLAY CROSSHANDS ALL THE TIME, IVOR!
I DONT UNDERSTAND IT EITHER.
AFTER THE RECITAL...
MAY I HAVE YOUR AUTOGRAPH, MISTER ZILOWKI?
CERTAINLY BOY!
...
SAY! WHAT IS THIS? WHY! THIS IS MIRROR WRITING!
AT THE WORD MIRROR ZILOWSKI WHO IS BUT A REFLECTION PANICS
SAY! WHAT'S EATING HIM? ALL I SAID WAS...
.. HOLY MACARONI! SOMETHING QUEER GOING ON! I'VE A STRANGE HUNCH ABOUT THIS TOO. WELL-
KIMOTA!
AT THE MAGIC KEY WORD, ATOMIC STRENGTH SMASHES DOWN AND MICKY IMMEDIATELY TAKES HIS OTHER FORM...
WOOF

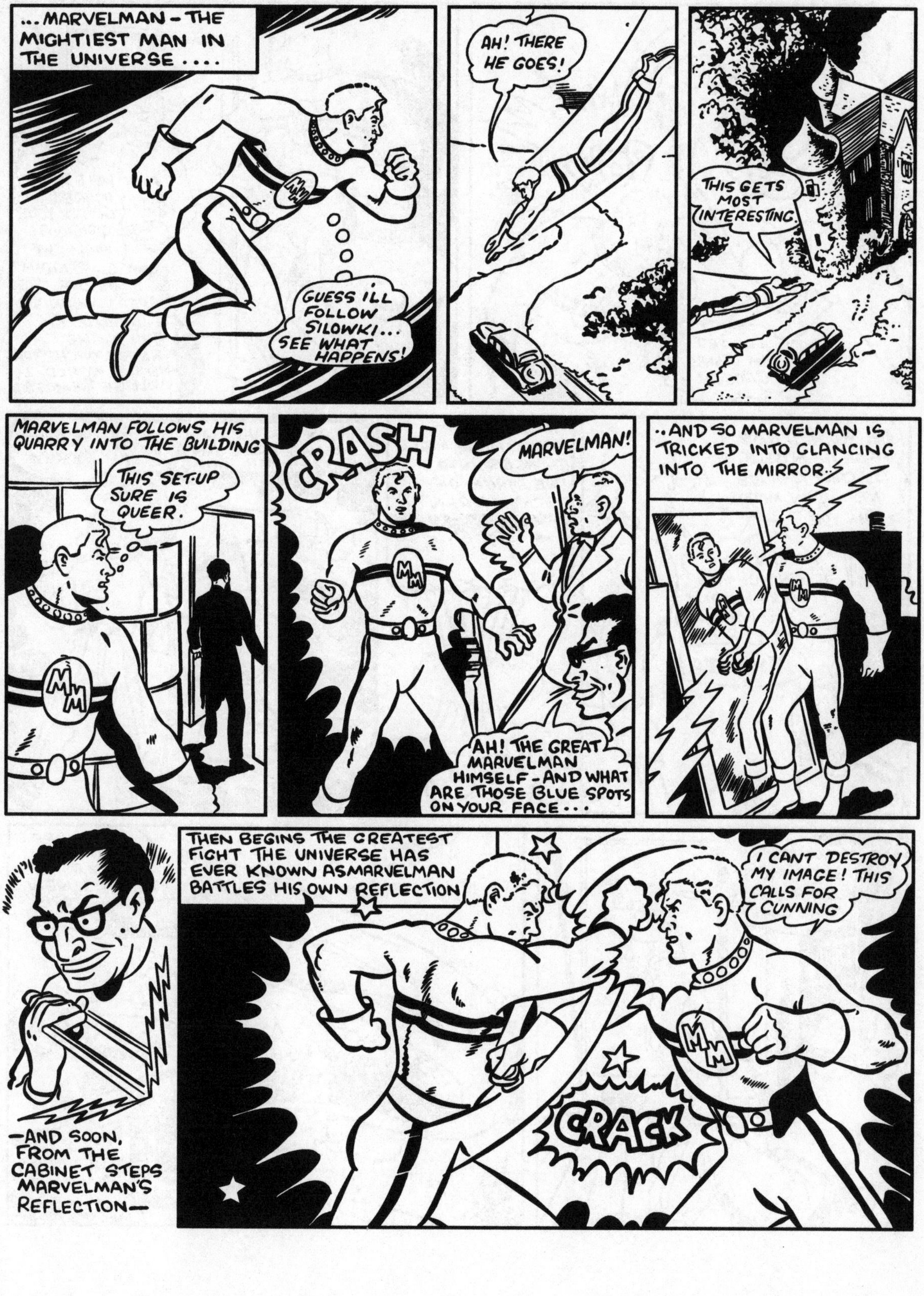
...MARVELMAN - THE MIGHTIEST MAN IN THE UNIVERSE....
GUESS I'LL FOLLOW SILOWKI... SEE WHAT HAPPENS!
AH! THERE HE GOES!
THIS GETS MOST INTERESTING.
MARVELMAN FOLLOWS HIS QUARRY INTO THE BUILDING
THIS SET-UP SURE IS QUEER.
CRASH
MARVELMAN!
AH! THE GREAT MARVELMAN HIMSELF - AND WHAT ARE THOSE BLUE SPOTS ON YOUR FACE...
..AND SO MARVELMAN IS TRICKED INTO GLANCING INTO THE MIRROR..
-AND SOON, FROM THE CABINET STEPS MARVELMAN'S REFLECTION-
THEN BEGINS THE GREATEST FIGHT THE UNIVERSE HAS EVER KNOWN ASMARVELMAN BATTLES HIS OWN REFLECTION
I CANT DESTROY MY IMAGE! THIS CALLS FOR CUNNING
CRACK

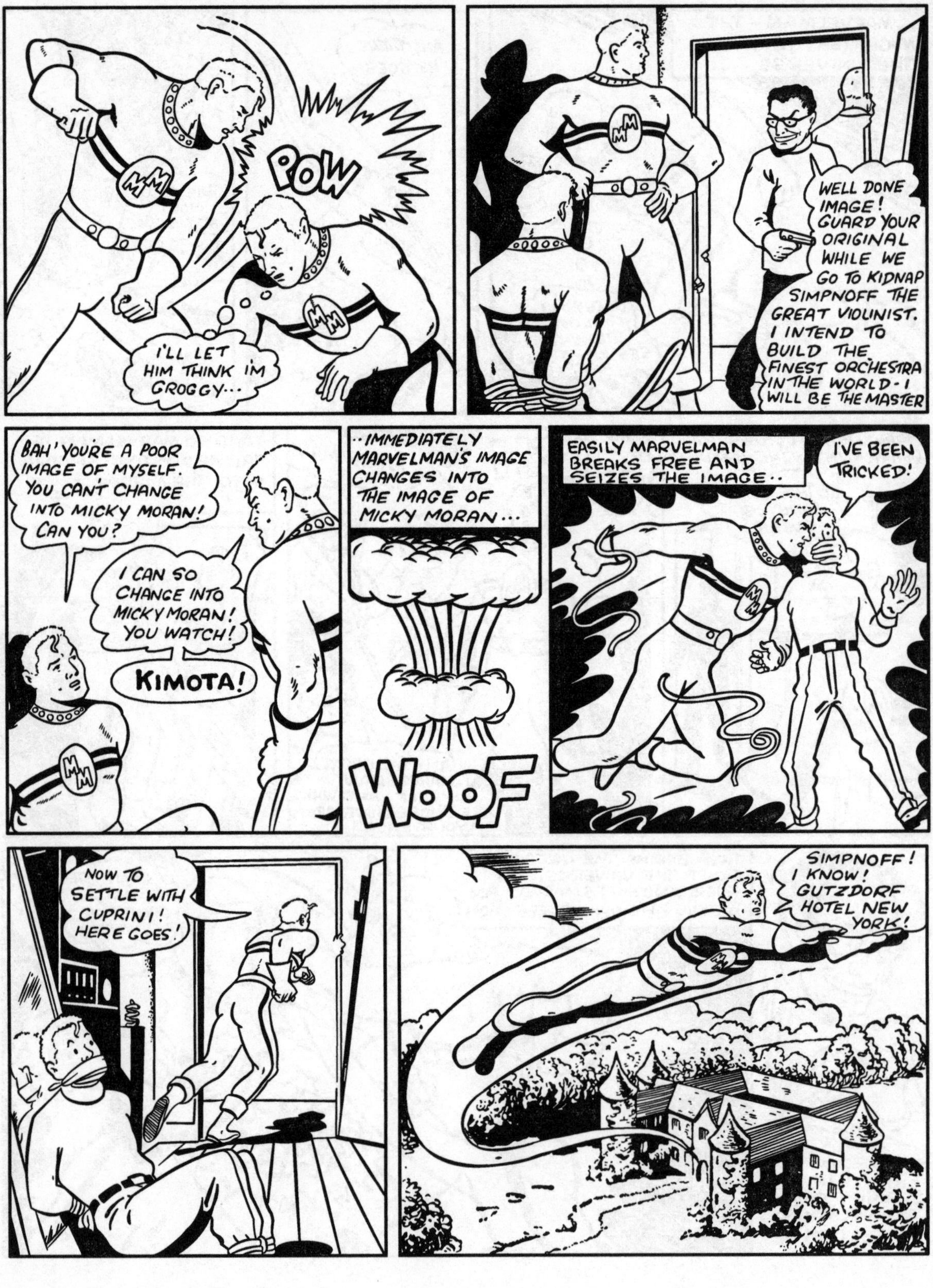
POW
I'LL LET HIM THINK I'M GROGGY...
WELL DONE IMAGE! GUARD YOUR ORIGINAL WHILE WE GO TO KIDNAP SIMPNOFF THE GREAT VIOLINIST. I INTEND TO BUILD THE FINEST ORCHESTRA IN THE WORLD - I WILL BE THE MASTER
BAH' YOU'RE A POOR IMAGE OF MYSELF. YOU CAN'T CHANGE INTO MICKY MORAN! CAN YOU?
I CAN SO CHANGE INTO MICKY MORAN! YOU WATCH!
KIMOTA!
..IMMEDIATELY MARVELMAN'S IMAGE CHANGES INTO THE IMAGE OF MICKY MORAN...
WOOF
EASILY MARVELMAN BREAKS FREE AND SEIZES THE IMAGE..
I'VE BEEN TRICKED!
NOW TO SETTLE WITH CUPRINI! HERE GOES!
SIMPNOFF! I KNOW! GUTZDORF HOTEL NEW YORK!

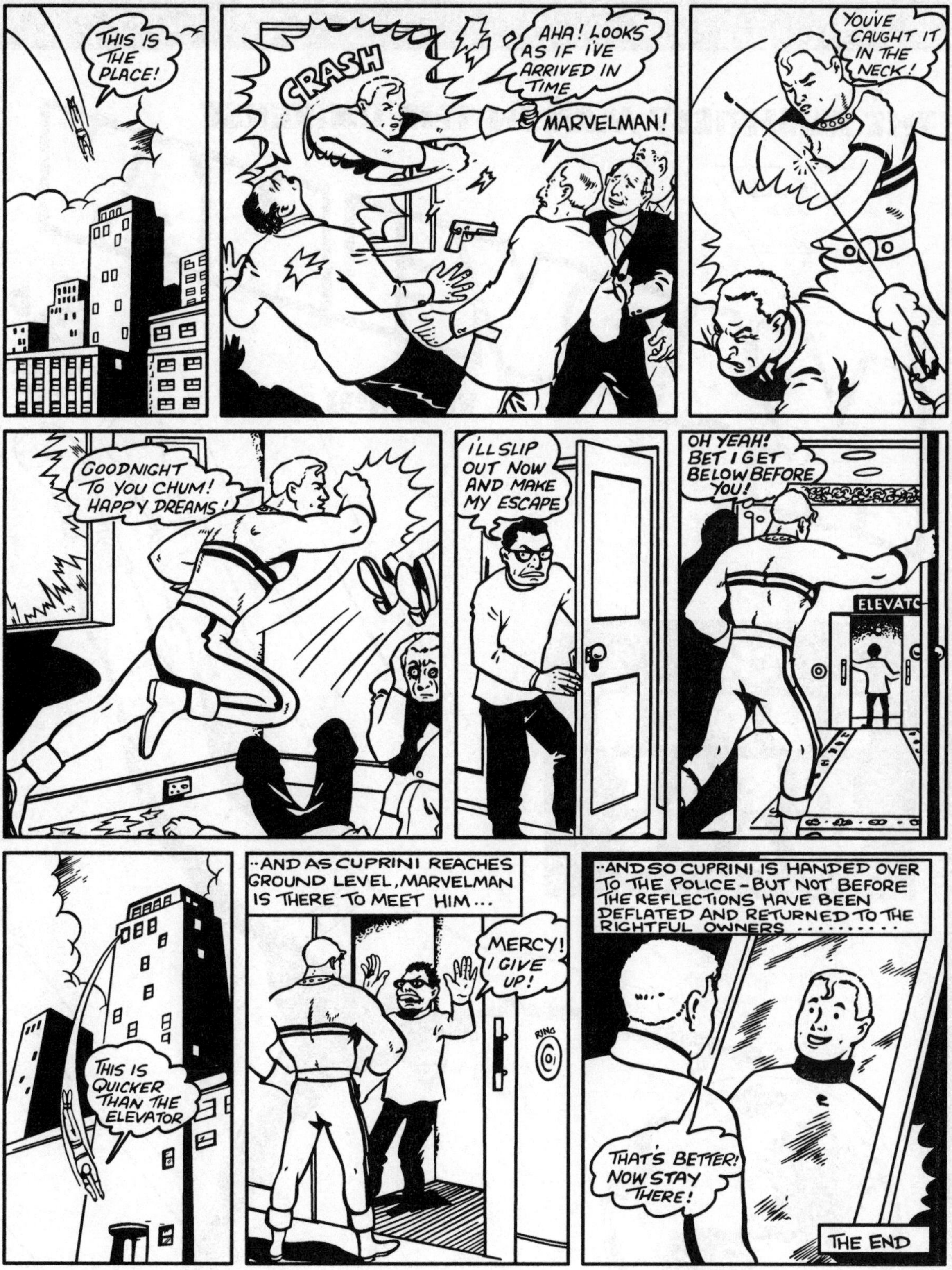
THIS IS THE PLACE!
CRASH
AHA! LOOKS AS IF I'VE ARRIVED IN TIME
MARVELMAN!
YOU'VE CAUGHT IT IN THE NECK!
GOODNIGHT TO YOU CHUM! HAPPY DREAMS!
I'LL SLIP OUT NOW AND MAKE MY ESCAPE
OH YEAH! BET I GET BELOW BEFORE YOU!
ELEVATO
THIS IS QUICKER THAN THE ELEVATOR
..AND AS CUPRINI REACHES GROUND LEVEL, MARVELMAN IS THERE TO MEET HIM...
MERCY! I GIVE UP!
RING
..AND SO CUPRINI IS HANDED OVER TO THE POLICE - BUT NOT BEFORE THE REFLECTIONS HAVE BEEN DEFLATED AND RETURNED TO THE RIGHTFUL OWNERS ....
THAT'S BETTER! NOW STAY THERE!
THE END

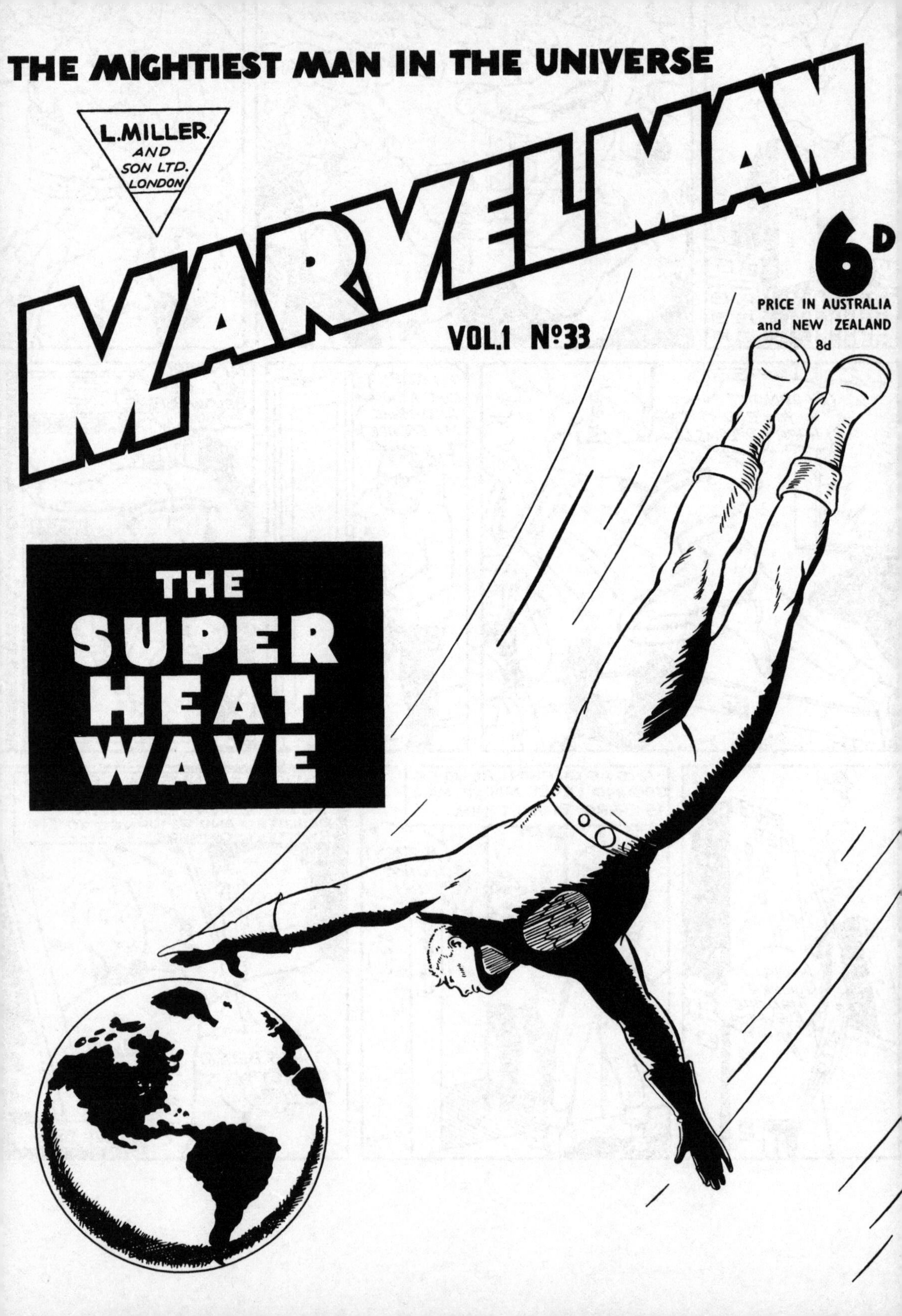
THE MIGHTIEST MAN IN THE UNIVERSE
L.MILLER AND SON LTD. LONDON
MARVELMAN
6D
PRICE IN AUSTRALIA and NEW ZEALAND 8d
VOL.1 No.33
THE SUPER HEAT WAVE

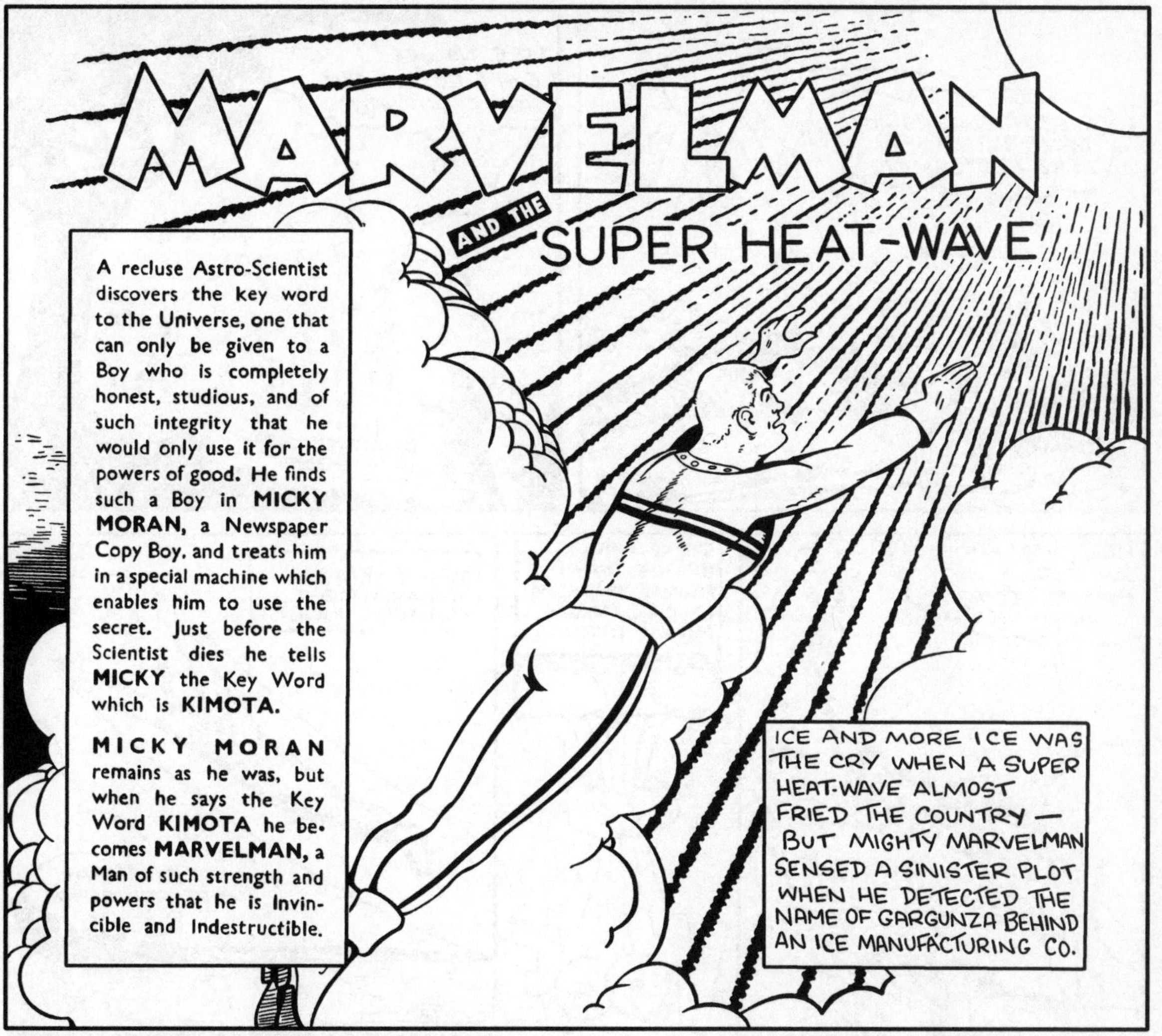
MARVELMAN
AND THE SUPER HEAT-WAVE
A recluse Astro-Scientist discovers the key word to the Universe, one that can only be given to a Boy who is completely honest, studious, and of such integrity that he would only use it for the powers of good. He finds such a Boy in MICKY MORAN, a Newspaper Copy Boy, and treats him in a special machine which enables him to use the secret. Just before the Scientist dies he tells MICKY the Key Word which is KIMOTA.
MICKY MORAN remains as he was, but when he says the Key Word KIMOTA he becomes MARVELMAN, a Man of such strength and powers that he is Invincible and Indestructible.
ICE AND MORE ICE WAS THE CRY WHEN A SUPER HEAT-WAVE ALMOST FRIED THE COUNTRY — BUT MIGHTY MARVELMAN SENSED A SINISTER PLOT WHEN HE DETECTED THE NAME OF GARGUNZA BEHIND AN ICE MANUFÁCTURING CO.

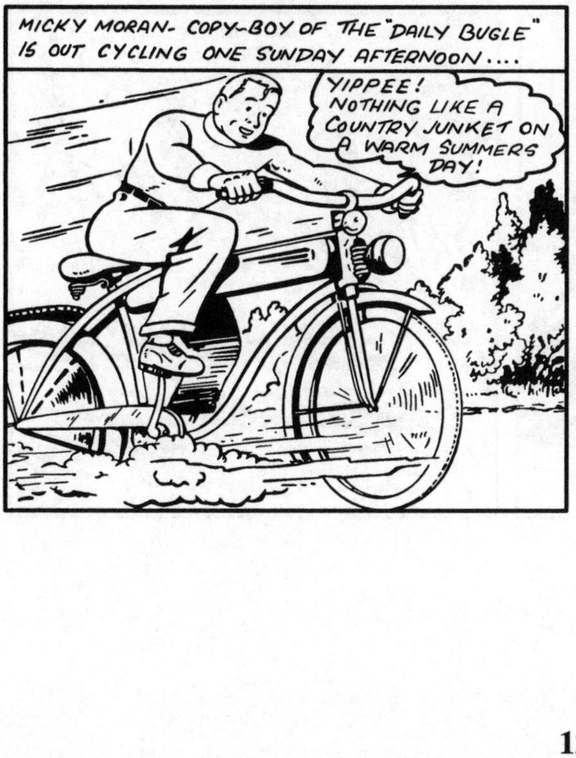
MICKY MORAN- COPY-BOY OF THE "DAILY BUGLE" IS OUT CYCLING ONE SUNDAY AFTERNOON....
YIPPEE! NOTHING LIKE A COUNTRY JUNKET ON A WARM SUMMERS DAY!

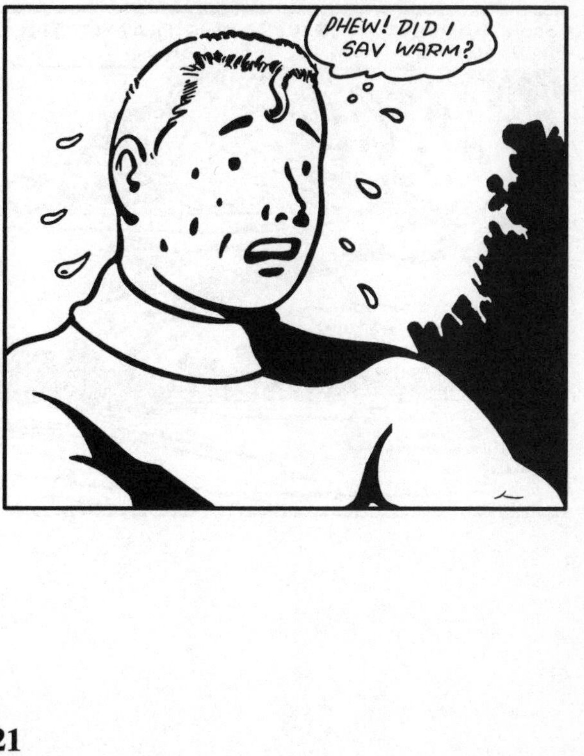
PHEW! DID I SAV WARM?

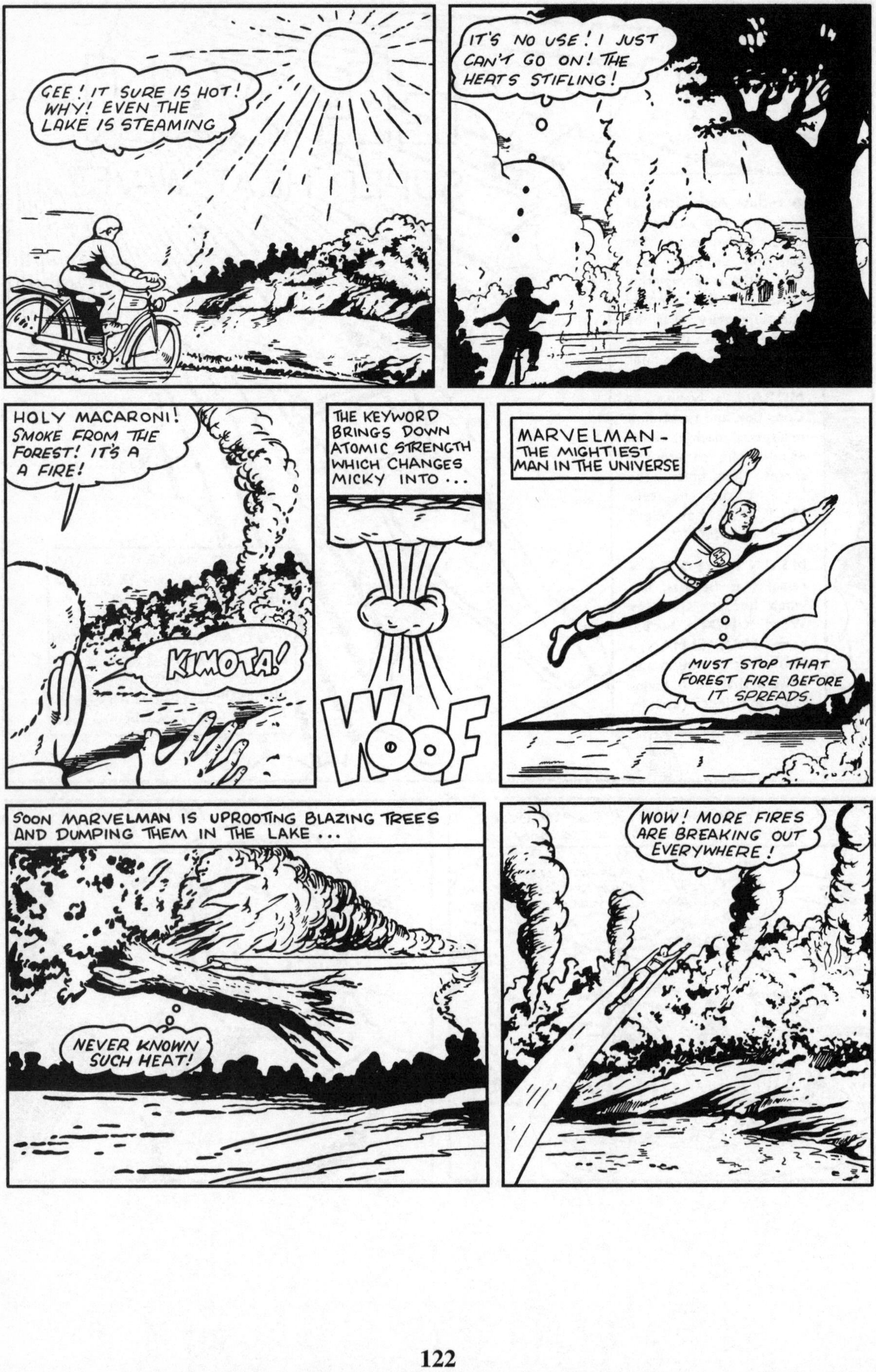
GEE! IT SURE IS HOT! WHY! EVEN THE LAKE IS STEAMING
IT'S NO USE! I JUST CAN'T GO ON! THE HEAT'S STIFLING!
HOLY MACARONI! SMOKE FROM THE FOREST! IT'S A FIRE!
KIMOTA!
THE KEYWORD BRINGS DOWN ATOMIC STRENGTH WHICH CHANGES MICKY INTO ...
WOOF
MARVELMAN - THE MIGHTIEST MAN IN THE UNIVERSE
MUST STOP THAT FOREST FIRE BEFORE IT SPREADS.
SOON MARVELMAN IS UPROOTING BLAZING TREES AND DUMPING THEM IN THE LAKE ...
NEVER KNOWN SUCH HEAT!
WOW! MORE FIRES ARE BREAKING OUT EVERYWHERE!

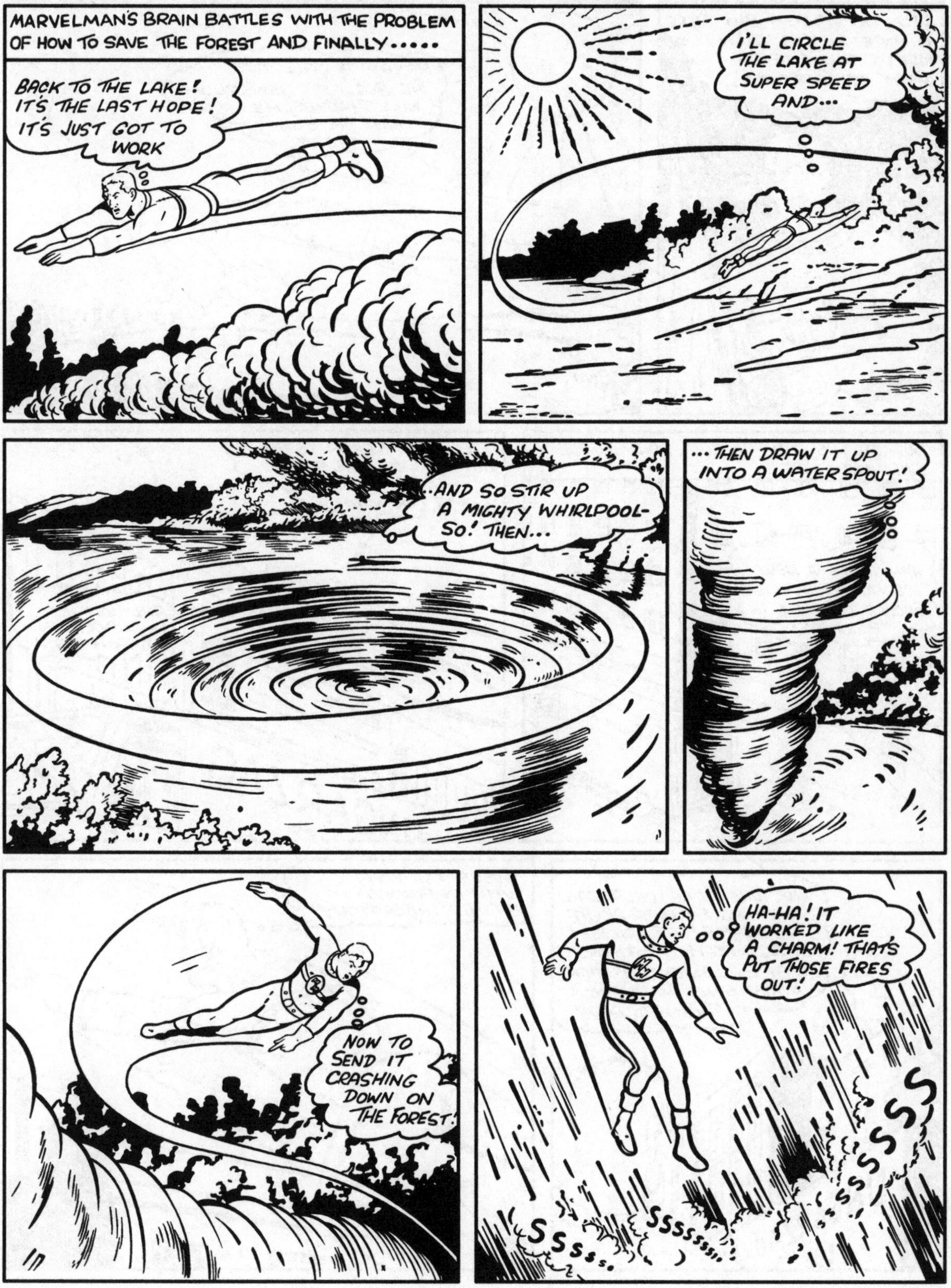
MARVELMAN'S BRAIN BATTLES WITH THE PROBLEM OF HOW TO SAVE THE FOREST AND FINALLY.....
BACK TO THE LAKE! IT'S THE LAST HOPE! IT'S JUST GOT TO WORK
I'LL CIRCLE THE LAKE AT SUPER SPEED AND...
...AND SO STIR UP A MIGHTY WHIRLPOOL- SO! THEN...
...THEN DRAW IT UP INTO A WATER SPOUT!
NOW TO SEND IT CRASHING DOWN ON THE FOREST!
HA-HA! IT WORKED LIKE A CHARM! THAT'S PUT THOSE FIRES OUT!
SSSSS
SSSSSSSS
SSSSSSS

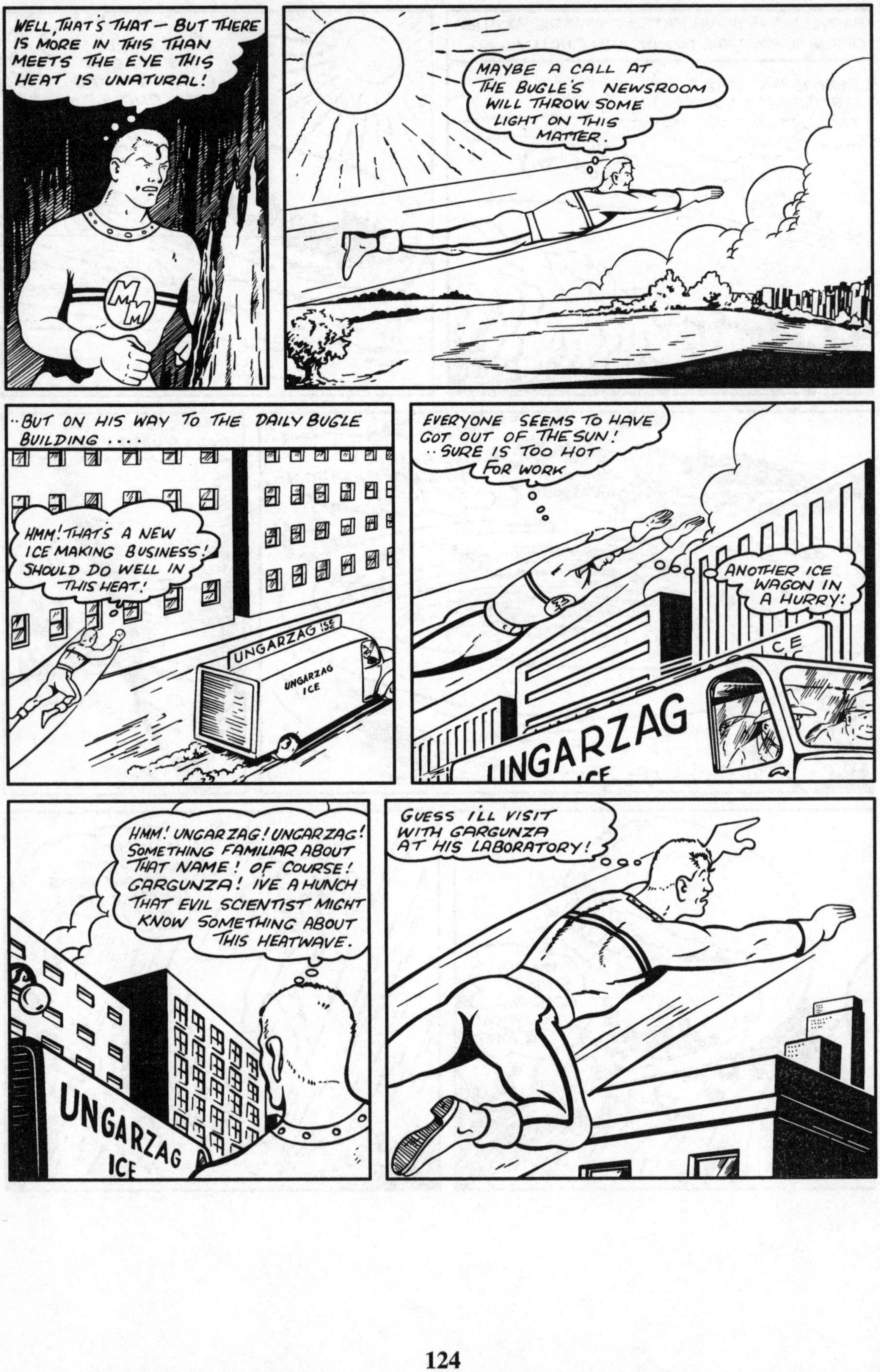

WELL, THAT'S THAT— BUT THERE IS MORE IN THIS THAN MEETS THE EYE THIS HEAT IS UNATURAL!
MAYBE A CALL AT THE BUGLE'S NEWSROOM WILL THROW SOME LIGHT ON THIS MATTER.
..BUT ON HIS WAY TO THE DAILY BUGLE BUILDING ....
HMM! THAT'S A NEW ICE MAKING BUSINESS! SHOULD DO WELL IN THIS HEAT!
UNGARZAG ICE
UNGARZAG ICE
EVERYONE SEEMS TO HAVE GOT OUT OF THE SUN! ..SURE IS TOO HOT FOR WORK
ANOTHER ICE WAGON IN A HURRY!
UNGARZAG
UNGARZAG
HMM! UNGARZAG! UNGARZAG! SOMETHING FAMILIAR ABOUT THAT NAME! OF COURSE! GARGUNZA! IVE A HUNCH THAT EVIL SCIENTIST MIGHT KNOW SOMETHING ABOUT THIS HEATWAVE.
UNGARZAG ICE
GUESS I'LL VISIT WITH GARGUNZA AT HIS LABORATORY!

MARVELMAN SOARS OVER THE CITY TO THE SCIENTIST'S LABORATORY......

SAY! THIS DOESN'T SEEM TO BE A LAB ANY LONGER. MAYBE GARGUNZA'S PULLED OUT!

HOLY MACARONI! I'M NOT SO SURE HE'S PULLED OUT

CRASH!

ALL THAT ICE MUST MEAN SOMETHING.

WHERE'S GARGUNZA?

NEVER HEARD OF IT? SOUNDS LIKE CHEESE!

QUIT STALLING!

HONEST INJUN. I ONLY KNOW THAT THIS SET-UP IS RUN BY A GUY CALLED NULLET! HE'S IN THE OFFICE BELOW

O.K. BUT IF THIS IS ANOTHER STALL I'LL BE RIGHT BACK

SAY BOSS! THAT CRASH WAS MARVELMAN BREAKING THROUGH THE WINDOW

BAH! THAT BLUE BABOON'S GOT NOTHING ON ME!

MARVELMAN STRIDES INTO THE ROOM..

HOLY MACARONI! IT'S AUGUSTUS NULLET THE BUSINESS TYCOON!

YES, INDEED, MARVELMAN. WHAT'S THE BIG IDEA BURSTING IN HERE LIKE THIS?

BUT GARGUNZA USED TO OCCUPY THESE PREMISES. I WAS CONVINCED...

HE MOVED OUT AGES AGO! SURELY YOU DON'T SUSPECT ME IN SUCH A DIABOLICAL PLOT THIS SUPER HEAT WAVE IS...

SAY! WHO SAID ANYTHING ABOUT A DIABOLICAL PLOT? WHO MENTIONED A SUPER-HEAT WAVE? YOU'VE GOT A CONSCIENCE, BROTHER!

YOU TALK TOO MUCH, BLABBERMOUTH — BUT NOW YOU CAN KEEP TALKING. LET'S HEAR SOME MORE.

POW!

HEY! WHAT GIVES?

MARVELMAN PILES INTO THE HOOLIGANS..

THOUGHT THERE WAS SOMETHING FUNNY ABOUT THIS SET-UP!

BIM

BAM

EASIEST WAY TO DISPOSE OF THIS MOB! NOW I CAN CONCENTRATE ON NULLET!

BIF

POW

BAM

THUD

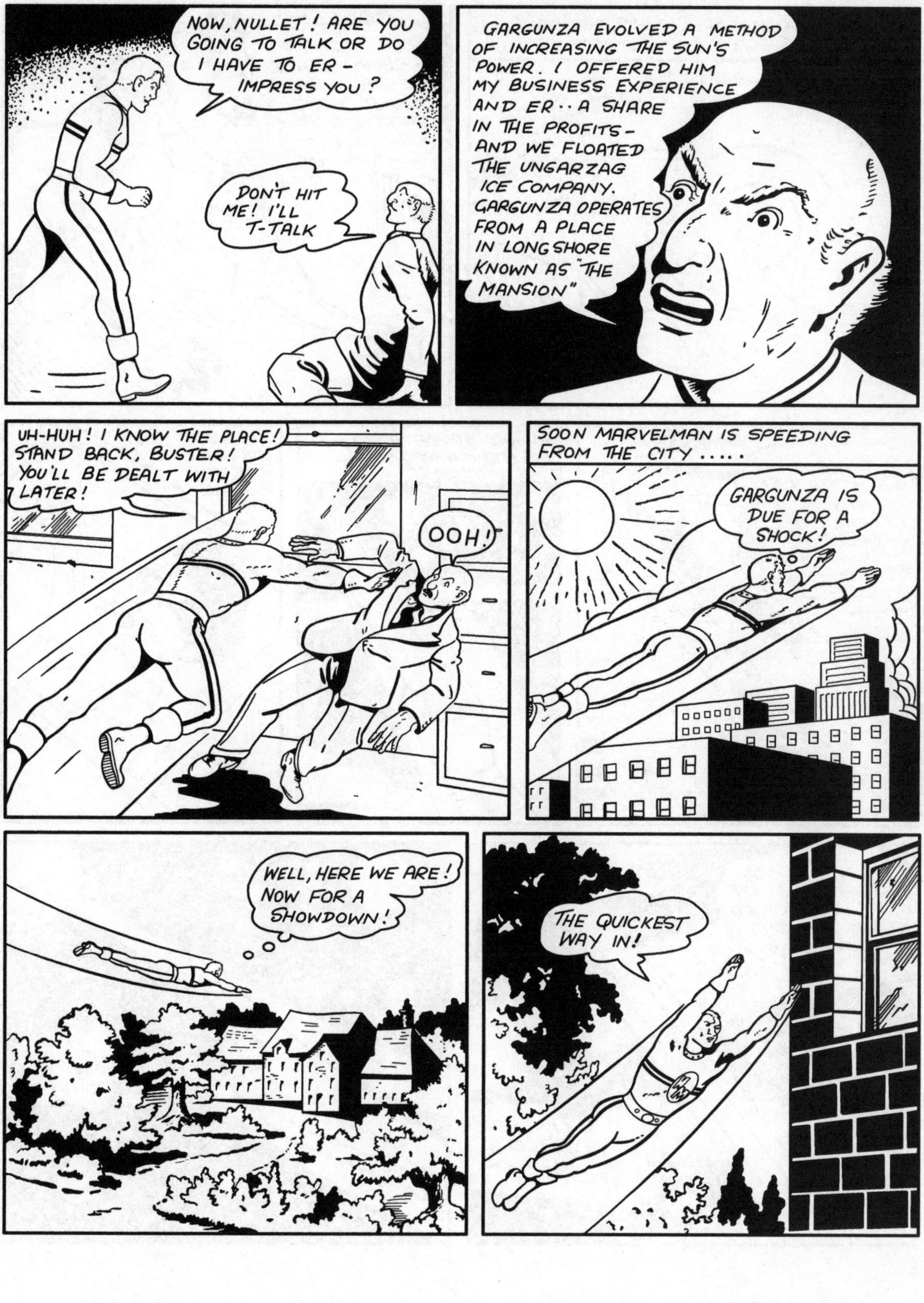

NOW, NULLET! ARE YOU GOING TO TALK OR DO I HAVE TO ER - IMPRESS YOU?
DON'T HIT ME! I'LL T-TALK
GARGUNZA EVOLVED A METHOD OF INCREASING THE SUN'S POWER. I OFFERED HIM MY BUSINESS EXPERIENCE AND ER.. A SHARE IN THE PROFITS - AND WE FLOATED THE UNGARZAG ICE COMPANY. GARGUNZA OPERATES FROM A PLACE IN LONGSHORE KNOWN AS "THE MANSION"
UH-HUH! I KNOW THE PLACE! STAND BACK, BUSTER! YOU'LL BE DEALT WITH LATER!
OOH!
SOON MARVELMAN IS SPEEDING FROM THE CITY....
GARGUNZA IS DUE FOR A SHOCK!
WELL, HERE WE ARE! NOW FOR A SHOWDOWN!
THE QUICKEST WAY IN!

BUT AS MARVELMAN BREAKS INTO THE MANSION, A SHATTERING EXPLOSION WRECKS THE PLACE..

HOLY MACARONI! I SHOULD HAVE GUESSED NULLET WOULD 'PHONE GARGUNZA TO TIP HIM OFF!

SO THAT'S IT! THE LITTLE RAT IS MAKING A GETAWAY IN A SPACESHIP!

SO INTO SPACE SHOOTS THE MIGHTIEST MAN IN THE UNIVERSE......

HAK-HAK! NULLET CAN TAKE THE RAP FOR ME

HAK-HAK! I THE GREAT GARGUNZA HAS OUTWITTED THAT BIG BLUE BLOCKHEAD!

AH! THERE HE GOES!

HE'S HEADING FOR THAT ASTEROID!

DOWN AT LAST! I SHALL BE SAFE HERE!
HAK-HAK!
NOW I'LL GIVE THE WORLD A NICE LITTLE ROASTING JUST FOR THE FUN OF IT- THEN LATER I'LL RETURN AS WORLD RULER!
GUESS I'LL TRAIL HIM AND SEE EXACTLY WHAT HE'S UP TO.
YES! A GOOD ROASTING WILL MAKE THE SO-CALLED WORLD LEADERS REALISE JUST HOW POWERFUL I AM!
SOON THE EVIL LITTLE SCIENTIST REACHES A STRANGE-LOOKING BUILDING....
MY GREATEST INVENTION!
UNAWARE OF MARVELMAN'S PRESENCE GARGUNZA LETS HIMSELF INTO THE BUILDING...
HAK-HAK-HAK!

GARGUNZA IS SOON BUSY........

I'LL FORCE THE EARTH'S TEMPERATURE UP TO BOILING

YOU EVIL LITTLE HORROR! WHAT FIENDISH MACHINE HAVE YOU CREATED THIS TIME..

YIPES!

O K.. YOU DEVIL! NOW OPEN UP OR I'LL KNOCK YOUR SKULL CLEAN THROUGH THE WALL!

I'LL TALK, YOU BIG BLUE BULLY! THIS DOME REFLECTS A RAY BETWEEN THE EARTH AND THE SUN WHICH I CAN MANIPULATE TO INCREASE OR DECREASE THE SUN'S POWER!

YOU RAT! YOU NEVER SEEM TO LEARN A LESSON!

CRASH!

B.F!

NEXT MARVELMAN WRECKS THE BUILDING AND THE HORRIBLE MACHINE----

WELL GARGUNZA! THAT'S THE LAST OF YOUR INVENTION!

MY POOR MACHINE!

I HOPE YOU HAVE LEARNED A LESSON THIS TIME NOT TO CONTINUE YOUR EVIL WAYS. YOUR BRAIN IS WASTED!

YES MARVELMAN- BUT REALLY IT WASN'T MY FAULT. NULLET INSTIGATED THE PLOT!

LATER

THE HEAT GARGUNZA CREATED WAS NOTHING COMPARED TO THE HEAT OF THAT ARGUMENT.

IT WAS YOU NULLET!

NUTS! YOU WERE TO BLAME!

THE END

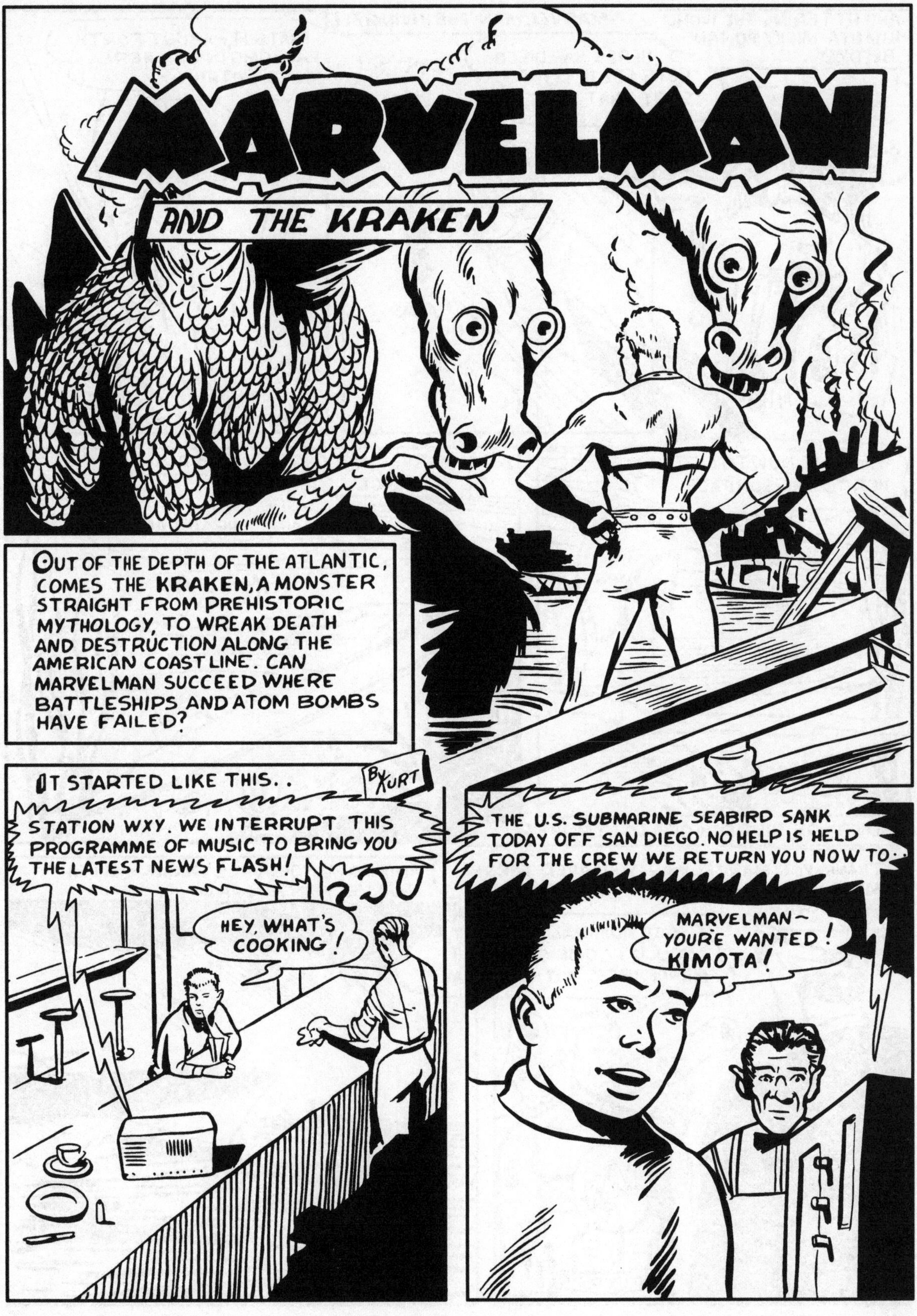
MARVELMAN
AND THE KRAKEN
OUT OF THE DEPTH OF THE ATLANTIC, COMES THE KRAKEN, A MONSTER STRAIGHT FROM PREHISTORIC MYTHOLOGY, TO WREAK DEATH AND DESTRUCTION ALONG THE AMERICAN COAST LINE. CAN MARVELMAN SUCCEED WHERE BATTLESHIPS AND ATOM BOMBS HAVE FAILED?
IT STARTED LIKE THIS. .
BY KURT
STATION WXY. WE INTERRUPT THIS PROGRAMME OF MUSIC TO BRING YOU THE LATEST NEWS FLASH!
HEY, WHAT'S COOKING!
THE U.S. SUBMARINE SEABIRD SANK TODAY OFF SAN DIEGO. NO HELP IS HELD FOR THE CREW WE RETURN YOU NOW TO. .
MARVELMAN~ YOU'RE WANTED! KIMOTA!

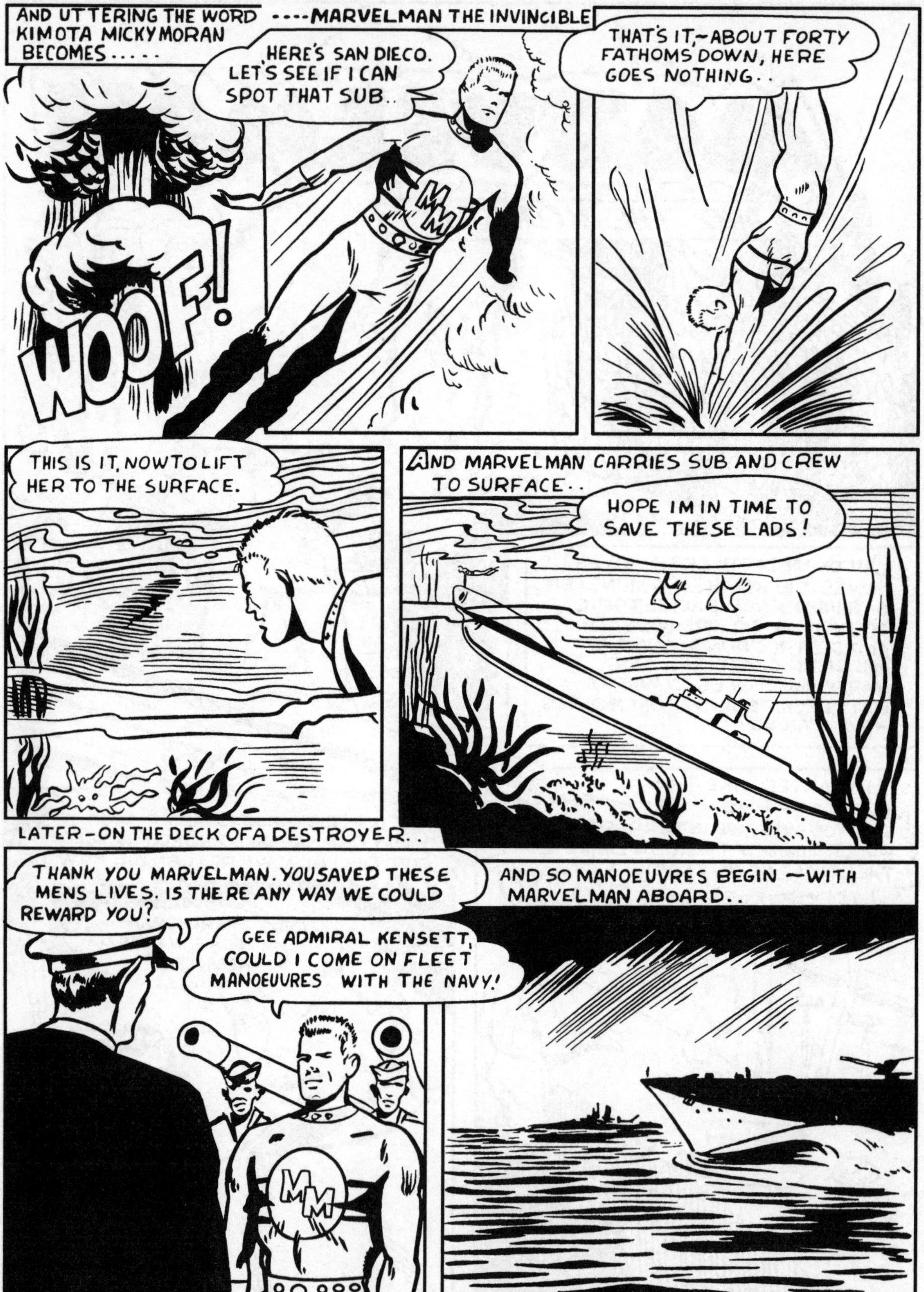
AND UTTERING THE WORD KIMOTA MICKY MORAN BECOMES.....
----MARVELMAN THE INVINCIBLE
HERE'S SAN DIEGO. LET'S SEE IF I CAN SPOT THAT SUB..
WOOF!
THAT'S IT,~ABOUT FORTY FATHOMS DOWN, HERE GOES NOTHING..
THIS IS IT, NOW TO LIFT HER TO THE SURFACE.
AND MARVELMAN CARRIES SUB AND CREW TO SURFACE..
HOPE IM IN TIME TO SAVE THESE LADS!
LATER-ON THE DECK OF A DESTROYER..
THANK YOU MARVELMAN. YOU SAVED THESE MENS LIVES. IS THERE ANY WAY WE COULD REWARD YOU?
GEE ADMIRAL KENSETT, COULD I COME ON FLEET MANOEUVRES WITH THE NAVY!
AND SO MANOEUVRES BEGIN —WITH MARVELMAN ABOARD..

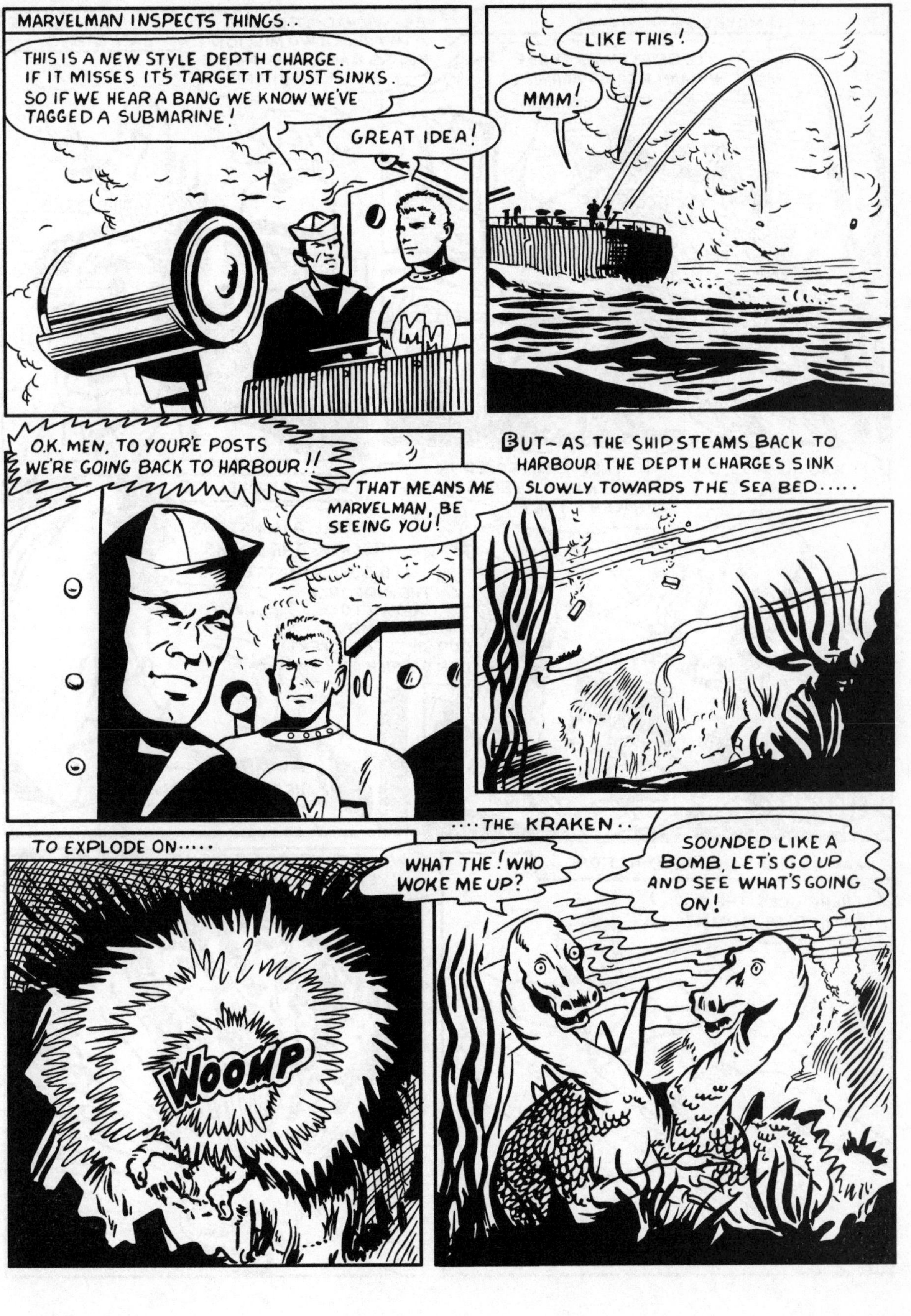
MARVELMAN INSPECTS THINGS..
THIS IS A NEW STYLE DEPTH CHARGE. IF IT MISSES IT'S TARGET IT JUST SINKS. SO IF WE HEAR A BANG WE KNOW WE'VE TAGGED A SUBMARINE!
GREAT IDEA!
LIKE THIS!
MMM!
O.K. MEN, TO YOUR'E POSTS WE'RE GOING BACK TO HARBOUR!!
THAT MEANS ME MARVELMAN, BE SEEING YOU!
BUT-AS THE SHIP STEAMS BACK TO HARBOUR THE DEPTH CHARGES SINK SLOWLY TOWARDS THE SEA BED.....
TO EXPLODE ON.....
WOOMP
....THE KRAKEN..
WHAT THE! WHO WOKE ME UP?
SOUNDED LIKE A BOMB, LET'S GO UP AND SEE WHAT'S GOING ON!

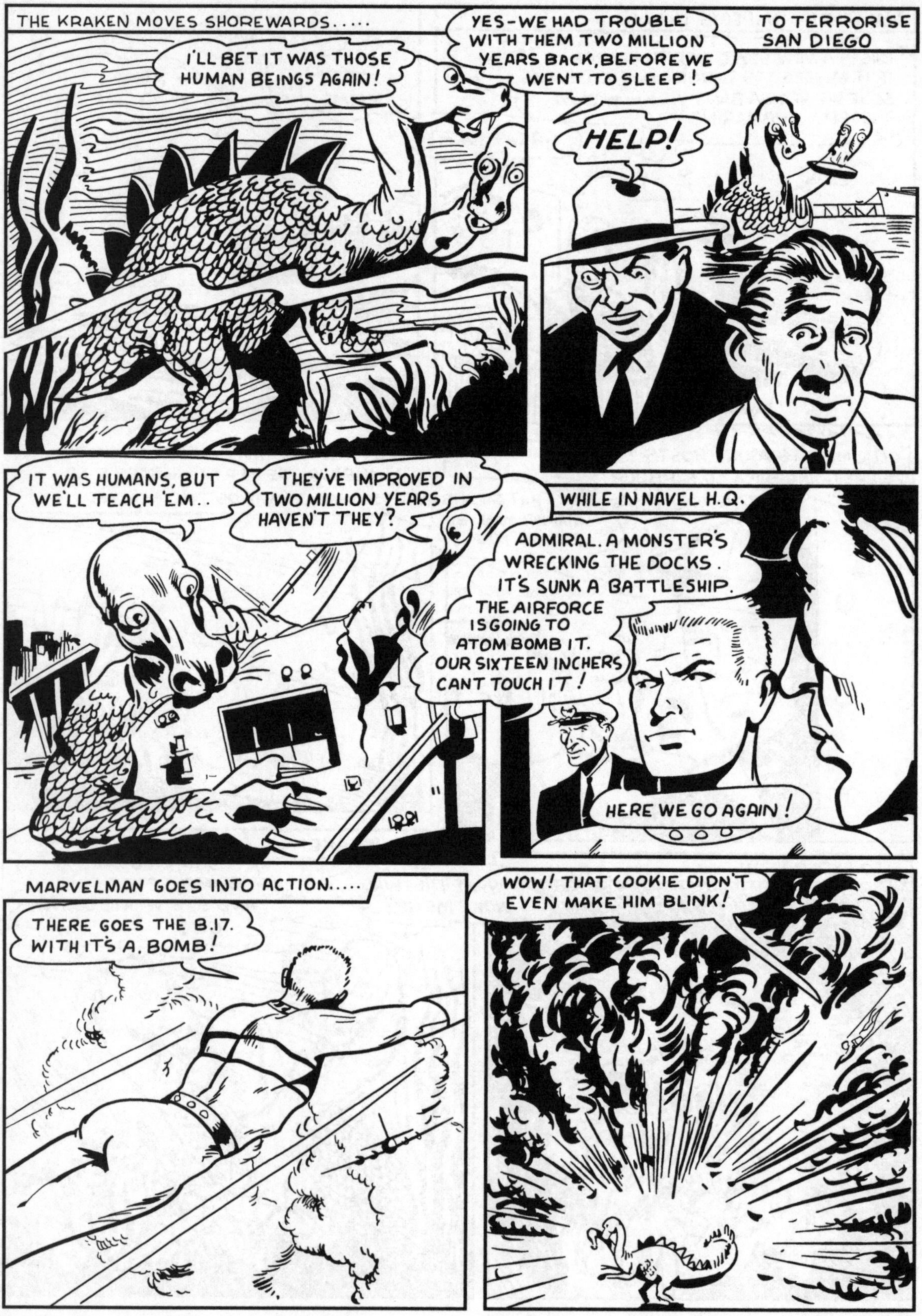
THE KRAKEN MOVES SHOREWARDS.....
I'LL BET IT WAS THOSE HUMAN BEINGS AGAIN!
YES-WE HAD TROUBLE WITH THEM TWO MILLION YEARS BACK, BEFORE WE WENT TO SLEEP!
TO TERRORISE SAN DIEGO
HELP!
IT WAS HUMANS, BUT WE'LL TEACH 'EM..
THEY'VE IMPROVED IN TWO MILLION YEARS HAVEN'T THEY?
WHILE IN NAVEL H.Q.
ADMIRAL. A MONSTER'S WRECKING THE DOCKS. IT'S SUNK A BATTLESHIP.
THE AIRFORCE IS GOING TO ATOM BOMB IT. OUR SIXTEEN INCHERS CANT TOUCH IT!
HERE WE GO AGAIN!
MARVELMAN GOES INTO ACTION.....
THERE GOES THE B.17. WITH IT'S A. BOMB!
WOW! THAT COOKIE DIDN'T EVEN MAKE HIM BLINK!

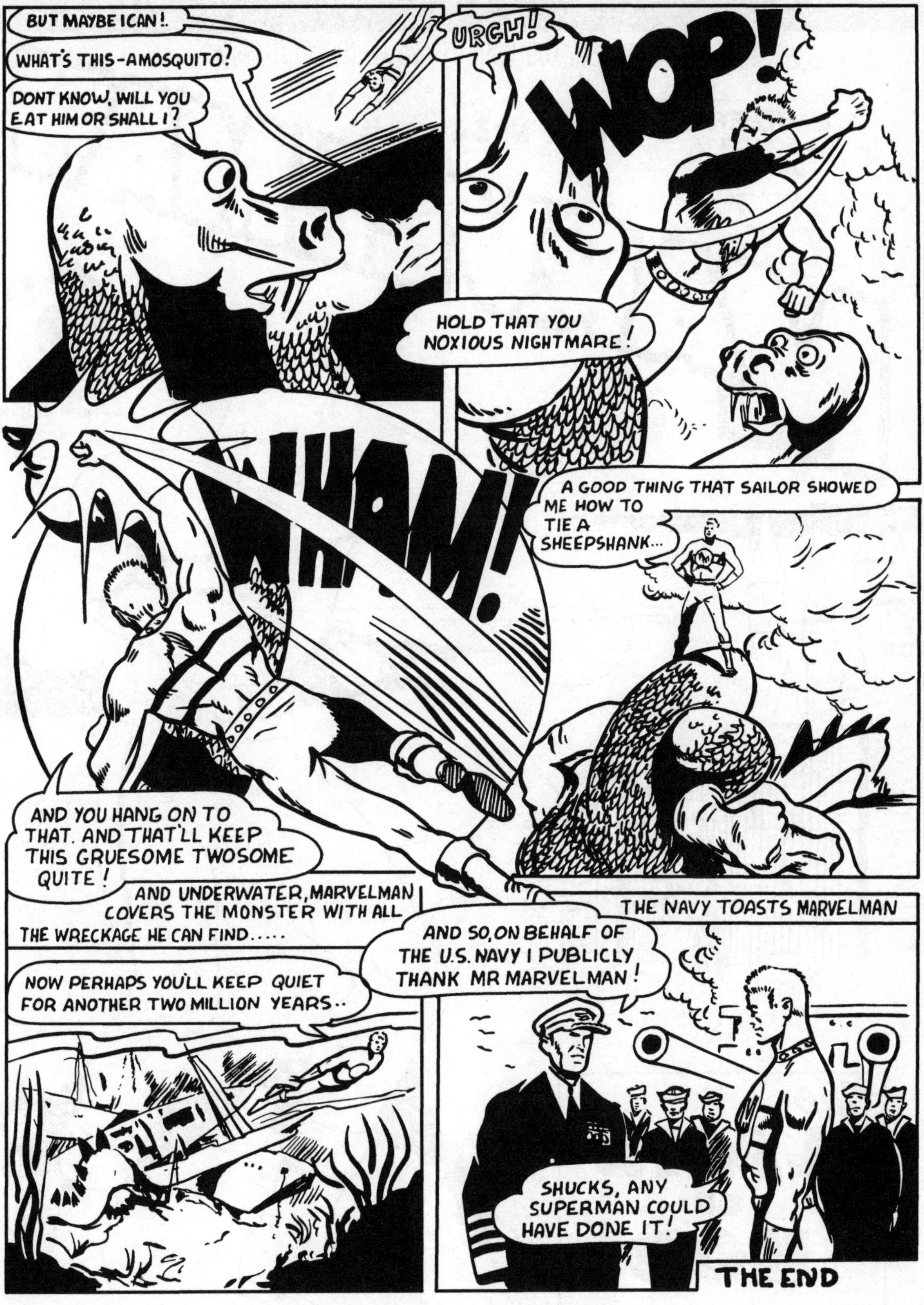

BUT MAYBE I CAN!.
WHAT'S THIS-A MOSQUITO?
DONT KNOW. WILL YOU EAT HIM OR SHALL I?
URGH!
WOP!
HOLD THAT YOU NOXIOUS NIGHTMARE!
WHAM!
AND YOU HANG ON TO THAT. AND THAT'LL KEEP THIS GRUESOME TWOSOME QUITE!
A GOOD THING THAT SAILOR SHOWED ME HOW TO TIE A SHEEPSHANK...
AND UNDERWATER, MARVELMAN COVERS THE MONSTER WITH ALL THE WRECKAGE HE CAN FIND.....
NOW PERHAPS YOU'LL KEEP QUIET FOR ANOTHER TWO MILLION YEARS..
THE NAVY TOASTS MARVELMAN
AND SO, ON BEHALF OF THE U.S. NAVY I PUBLICLY THANK MR MARVELMAN!
SHUCKS, ANY SUPERMAN COULD HAVE DONE IT!
THE END

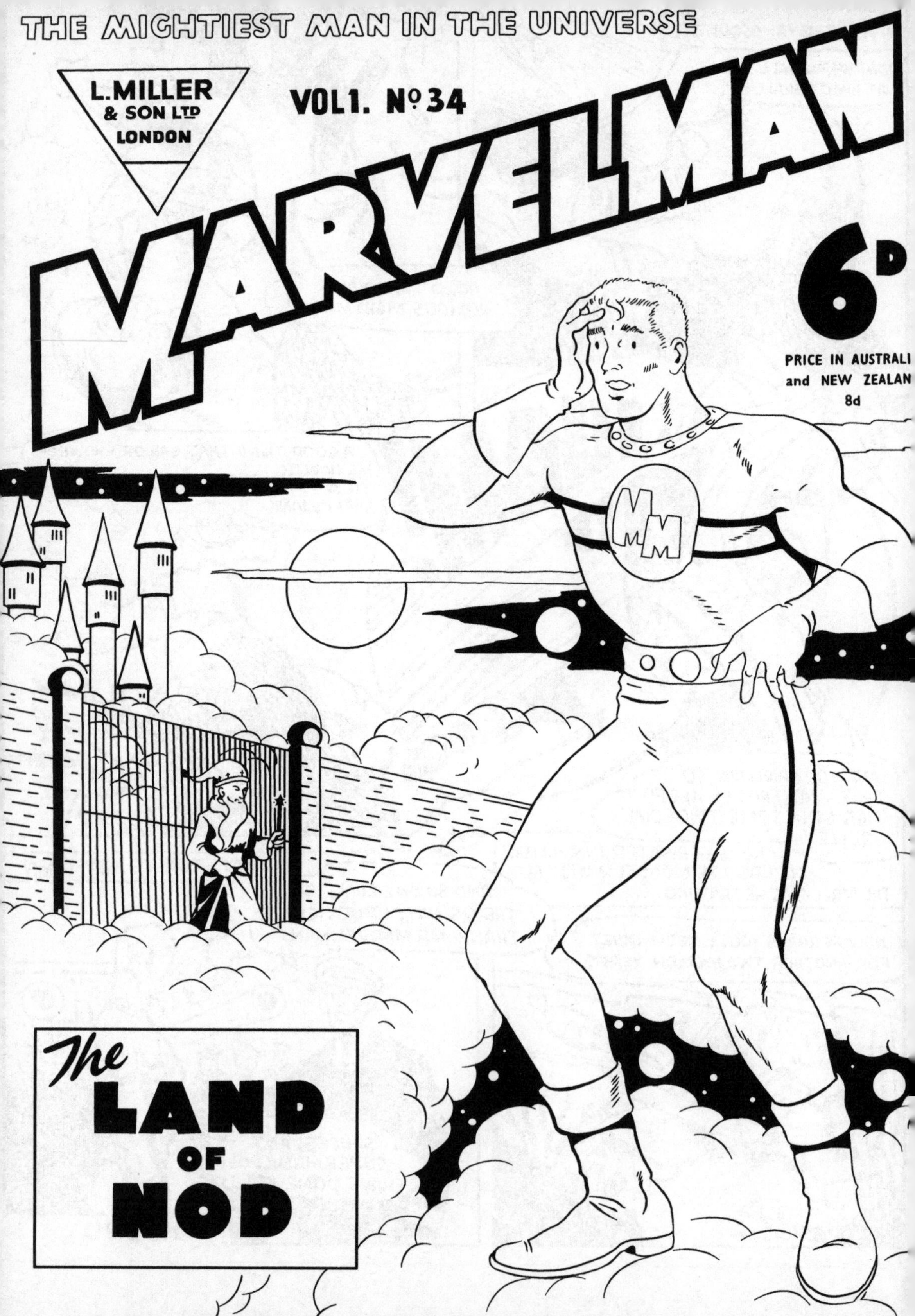
THE MIGHTIEST MAN IN THE UNIVERSE
L.MILLER
& SON LTD
LONDON
VOL1. No 34
MARVELMAN
6D
PRICE IN AUSTRALI
and NEW ZEALAN
8d
MM
The
LAND
OF
NOD

MARVELMAN

AND
THE LAND OF NOD

A recluse Astro-Scientist discovers the key word to the Universe, one that can only be given to a Boy who is completely honest, studious, and of such integrity that he would only use it for the powers of good. He finds such a Boy in **MICKY MORAN,** a Newspaper Copy Boy, and treats him in a special machine which enables him to use the secret. Just before the Scientist dies he tells **MICKY** the Key Word which is **KIMOTA.**

MICKY MORAN remains as he was, but when he says the Key Word **KIMOTA** he becomes **MARVELMAN,** a Man of such strength and powers that he is Invincible and Indestructible.

EVERYBODY NEEDS SLEEP AND WHEN KING NOD REFUSES TO ALLOW PEOPLE TO HAVE THEIR MUCH NEEDED REST, HE SETS A PROBLEM THAT ONLY THE GREAT MARVELMAN CAN SOLVE

MICKY MORAN - COPYBOY ON THE DAILY BUGLE IS FINDING IT HARD TO FALL ASLEEP.

GEE! I NEVER KNEW SUCH A NIGHT! I JUST CAN'T SLEEP

MAYBE A GLASS OF WATER WILL HELP. IF I DON'T GET SOME SLEEP SOON, I'LL BE FIT FOR NOTHING IN THE MORNING

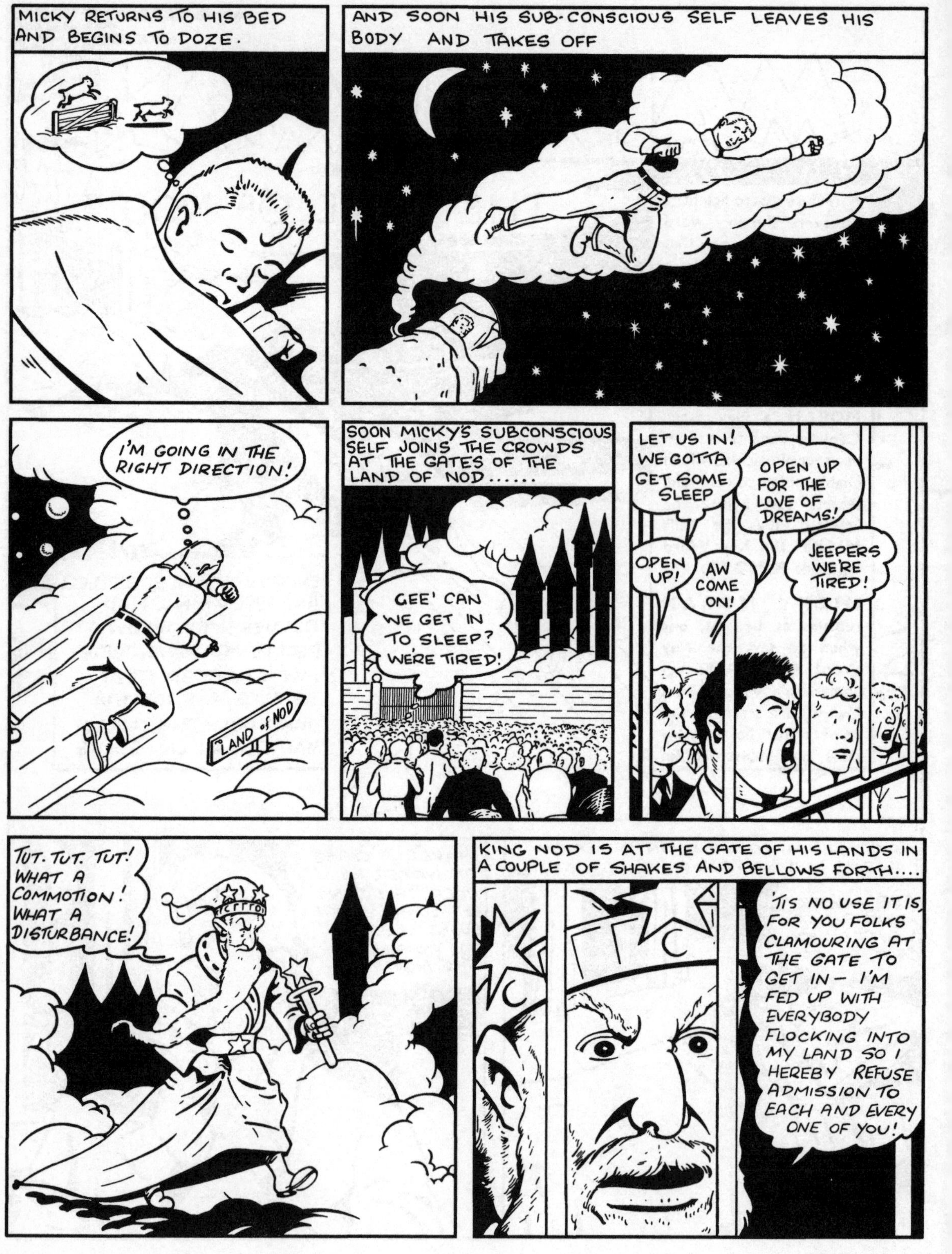
MICKY RETURNS TO HIS BED AND BEGINS TO DOZE.
AND SOON HIS SUB-CONSCIOUS SELF LEAVES HIS BODY AND TAKES OFF
I'M GOING IN THE RIGHT DIRECTION!
LAND of NOD
SOON MICKY'S SUBCONSCIOUS SELF JOINS THE CROWDS AT THE GATES OF THE LAND OF NOD......
GEE' CAN WE GET IN TO SLEEP? WE'RE TIRED!
LET US IN! WE GOTTA GET SOME SLEEP
OPEN UP FOR THE LOVE OF DREAMS!
OPEN UP!
AW COME ON!
JEEPERS WE'RE TIRED!
TUT. TUT. TUT! WHAT A COMMOTION! WHAT A DISTURBANCE!
KING NOD IS AT THE GATE OF HIS LANDS IN A COUPLE OF SHAKES AND BELLOWS FORTH....
'TIS NO USE IT IS, FOR YOU FOLKS CLAMOURING AT THE GATE TO GET IN – I'M FED UP WITH EVERYBODY FLOCKING INTO MY LAND SO I HEREBY REFUSE ADMISSION TO EACH AND EVERY ONE OF YOU!

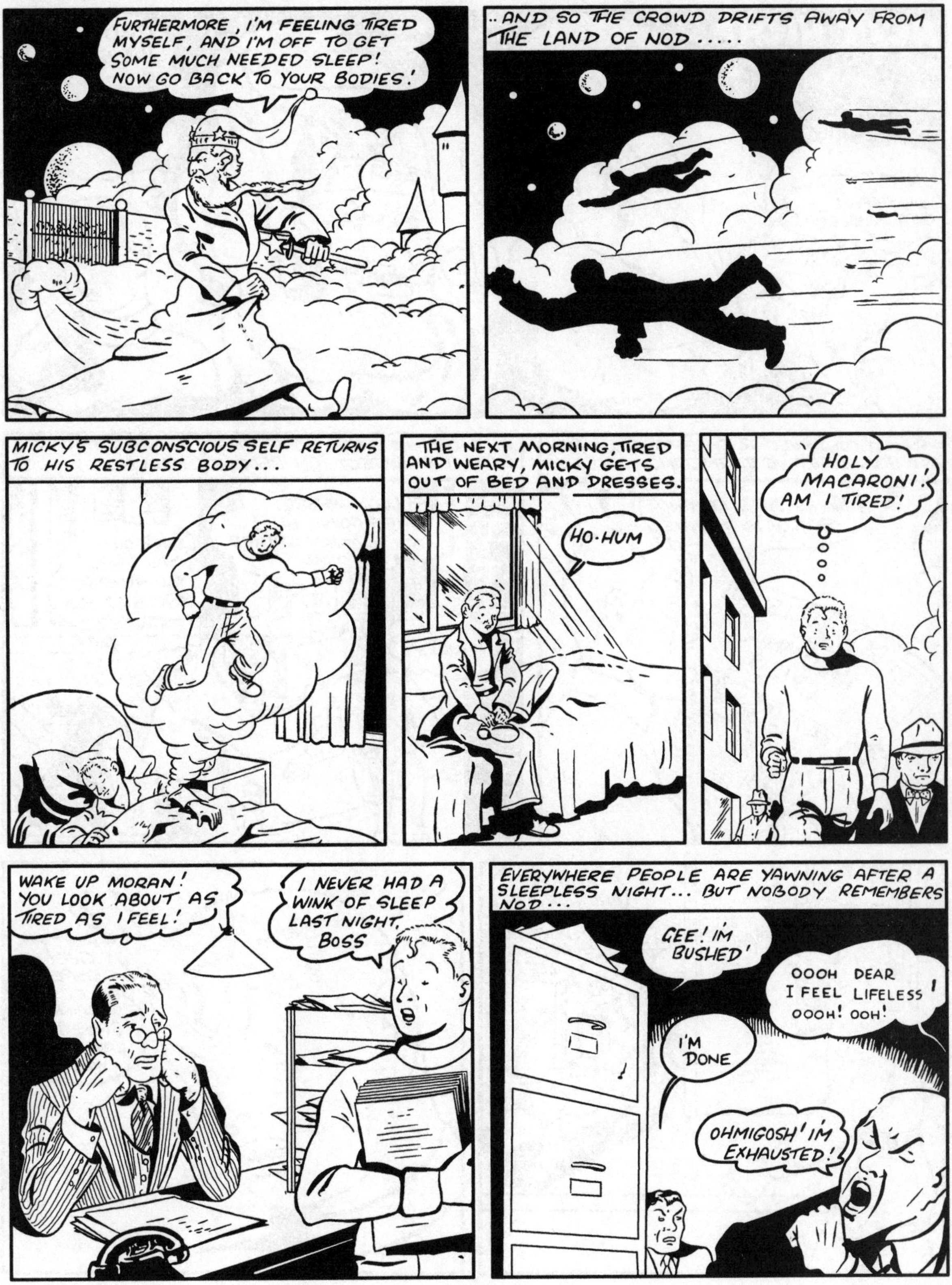
FURTHERMORE, I'M FEELING TIRED MYSELF, AND I'M OFF TO GET SOME MUCH NEEDED SLEEP! NOW GO BACK TO YOUR BODIES!
..AND SO THE CROWD DRIFTS AWAY FROM THE LAND OF NOD.....
MICKY'S SUBCONSCIOUS SELF RETURNS TO HIS RESTLESS BODY...
THE NEXT MORNING, TIRED AND WEARY, MICKY GETS OUT OF BED AND DRESSES.
HO-HUM
HOLY MACARONI! AM I TIRED!
WAKE UP MORAN! YOU LOOK ABOUT AS TIRED AS I FEEL!
I NEVER HAD A WINK OF SLEEP LAST NIGHT, BOSS
EVERYWHERE PEOPLE ARE YAWNING AFTER A SLEEPLESS NIGHT... BUT NOBODY REMEMBERS NOD...
GEE! I'M BUSHED!
OOOH DEAR I FEEL LIFELESS! OOOH! OOH!
I'M DONE
OHMIGOSH I'M EXHAUSTED!

NEXT NIGHT..
JUST CAN'T GET TO SLEEP!
NO!
OOOH I'M SO SLEEEEEEPY!
INSOMNIA CONTINUES TO SWEEP THE COUNTRY AND SOON EVERYONE IS SUFFERING ....
THINGS ARE GETTING REALLY DESPERATE!
DAILY BUGLE
3¢
INSOMNIA CRISIS
PRESIDENT TO BROADCAST
AND ON HIS WAY HOME THAT, EVENING MICKY SEES THE EFFECT ON PEOPLE'S NERVES .....
LOOK WHERE YOU'RE GOING KID! YOU ALMOST WALKED INTO ME
LOOK OUT, YOU DOPE! YOU ALMOST KNOCKED ME DOWN
AW! PHOOEY!
DR. QUACK.
BEAT IT BROTHER! I'M TIRED OF HANDING OUT SLEEPING PILLS!
POW
GEE! TEMPER'S ARE GETTING STRAINED. SUCH THINGS CAN LEAD TO WARS!

GUESS THIS IS SOMETHING MARVELMAN SHOULD LOOK INTO

KIMOTA!

AT THE KEYWORD, ATOMIC STRENGTH CRASHES DOWN ON MICKY, TRANSFORMING HIM INTO HIS OTHER SELF....

WWOOF

..MIGHTY MARVELMAN.

WELL, YOUNG MICKY CAN'T SLEEP — MAYBE I CAN.

THERE'S ONE WAY TO FIND OUT!

...SOON, AS MARVELMAN DOZES, HIS SUBCONSCIOUS SELF LEAVES HIS BODY

OH, FOR SOME SLEEP!

HOPE I CAN GET IN! I'M BUSHED!

TO LAND OF NOD

AS IT IS REALLY QUITE EARLY, NO CROWD HAS GATHERED, AS YET AT THE GATES OF NOD!

HO-HUM!

LET ME IN! OPEN UP! C'MON!
BANG!
RATTLE!
TUT-TUT-TUT! .. AND TUT AGAIN! TSK-TSK! FOR THE LOVE OF SLEEP!
AH! AT LAST! HERE COMES THE KING OF NOD!
O.K! NOW LET'S HAVE LESS OF THIS NONSENSE! OPEN UP AND STOP THIS STUPIDITY!
I WILL NOT! I WILL NOT! SCRAM, YOU BIG BLUE BABOON!
THE SUBCONCIOUS SELF OF MARVELMAN RE-ACTS.
O.K! IF YOU WON'T PLAY BALL..
CRACK!
OW!
OUT OF THE WAY KING MISERY. I WANT SOOM SLEEP!
BIF!
ONCE INSIDE THE LAND OF NOD, THE SUBCONSCIOUS MARVELMAN FALLS ASLEEP..
Z Z Z Z Z Z Z Z Z Z Z

TSK-TSK! HE'S IN SO I GUESS HE MIGHT AS WELL STAY IN!

SOON, KING NOD IS BUSILY ENGAGED, REPAIRING THE GATES.

MUST GET THIS FIXED BEFORE THE CROWDS START ROLLING UP!

BUT SOON THE SUBCONSCIOUS SELVES BEGIN TO ARRIVE!

SCRAM! I'M NOT THROUGH YET!

POW

LOOK! THE GATES ARE OPEN! LOOKS LIKE WE'RE GOING TO GET SOME SLEEP AT LAST!

GOODY!

BUT OH! OH! OH!

AH! JUST IN TIME! THAT'LL KEEP 'EM OUT!

MEANWHILE, MARVELMAN HIMSELF SLEEPS, AS DOES HIS SUBCONSCIOUS SELF IN THE LAND OF NOD... BUT...

ZZZ- MUST GET KING NOD TO OPEN THE GATES- MUST GET...

... KING NOD TO OPEN THE GATES ... MUST GET THOSE GATES OPEN...MAYBE MICKY CAN...KIM...

KIMOTA!

AT THE KEYWORD ATOMIC STRENGTH CHANGES MARVELMAN BACK TO MICKY MORAN..

WOOF

143

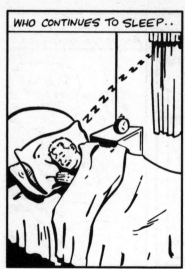

WHO CONTINUES TO SLEEP..

WHILE MARVELMANS SUB-CONSCIOUS SELF IS CHANGED INTO MICKY'S SUBCONSCIOUS SELF.

SOON..

TSK - TSK! HOW IN NOD DID THAT LAD GET IN HERE?

WAKE UP YOU! WHERE DID THAT BIG BLUE OAF GET TO?

OOH!

SCRAM!

BUT I WANT TO SLEEP!

I'M TIRED!

YEAH! SO AM I! OF YOU PEOPLE!

BF!

WITH THE RETURN OF HIS SUBCONSCIOUS SELF, MICKY AWAKES...

HOLY MACARONI! MARVELMAN FELL ASLEEP AND I WAKE UP!

NATURALLY, MICKY CANNOT REMEMBER HIS SUBCONSCIOUS TRIP TO NOD — BUT...

WELL, I DON'T REMEMBER WHAT HAPPENED, BUT MAYBE MARVELMAN HIMSELF, DOES *KIMOTA!*

...DOWN COMES ATOMIC STRENGTH TO ONCE MORE CHANGE MICKY INTO MARVELMAN..

WOOF

AND...

HOLY MACARONI! I CAN REMEMBER IT ALL NOW! THE LAND OF NOD... KING NOD

MARVELMAN HIMSELF, THE MIGHTIEST MAN IN THE UNIVERSE IS ABLE TO BREAK THROUGH THE BOUNDS OF THE SUBCONSCIOUS....

WELL, KING NOD, THIS TIME IT'S MYSELF YOU'LL BE MEETING — NOT JUST MY MERE SUBCONSCIOUS SELF!

UH-HUH! IT WON'T BE LONG NOW!

TO LAND of NOD

GATES DON'T HINDER ME!

JUST AS I THOUGHT! THE LAND OF NOD CAN'T AFFECT ME!

HEY, THERE! I WANT YOU, KING NOD!

IT'S THAT BIG BLUE APE AGAIN!

145

SLY KING NOD IS QUICK TO REALISE THAT THIS IS NO ORDINARY SUBCONSCIOUS MORTAL..
I'M SCRAMMING!
LOOKS LIKE YOU'VE GOT TO BE TAUGHT A LESSON!
SLAM
BAH! BEAT ME AS YOU WILL. YOUR BLOWS HARM ME NOT! I AM NOT A CONSCIOUS MORTAL AND I REFUSE TO BOW TO YOUR MORTAL STRENGTH!
BUT MARVELMAN KNOWS THE WAY TO DEAL WITH KING NOD!
O.K. WE'LL SEE HOW YOU LIKE THE WORLD OF THE CONSCIOUS
OH NO!
TAKE ME BACK O MIGHTY BLUE SIR! I CANNOT EXIST OUTSIDE OF NOD! I REPENT! THE GATES WILL BE OPENED AND NONE SHALL BE TURNED AWAY! PLEASE, O MIGHTY SIR!
RIGHT! NOW YOU'VE LEARNED YOUR LESSON JUST REMEMBER THIS..
MARVELMAN RETURNS THE KING TO NOD..
TRY YOUR TRICKS AGAIN AND I'LL BE RIGHT BACK!
I'LL NOT ATTEMPT TO HIBERNATE AGAIN— I PROMISE!
MARVELMAN GOES HOME..
QUIET! GOOD! EVERYBODY IS NOW ENJOYING MUCH NEEDED SLEEP!
THE END!

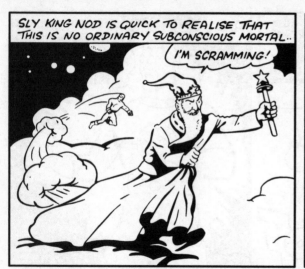

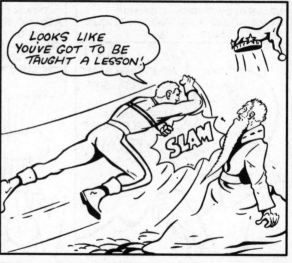

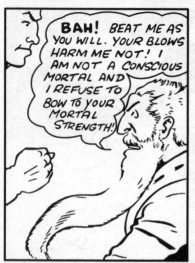

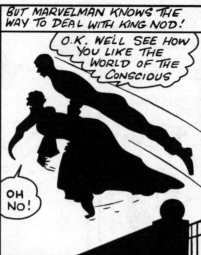

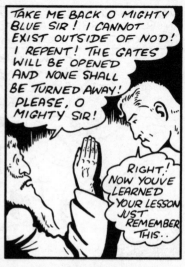

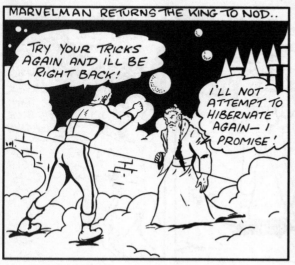

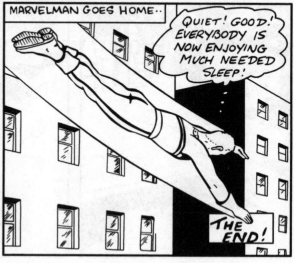

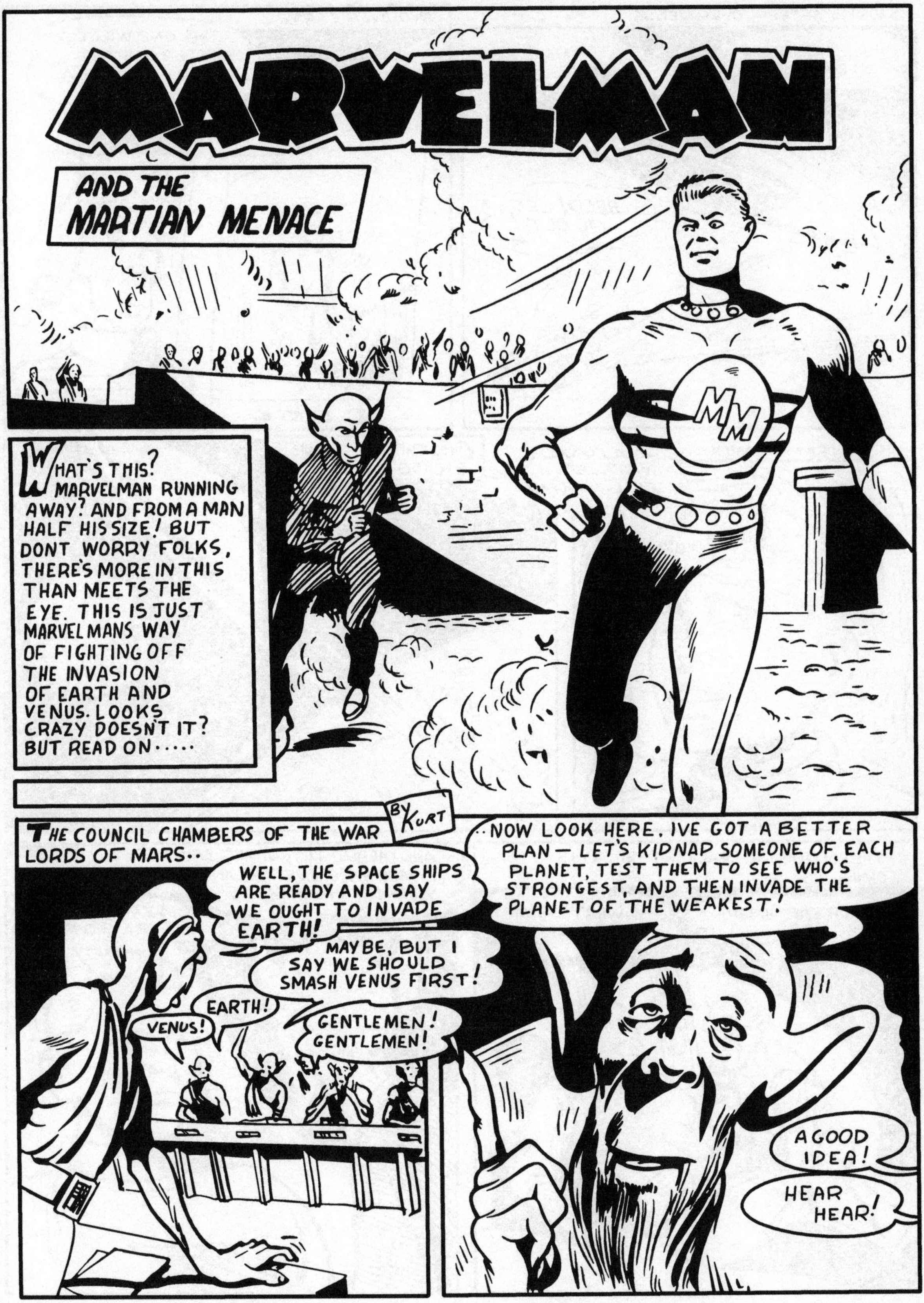
MARVELMAN
AND THE MARTIAN MENACE
WHAT'S THIS? MARVELMAN RUNNING AWAY? AND FROM A MAN HALF HIS SIZE! BUT DONT WORRY FOLKS, THERE'S MORE IN THIS THAN MEETS THE EYE. THIS IS JUST MARVELMANS WAY OF FIGHTING OFF THE INVASION OF EARTH AND VENUS. LOOKS CRAZY DOESN'T IT? BUT READ ON.....
MM
BY KURT
THE COUNCIL CHAMBERS OF THE WAR LORDS OF MARS..
WELL, THE SPACE SHIPS ARE READY AND I SAY WE OUGHT TO INVADE EARTH!
MAYBE, BUT I SAY WE SHOULD SMASH VENUS FIRST!
EARTH!
VENUS!
GENTLEMEN! GENTLEMEN!
..NOW LOOK HERE. IVE GOT A BETTER PLAN — LET'S KIDNAP SOMEONE OF EACH PLANET, TEST THEM TO SEE WHO'S STRONGEST, AND THEN INVADE THE PLANET OF THE WEAKEST!
A GOOD IDEA!
HEAR HEAR!

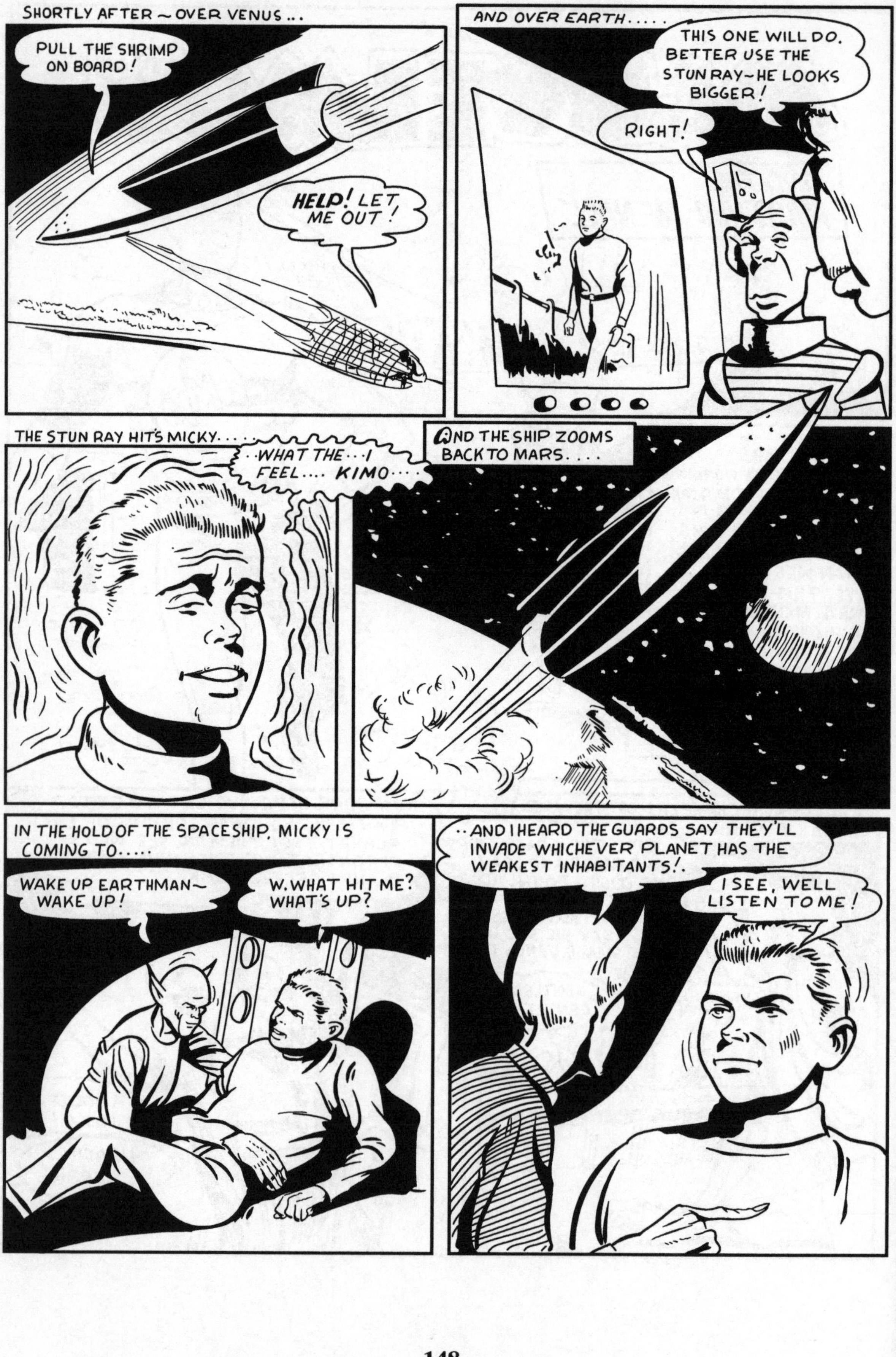
SHORTLY AFTER ~ OVER VENUS...
PULL THE SHRIMP ON BOARD!
HELP! LET ME OUT!
AND OVER EARTH.....
THIS ONE WILL DO. BETTER USE THE STUN RAY~HE LOOKS BIGGER!
RIGHT!
THE STUN RAY HIT'S MICKY.....
..WHAT THE...I FEEL.... KIMO...
AND THE SHIP ZOOMS BACK TO MARS...
IN THE HOLD OF THE SPACESHIP, MICKY IS COMING TO.....
WAKE UP EARTHMAN~ WAKE UP!
W. WHAT HIT ME? WHAT'S UP?
..AND I HEARD THE GUARDS SAY THEY'LL INVADE WHICHEVER PLANET HAS THE WEAKEST INHABITANTS!.
I SEE, WELL LISTEN TO ME!

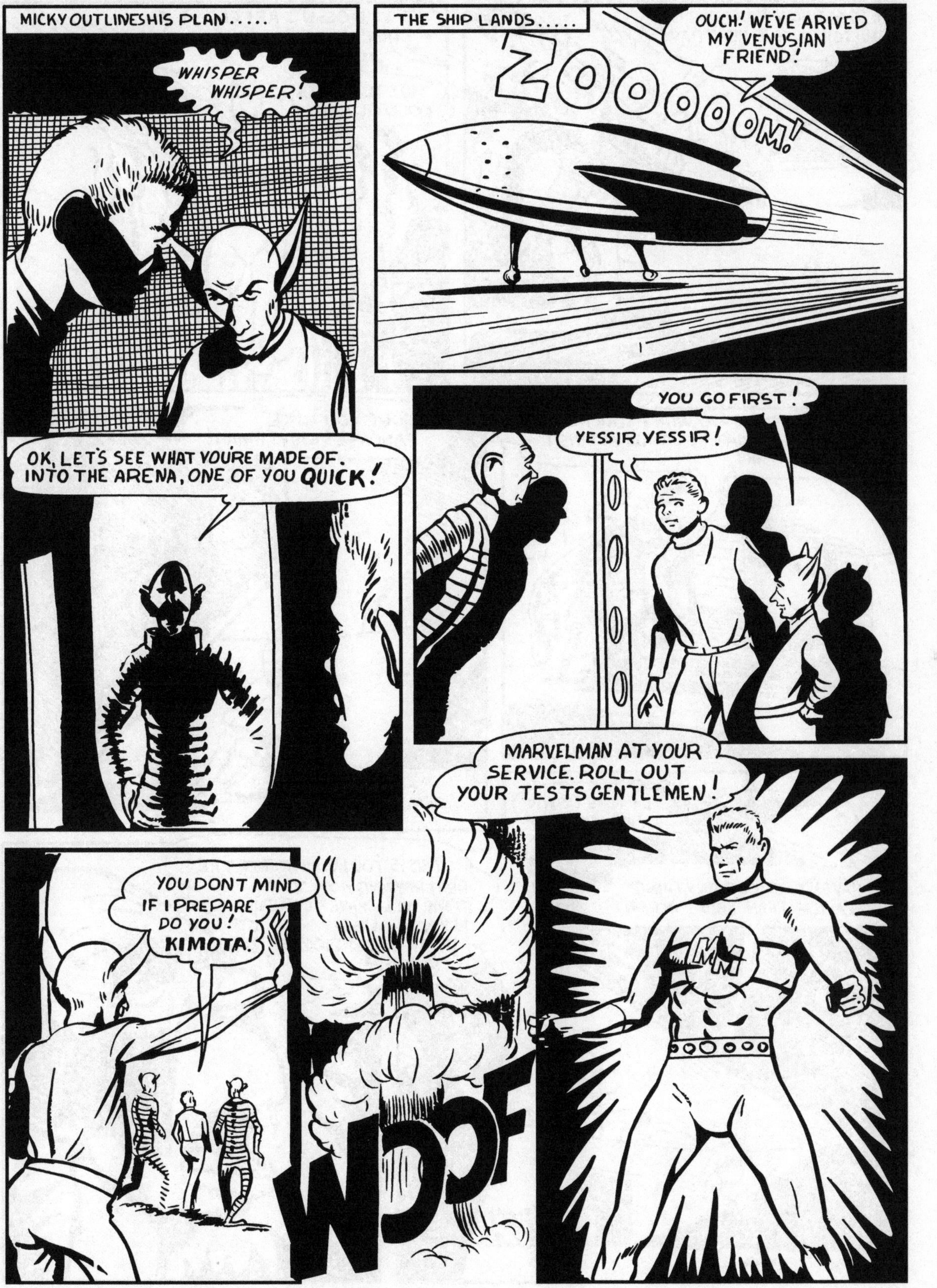
MICKY OUTLINESHIS PLAN.....
WHISPER WHISPER!
THE SHIP LANDS.....
OUCH! WE'VE ARIVED MY VENUSIAN FRIEND!
ZOOOOOOM!
OK, LET'S SEE WHAT YOU'RE MADE OF. INTO THE ARENA, ONE OF YOU QUICK!
YOU GO FIRST!
YESSIR YESSIR!
YOU DONT MIND IF I PREPARE DO YOU! KIMOTA!
WOOF
MARVELMAN AT YOUR SERVICE. ROLL OUT YOUR TESTS GENTLEMEN!

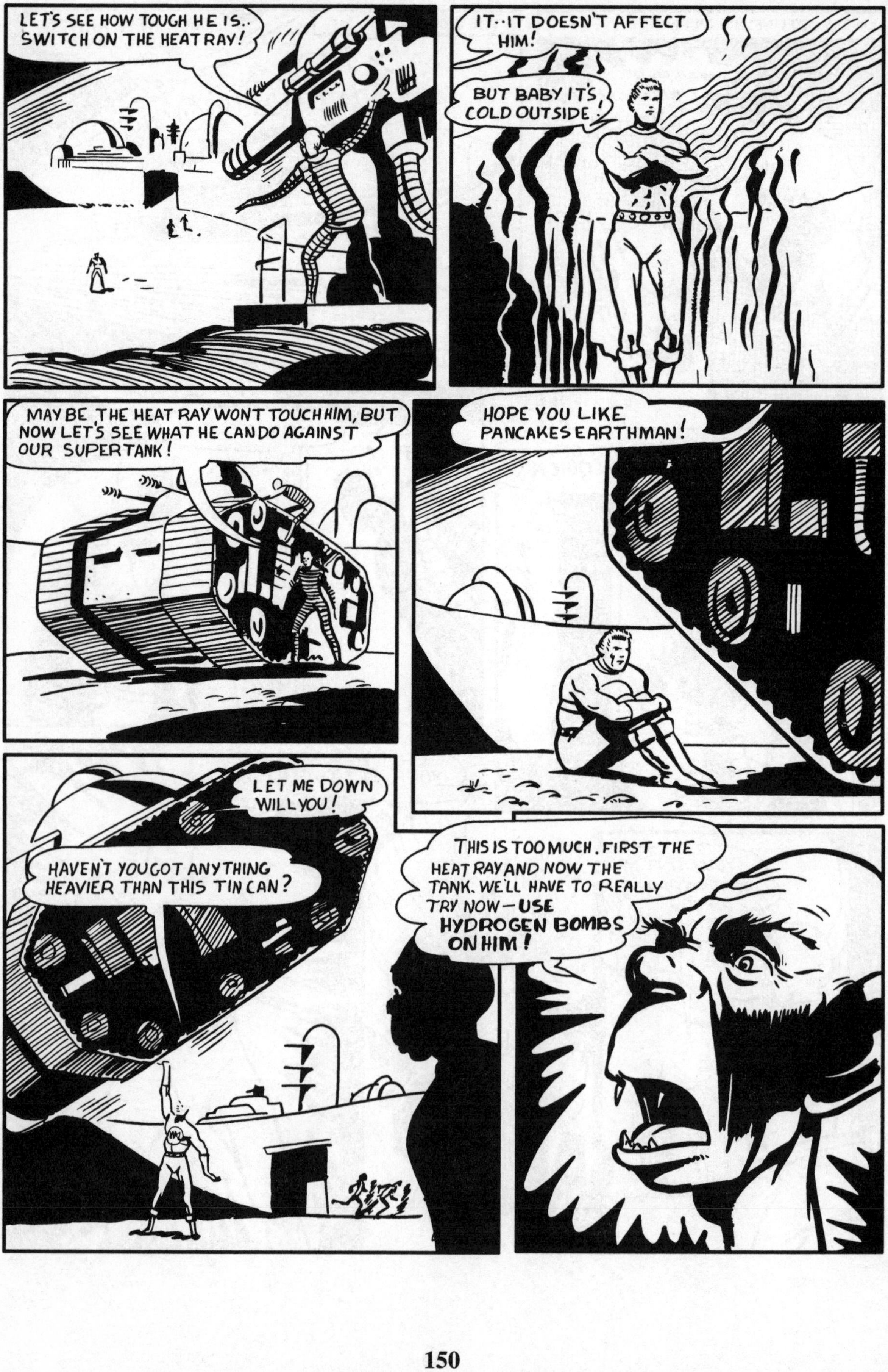
LET'S SEE HOW TOUGH HE IS.. SWITCH ON THE HEAT RAY!
IT..IT DOESN'T AFFECT HIM!
BUT BABY IT'S COLD OUTSIDE!
MAY BE THE HEAT RAY WONT TOUCH HIM, BUT NOW LET'S SEE WHAT HE CAN DO AGAINST OUR SUPERTANK!
HOPE YOU LIKE PANCAKES EARTHMAN!
LET ME DOWN WILL YOU!
HAVEN'T YOU GOT ANYTHING HEAVIER THAN THIS TIN CAN?
THIS IS TOO MUCH. FIRST THE HEAT RAY AND NOW THE TANK. WE'LL HAVE TO REALLY TRY NOW—USE HYDROGEN BOMBS ON HIM!

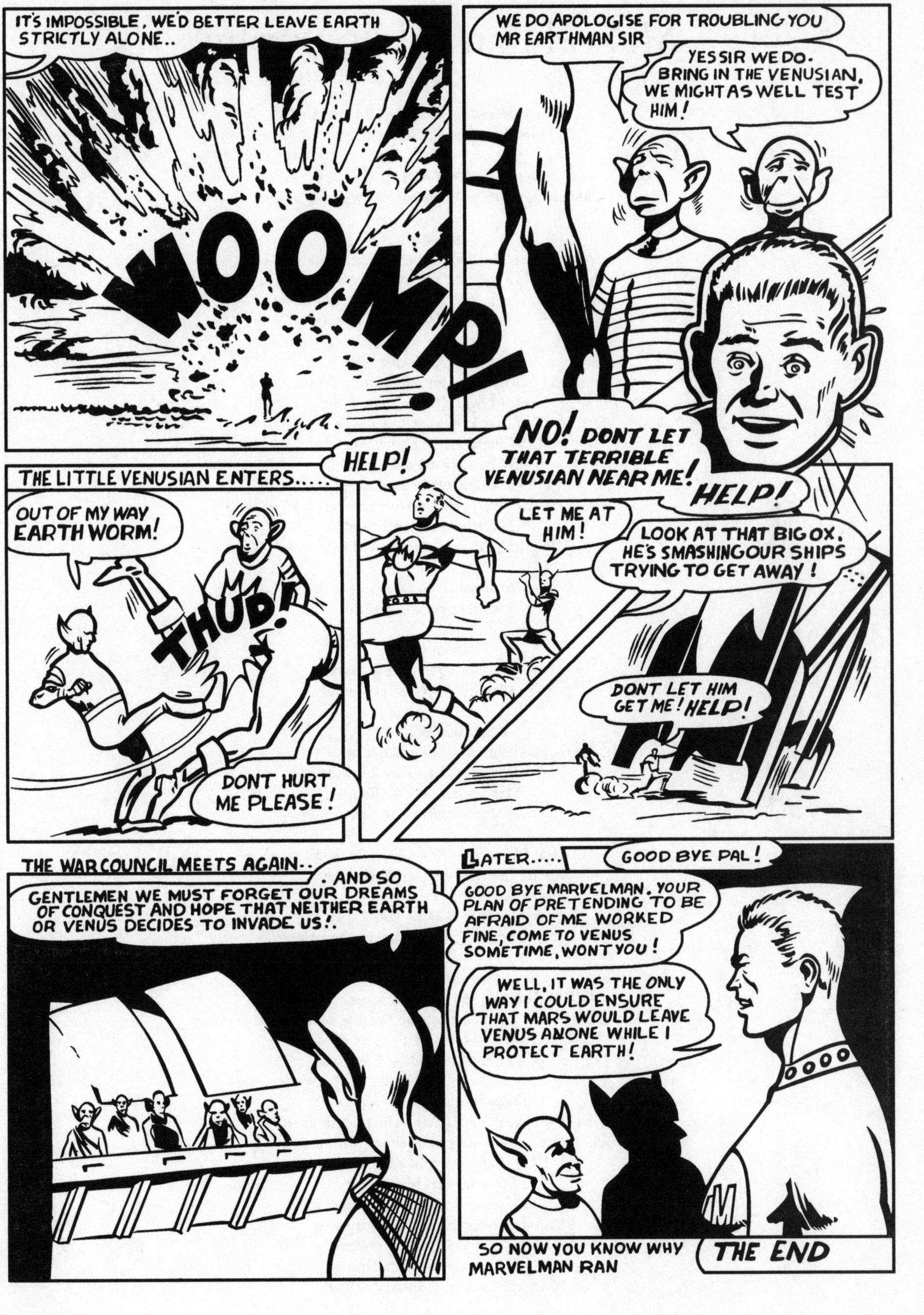
IT'S IMPOSSIBLE, WE'D BETTER LEAVE EARTH STRICTLY ALONE..
WOOMP!
WE DO APOLOGISE FOR TROUBLING YOU MR EARTHMAN SIR
YES SIR WE DO. BRING IN THE VENUSIAN, WE MIGHT AS WELL TEST HIM!
NO! DONT LET THAT TERRIBLE VENUSIAN NEAR ME!
HELP!
THE LITTLE VENUSIAN ENTERS.....
OUT OF MY WAY EARTH WORM!
THUD!
DONT HURT ME PLEASE!
HELP!
LET ME AT HIM!
LOOK AT THAT BIG OX. HE'S SMASHING OUR SHIPS TRYING TO GET AWAY!
DONT LET HIM GET ME! HELP!
THE WAR COUNCIL MEETS AGAIN..
. AND SO GENTLEMEN WE MUST FORGET OUR DREAMS OF CONQUEST AND HOPE THAT NEITHER EARTH OR VENUS DECIDES TO INVADE US!.
LATER.....
GOOD BYE PAL!
GOOD BYE MARVELMAN. YOUR PLAN OF PRETENDING TO BE AFRAID OF ME WORKED FINE, COME TO VENUS SOMETIME, WONT YOU!
WELL, IT WAS THE ONLY WAY I COULD ENSURE THAT MARS WOULD LEAVE VENUS ANONE WHILE I PROTECT EARTH!
SO NOW YOU KNOW WHY MARVELMAN RAN
THE END

Marvelman Bibliography

Captain Marvel #19 — Dec. 23, 1953
First mention of Marvelman

Captain Marvel #24 — Jan. 27, 1954
Title change to *The Marvelman, Captain Marvel*

Marvelman
#25 — Feb. 3, 1954 — First issue, weekly.
#102 — July 30, 1955 — First appearance of Kid Marvelman
#336 — Feb. 3, 1960 — Title goes monthly
#370 — February 1963 — Last issue

Marvelman Annual
1954 (softcover) Marvelman standing
1955 (softcover) Marvelman flying
1956 (hardcover) yellow cover
1957 (hardcover) pink cover
1958 (hardcover) red cover
1959 (hardcover) orange cover
1960 (hardcover) yellow cover (racing car)
1961 (card cover) with cape
1962 (card cover) printed as 1963

Marvelman Family Annual
1963 (card cover) only issue

Marvelman Family
#1 — October 1956 — First issue
#30 — October 1959 — Last issue

Magic Painting Books
Marvelman — The Magician
Marvelman — The Giant Flower
Young Marvelman — The Reindeer
Young Marvelman — In Space

Captain Marvel Jr. #19 — Dec. 23, 1953
First mention of Young Marvelman

Captain Marvel Jr. #24 — Jan. 27, 1954
Title change to *The Young Marvelman, Captain Marvel Jr.*

Young Marvelman
#25 — Feb. 3, 1954 — First issue, weekly
#37 — April 21, 1954 — First Marvelman/Young Marvelman team-up
#336 — Feb. 3, 1960 — Title goes monthly
#370 — February 1963 — Last issue

Young Marvelman Annual
1954 (softcover) Young Marvelman with alien
1955 (softcover) Young Marvelman with dagger
1956 (hardcover) black cover
1957 (hardcover) blue cover
1958 (hardcover) yellow cover
1959 (hardcover) blue cover (airplane)
1960 (hardcover) white cover
1961 (card cover) with cape
1962 (card cover) printed as 1963

Marvelman Jr. Annual
1963 (card cover) only issue